A Basic
Guide to
Exporting

Compiled by
U.S. Department
of Commerce

Printed on recyclable paper

NTC Business Books
a division of *NTC Publishing Group* • Lincolnwood, Illinois USA

1995 Printing

This NTC edition, first published in 1989 by
NTC Business Books, a division of
NTC Publishing Group, 4255 West Touhy Avenue,
Lincolnwood (Chicago), Illinois 60646-1975,
is an unabridged publication of *A Basic Guide to
Exporting*, compiled by the United States
Department of Commerce, International Trade
Administration, U.S. and Foreign and Commercial
Service, and revised and updated by
TransNational, Inc., of Washington, DC, under
contract with the Department of Commerce,
September 1986.
Manufactured in the United States of America.
Library of Congress Catalog Card Number: 88-63900

4 5 6 7 8 9 VP 9 8 7 6

Table of contents

Department of Commerce
Department of Agriculture
Agency for International Development
Trade and Development Program
State and local government assistance
Business and service organization contacts
Promotion in publications and other media

Planning the itinerary
Other preparation
Business preparations for international travel
Assistance from U.S. Embassies and Consulates
Carnets
Cultural factors

Part B.   Making the sale

Responding to inquiries
Separating the wheat from the chaff
Business practices in international selling
Building a working relationship

Foreign market objectives
Costs
Market demand
Competition
Pricing summary
Quotations and "pro forma" invoices
Terms of sale

Major considerations in financing
Commercial banks
Types of bank financing
Federal government export financing programs
State and local export finance programs
Export trading companies and export management companies
Other private sources

Export regulations
Customs benefits for exporters
Foreign sales corporation
Commerce assistance related to the Multilateral Trade Negotiations
Patent, trademark, copyright, and trade secret considerations

Part C.   After the sale

Freight forwarders
Packing
Labeling
Documentation
Shipping
Insurance

Cash in advance
Open account
Consignment sales
Drafts and letters of credit
Foreign exchange
Countertrade and barter
Decreasing credit risks through credit checks
Collection problems: What to do when something goes wrong

Maintenance, repair, and training
Feedback and customer relations

Technology licensing
Wholly owned branch and subsidiary operations
Joint ventures

Appendices

Overview

Why export?

A few years ago, many presently successful exporters had little or no interest in exporting due to the complexities involved. Today, however, they find it worth the effort. International business represents a substantial part of their total sales volume and profits. They are finding that, by selling internationally, they can improve economies of scale in production, in marketing, and in distribution. As a result, the exporter can spread fixed costs over more products, which reduces the costs of production and increases profits. Lower cost can also mean a lower sales price that, in turn, can open up new markets and further increase volume. Increased production can also mean using slack capacity.

Equally important, the ability of U.S.-made products to compete for sales domestically, as well as overseas, increases as a company responds to preferences of overseas customers and innovations of foreign competitors. Many important new developments are occurring in foreign manufacturing that may threaten the marketing position of products overseas and in the United States. By marketing products overseas, a U.S. company can gain advance intelligence on these new developments rather than be caught unprepared for the loss of domestic market share to foreign competition.

Exporting is also important for the United States as a nation. The steady erosion of the U.S. share of total world exports during the 1960's and 1970's has had more than purely statistical repercussions. It has had a major impact on our economy and our citizens. One billion dollars of trade activity creates close to 40,000 jobs, directly and indirectly. It generates an additional $2 billion in gross national product and $400 million in additional State and Federal revenue.

These advantages make exporting well worth the effort, despite its initial complexities.

How does exporting differ from domestic selling?

For some firms, international marketing may not be all that different from domestic selling. If, for example, a company chooses to sell to another company that then sells the products abroad, the original seller probably notices little difference between that sale and other domestic sales. This is one of several methods of selling abroad that can minimize the difference between foreign and domestic sales.

On the other hand, as direct involvement in exporting increases, effort and investment of time and money increase, and so do the opportunities for higher profits—if a company is at a stage where a higher level of investment is now feasible. Direct exporting requires gaining knowledge of foreign buyer needs and tastes, as well as different and more complex channels of distribution. Communications becomes more important because of greater distances, different time zones, languages, and customs. Business practices, taxes, government regulations, laws, currency, transportation systems—all are different because of distance and the need to cross international borders. Credit terms, financing needs, and collection times are also different; payment often takes longer because of longer time required for shipping or because of currency exchange problems in certain countries.

There are obviously real costs and risks associated with direct exporting. Apprehensions about these factors may keep potential exporters from exploring the options available. Yet the costs and risks of exporting can be less than those of selling domestically, and, more important, profits can be higher.

Reasons for exporting

- Increase overall sales volume.
- Enlarge sales base to spread out fixed costs.
- Use excess production capacity.
- Compensate for seasonal fluctuations in domestic sales.
- Find new markets for products with declining U.S. sales.
- Exploit existing advantages in untapped markets.
- Take advantage of high-volume foreign purchases.
- Learn about advanced technical methods used abroad.
- Follow domestic competitors who are selling overseas.
- Acquire knowledge about international competition.
- Test opportunities for overseas licensing or production.
- Contribute to the company's general expansion.
- Improve overall return on investment. Create more jobs.

The purpose and use of the BASIC GUIDE TO EXPORTING

The BASIC GUIDE TO EXPORTING has been designed to provide information needed to export profitably. It tells what decisions have to be made, what knowledge is needed to make them, and where to get the necessary information. In addition to a written guide such as this, personal advisors are also essential. Throughout the book numerous references are made to persons who can assist, often at no cost. For example, the U.S. and Foreign Commercial Service of the Department of Commerce has District Offices located in 48 cities in the United States. Each office has skilled trade specialists who can provide both general and specialized assistance to individual companies. These professionals are also very familiar with the many other resources available within their area and can refer exporters to those resources.

Chapter 1 of the BASIC GUIDE presents several general factors that should be considered when a company is preparing its overall plans for exporting. Chapter 2 describes many sources of assistance within the U.S. Department of Commerce, other Federal agencies, local governments, and private organizations. Chapter 2 can help to quickly identify the most useful organization to contact for particular needs. The remaining chapters of the BASIC GUIDE break the export process into several of its components in order to provide basic information on each. Finally, the appendices contain information that can be used to locate helpful people and organizations in Washington, DC, in every State, and in many foreign countries. Like most guidebooks, the BASIC GUIDE may be read from cover to cover as a thorough introduction to exporting, or it may be used as a reference to obtain information on particular topics.

Before
the sale

Export strategy

Assessing a product's export potential

There are several ways to measure a product's potential in overseas markets. One of the most important is its success in domestic markets. If a company is successful in selling a product in the U.S. market, there is a good chance that it will be successful in selling in markets abroad, wherever similar needs and conditions exist. In markets that differ significantly from the U.S. market, some products may have limited potential. Significant differences may relate to climate and environmental factors, local availability of raw materials or product alternatives, lower wage costs, and lower purchasing power. If a product is successful in the United States, its success in export markets may necessitate a careful analysis of why it sells here and then the selection of similar markets abroad. In this way, little or no product modification is required.

If a product is not new or unique, preliminary and low cost market research is probably already available that can facilitate the assessment of its overseas market potential (see Chapter 3 for more information on market research techniques and resources). Trade statistics, available in many local libraries, can give a preliminary indication of markets for a particular product in most countries. If a product is unique and has important advantages that are hard to duplicate abroad, market data may not be available, yet chances are very good for finding an export market.

Finally, even if the sales of a product are now declining in the United States, sizeable export markets may exist, especially if the product once did well in the United States but is now losing market share to more technically advanced products. Although the United States is a world leader in introducing new technology, there is often a significant time lag between the demand for new products in the United States and in some other countries. Countries that are less developed may not need ''state-of-the-art'' technology and may instead have a surprisingly healthy demand for U.S. products that are older, less expensive, and less sophisticated.

Making the export decision

Once a company determines that it has exportable products, it must still consider other factors, such as:

- What does the company want to gain from exporting? Is exporting consistent with other company goals?
- What demands will exporting place on the company's key resources—management, personnel, production capacity and finance—and how will these demands be met?
- Are the expected benefits worth the costs or would company resources be better used for developing new domestic business?

A more detailed list of questions can be found in Table 1. Answers to the questions listed there can help a company to decide not only whether or not to export, but, if so, what methods of exporting should be initially used.

The value of planning

Many companies begin export activities without a careful screening of markets or options for market entry. While these companies may encounter a measure of success, they may overlook better export opportunities. In the event that early export efforts are not successful, the company may unwisely abandon exporting altogether. Formulating an export strategy, based on good information and assessment, makes it more likely that the best among several options will be chosen, that resources will be used effectively, and that efforts will be carried through to completion.

The purpose of the export plan is to assemble facts, constraints, and goals, and to create an action statement. The statement includes specific objectives; it sets forth time schedules for implementation; and it marks milestones in order to measuring the degree of success and helping motivate personnel.

The basic elements of a plan need not be elaborate or detailed—nor should they be the first time around. However, at a minimum, the following questions should be answered:

1. What countries are targeted for sales development?
2. What strategy is to be exploited in these markets?
3. What specific operational steps must be taken and when?
4. How many dollars and how much management time can be committed to each element of an export plan?
5. What will be the framework for implementing different elements of the plan?
6. How will results be evaluated and used to modify efforts?

One key to developing a successful plan is the participation of all personnel who will be affected and involved in the exporting process. All aspects of an export plan should be agreed upon by those who will ultimately execute them.

A clearly written marketing strategy offers five immediate benefits:

1. Written plans help ensure a commitment to exporting for an evaluation of results.

2. Written plans display their strengths and weaknesses more readily. This will be of great help in formulating and polishing an export strategy.

3. Written plans are not as easily forgotten, overlooked, or ignored by those charged with executing them. If deviation from the original plan occurs, it is likely to be due to a deliberate choice to do so.

4. Written plans are easier to communicate to others and are less likely to be misunderstood.

5. Written plans allocate responsibilities and provide for an evaluation of results.

All of the advantages of written plans listed here are important, but the first is especially noteworthy. Unless top management is willing to commit itself to the steps of a clearly written plan, it is all too easy to let initial efforts die for lack of follow-through.

The planning process and the result

A crucial first step in planning is to develop broad consensus among key management officials on the company's goals, objectives, capabilities, and constraints. Answering the questions listed in Table 1 is one way to start.

The first time an export plan is made, the efforts should be kept simple. The initial planning efforts can generate much information and insight that can later be incorporated into more sophisticated planning.

Once the groundwork has been laid, the export plan should be written. It need only be a few pages long, especially for a first draft, since important information may not yet be available. The plan should be a working document that can be used actively as a management tool. The objectives in the plan should be used to measure the success of different strategies when compared to actual results. As more information and experience are gained, the company can modify the plan and make it more specific.

A detailed plan is recommended for companies that intend to export directly. Companies choosing indirect export methods may need much simpler plans. An outline of an export plan is included in Table 2.

Approaches to exporting

The way a company chooses to export its products can have a significant effect on its export plan and specific marketing strategies. The basic distinction among approaches to exporting concerns the level of involvement of the firm in the export process. There are at least four approaches, which may be used alone or in combination:

1. *Filling orders from domestic buyers* who then export the product. These sales are indistinguishable from other domestic sales as far as the original seller is concerned. Someone else has decided the product in question meets foreign demand. That party takes all the risk and handles all of the exporting details, in some cases without even the awareness of the original seller. Many companies take a stronger interest in exporting when they discover that their product is already being sold overseas.

2. *Seeking out domestic buyers* who represent foreign end-users or customers. There are a large number of U.S. and foreign corporations, general contractors, foreign trading companies, foreign government agencies, foreign distributors and retailers, and others in the United States who purchase for export. These buyers are a large market for a wide variety of goods and services. In this case, a company may know its product is being exported, but, as above, the risk is on the buyer of whether or not the product meets foreign demand. The buyer also handles all the details.

3. *Exporting indirectly through intermediaries.* With this approach, a company engages the services of an intermediary firm capable of finding foreign markets and buyers for its products. Export management companies (EMC's), Export Trading Companies (ETC's), international trade consultants, and other intermediaries can give the exporter access to well established expertise and trade contacts. Yet, the exporter can still retain considerable control over the process and can realize some of the other benefits of exporting, such as learning more about foreign competitors, new technologies and other market opportunities. While risks increase with this option, so do the potential profits.

4. *Exporting directly.* This approach means nearly total involvement in the process. That is, almost complete control is exercised from market research and planning through foreign distribution. It also involves significant commitment of management time to achieve success. This approach is not appropriate for everyone nor for every foreign market, but for some it represents the best way to achieve maximum profits and plan for long-term growth.

The first two approaches above represent substantial markets and proportions of sales, perhaps as much as 30 percent of U.S. exports. They do not, however, involve the firm in the export process. For this reason the GUIDE concentrates on the latter two. (For information on how to contact domestic buyers for overseas markets, refer to *How to Build an Export Business,* Minority Business Development Agency, U.S. Department of Commerce.)

If the nature of the company's goals and resources makes an indirect method of exporting the best choice, it is conceivable that little further planning is needed. In such a case, the main task is to find and select a suitable intermediary firm that can then handle most or all other details. For firms that are new to exporting or those that are not ready or able to commit staff and funds to more complex export activities, indirect methods of exporting may be more appropriate. A firm may choose to gradually increase its level of activity and to adopt more direct methods of exporting later after experience is gained and sales volume appears to justify added investment. If a company is already prepared to adopt more direct methods of distribution, then a more direct method is often more profitable.

For more information on different approaches to exporting and their advantages and disadvantages, see Chapter 4. Consulting advisors before making these decisions can be helpful. The next chapter presents information on a variety of organizations that can provide this type of help, in many cases at no cost.

Table 1
The export decision—management issues

I. Experience

1. With what countries has business already been conducted (or from what countries have inquiries already been received)?
2. Which product lines are mentioned most often?
3. List the sale inquiry of each buyer by product, by country.
4. Is the trend of sales/inquiries up or down?
5. Who are the main domestic and foreign competitors?
6. What general and specific lessons have been learned from past export experiences?

II. Management & personnel

1. Who will be responsible for the export department's organization and staff?
2. How much senior management time—
   a. Should be allocated?
   b. Could be allocated?
3. What are management's expectations for the effort?
4. What organization structure is required to ensure that export sales are adequately serviced? (Note the political implications, if any.)
5. Who will follow through after the planning is accomplished?

III. Production capacity

1. How is the present capacity being used?
2. Will filing export orders hurt domestic sales?
3. What will be the cost of additional production?
4. Are there fluctuations in the annual workload? When? Why?
5. What minimum order quantity is required?
6. What would be required to design and package products specifically for export?

IV. Financial capacity

1. What amount of capital can be tied up in exports?
2. What level of export department operating costs can be supported?
3. How are the initial expenses of export efforts to be allocated?
4. What other new development plans are in the works that may compete with export plans?
5. By what date must an export effort pay for itself?

Table 2
Outline for an export plan

Table of contents

Executive summary (one or two pages maximum)

Introduction: Why a company should export

Part I—An export policy commitment statement

Part II—The situation/background analysis

- Product
- Operations
- Personnel and export organization
- Resources of the firm
- Industry structure, competition and demand

Part III—The marketing component

- Identification, evaluation and selection of target markets
- Product selection & pricing
- Distribution method
- Terms and conditions
- Internal organization & procedures
- Sales goals: Profit (loss) forecasts

Part IV—Tactics: Action steps

- Countries where firm has special advantages (e.g. family ties)
- Primary target countries
- Secondary target countries
- Indirect marketing efforts

Part V—An export budget

- Pro forma financial statements

Part VI—An implementation schedule

- Followup
- Periodic operational/management review (measuring results against Plan)

Addenda—background data on target countries & market

- Basic market statistics: Historical & projected
- Background facts
- Competitive environment

Export advice

For companies making initial plans to export or to export in new areas, considerable advice and assistance is available at little or no cost. It is easy, through lack of experience, to overestimate the problems involved in exporting or to get embroiled in difficulties that can be avoided. For these and other good reasons, it is important to get expert counseling and assistance from the beginning.

This chapter gives a brief overview of sources of assistance available through Federal, State, and local government agencies and in the private sector. Other chapters in this book give more information on the specialized services of these organizations and how to use them. Information on where to find these organizations can be found in the appendices.

Some readers may initially feel overwhelmed by the number of sources of advice available. While having many sources to choose from can be advantageous, it can also be difficult to decide where to start. Some advice from experienced exporters may be helpful in this regard: Although it is not necessary to go to all of these resources, it is valuable to at least know something about each of them and to get to know several on a personal basis. Each individual or organization contacted can contribute different perspectives based on different experience and skills.

Department of Commerce

The scope of services provided by the U.S. Department of Commerce to exporters is vast but often overlooked by many businesses. The primary organization within the Department dealing with U.S. exports is the International Trade Administration (ITA).

Although ITA itself has many important divisions, each with a variety of services and products, the process of using these services has been streamlined. In each local area, it is only necessary to contact a single agency: The District Office of the U.S. and Foreign Commercial Service. Through the local District Office, the exporter has access to all assistance available through ITA and to trade information gathered overseas by US&FCS commercial officers in U.S. embassies and consulates.

Domestic assistance

U.S. and Foreign Commercial Service District Offices

The domestic arm of U.S. and Foreign Commercial Service (US&FCS) has 48 District Offices and 24 branch offices located in industrial and commercial centers throughout the United States and Puerto Rico. These offices provide information and counseling to the business community. Each District Office can give information about:

- Trade and investment opportunities abroad.
- Foreign markets for U.S. products and services.
- Services to locate and evaluate overseas buyers and representatives.
- Financing aid to exporters.
- U.S. Export-Import Bank.
- Tax advantages of exporting.
- International trade exhibitions.
- Export documentation requirements.
- Economic statistics of foreign countries.
- U.S. export licensing and foreign nation import requirements.

A key element in the aid offered by the District Office is the professional counseling provided by trade specialists to interested firms. Each office is headed by a director and is supported by a contingent of trade specialists and other staff. These professionals can first help a company's decision makers gain a basic understanding of profitable opportunities in exporting and assist them in evaluating the company's market potential overseas.

The next step may be to guide the company through the entire process from evaluating and choosing a market to making its first shipment. Once a firm has made its first overseas sale, chances are good the company will want to make more. The US&FCS District Offices and overseas commercial posts can actively identify additional sales leads for the firm and search for new market opportunities.

To encourage and assist U.S. businesses to enter international trade, US&FCS trade specialists draw upon the resources of the entire Department of Commerce for many export marketing aids and services. These services, many of which are described later in this publication, include the following:

- Market research.
- Assistance in promoting U.S. products in overseas markets.
- Computerized trade opportunities.
- Help in locating overseas agents or distributors.
- Trade missions and introductions between foreign buyers and U.S. firms.

- Export seminars and conferences.
- Participation in major international trade fairs.
- Customer evaluations.

Most District Offices maintain an extensive business library containing the Department's latest reports and statistical data.

The nearest District Office should be the starting point for any company that needs international marketing assistance or technical product information. Specialists there can assist local business not only with the Department of Commerce's varied resources and services, but also with matters pertaining to other government agencies. See Appendix V for a complete list of all US&FCS District Offices, including addresses and telephone numbers.

District Export Councils

In addition to the services of its District Offices, the U.S. Department of Commerce gives the exporter direct contact with seasoned exporters experienced in all phases of export trade through its District Export Councils (DEC's). There are 51 DEC's in the United States comprised of approximately 1,700 business and trade experts who serve without compensation and can help U.S. firms enter into the export field.

These DEC's assist in many of the workshops, seminars, and clinics on exporting arranged by the District Offices in cooperation with chambers of commerce, trade associations, banks, trade schools, colleges, and the Small Business Administration. They also arrange for private consultation between experienced and prospective exporters. District Office Directors, who serve as the Executive Secretaries of the DEC's in their respective regions, can provide details on this program.

Export seminars and educational programming

In addition to individual counseling sessions, a very effective method of informing the local business communities of the importance of international trade is through the conference and seminar program. Each year, the US&FCS District Offices conduct approximately 5,000 conferences, seminars, and workshops on topics such as: How to export, documentation and licensing procedures, country-specific market opportunities, export trading companies, and the Caribbean Basin Initiative. The seminars are usually held in conjunction with DEC's, local chambers of commerce, State agencies, and World Trade Clubs. For information on scheduled seminars across the country, or for educational programming assistance, contact the nearest US&FCS District Office.

Assistance available from Department of Commerce specialists in Washington, DC

Visitors to Washington, DC, can receive personal business counseling at the U.S. Department of Commerce. The Export Counseling Center (ECC) within the U.S. and Foreign Commercial Service, ITA, offers guidance on the resources of the Department. Counselors can also schedule appointments with appropriate officials in ITA and other agencies.

In addition, ECC staff can direct visitors to the extensive reference materials related to international trade maintained in ITA libraries. The Foreign Trade Reference Room contains one of the most comprehensive collections of trade statistics in the world.

Other collections contain market research data and a wide range of information on major foreign projects under consideration by international financial institutions and development banks.

Visitors to Washington who would like to obtain appointments or export advice should contact: Export Counseling Center, Room 1066, International Trade Administration, Department of Commerce, Washington, DC 20230. Telephone: (202) 377-3181.

Overseas marketing information and assistance

US&FCS overseas posts

Much of the information about trends and actual trade leads in foreign countries is gathered on site by the commercial officers of the US&FCS. About half of the approximately 175 US&FCS American officers working in 66 countries (with 126 offices) have been hired directly from the private sector, many with international trade experience. All understand firsthand the problems encountered by U.S. companies in their efforts to trade abroad. In addition, a valued asset of the US&FCS is a group of about 500 foreign nationals who provide continuity in commercial programs. Commercial service staff provide a range of services to help companies sell overseas. These include background information on foreign companies, agency-finding services, market research, business counseling, assistance in making appointments with key buyers and government officials, and representations on behalf of companies who are being victimized by trade barriers.

An important function of US&FCS posts is to continually seek out trade and investment opportunities that can benefit U.S. firms. This information is regularly distributed to U.S. firms through the US&FCS' Trade Opportunity Program (TOP). Foreign posts can also actively identify specific overseas buyers and representatives for a U.S. exporter through the Agent/Distributor Service (A/DS) and through distribution of product and service announcements in *Commercial News USA*. The US&FCS operates Export Development Offices to coordinate promotional events for certain posts. (See Chapter 7 for more information on these programs.)

Country desk officers

Country desk officers are another excellent source of information on trade potential in specific countries. These officers are stationed in Washington, DC, under the Assistant Secretary for International Economic Policy (IEP). Every country in the world has a country desk officer assigned to it. These specialists can look at the needs of an individual U.S. firm wishing to sell in a particular country in the full context of that country's overall economy, trade policies, and political situation, and also in light of U.S. policies toward that country.

Desk officers keep up-to-date on the economic and commercial conditions in their assigned countries. Each collects information on the country's regulations, tariffs, business practices, economic and political developments, trade data and trends, market size, and growth. In this way, each keeps tabs on the country's potential as a market for U.S. products, services, and investments.

Country desk officers seek to remove obstacles to U.S. commercial activities in their assigned countries. They develop and recommend trade and investment policy positions for the Department of Commerce and represent the Department in government discussions of the issues. They participate in negotiations of trade and investment agreements, drawing on their country expertise and the policy guidance they have received during government deliberations. They prepare or review Department of Commerce publications on individual countries such as *Overseas Business Reports* and *Foreign Economic Trends*. Often, they work with the 48 US&FCS District Offices in counseling business representatives and arranging seminars on trade and investment in their assigned countries. (See Appendix IV for list of country desks officers.)

Assistance to specific industries

The offices under the Assistant Secretary for Trade Development work to promote trade interests of the U.S. industry. The offices are divided into seven major industry sectors: Aerospace; Automotive Affairs and Consumer Goods; Basic Industries; Capital Goods and International Construction; Science and Electronics; Services; and Textiles and Apparel. Within each sector are specialists for various industries. These specialists work with representatives from industry and trade associations to identify obstacles and trade opportunities by product, industry sector, and market, and to develop plans for international marketing and policy negotiations. (see Appendix IV for a list of specialists in each industry.) Reports on competitive strengths and weaknesses of selected U.S. industries in domestic and international markets have been prepared and are available at low cost either from US&FCS District Offices or from the U.S. Government Printing Office.

Rounding out Trade Development are two units that cover issues that cut across industry sectors:

Trade Information and Analysis gathers, analyzes, and disseminates trade and investment data for use in trade promotion and policy formulation; and Trade Adjustment Assistance, which enables firms that have been hurt by imported products to adjust to international competition. Companies that are eligible for Trade Adjustment Assistance may receive technical consulting to help upgrade operations in such areas as marketing, product engineering, information systems, export promotion, and energy management. The Federal Government may assume up to 75 percent of the cost of these services. For more information, contact the nearest US&FCS District Office or call: (202) 377-4031.

Export Administration

The Assistant Secretary for Trade Administration is responsible for U.S. Export Controls (see Chapter 12). Assistance in complying with export controls can be obtained directly from local US&FCS District Offices or from the Export Assistance Division of ITA's Office of Export Administration in Washington, DC. Telephone: (202) 377-4811.

Minority Business Development Agency (MBDA)

Minority-owned businesses can receive special assistance within the Department from the Minority Business Development Agency. The MBDA is a separate agency within the Department of Commerce that promotes the expansion of minority-owned business. The Agency can provide a variety of services to minority businesses including export assistance. In particular, MBDA's Minority Export Development Consultant program makes private consultant services available at minimal cost to minority firms desiring to export.

Nine consultant organizations have been funded throughout the United States and Puerto Rico to help individual minority-owned companies develop export marketing plans, identify potential markets and trade leads, and provide the technical assistance necessary to complete international transactions, including documentation, short-term financing, and shipping organization in a specific area. Contact: Minority Business Development Agency, U.S. Department of Commerce, Washington, DC 20230. Telephone: (202) 377-2881.

Small Business Administration

Through its field offices in cities throughout the United States (see Appendix V), the U.S. Small Business Administration (SBA) provides counseling to potential and current small-business exporters. These services, available at no cost to eligible recipients, include the following:

- *Export counseling.* Export counseling services are furnished to potential and current small business exporters by executives, advanced business students, and professional consultants. Members of the Service Corps of Retired Executives (SCORE) and the Active Corps of Executives (ACE), with years of practical experience in international trade, assist small firms in evaluating their export potential and strengthening their domestic operations by identifying financial, managerial, or technical problems. These advisors also can help small firms develop and implement basic export marketing plans, which show where and how to sell goods abroad.

- **Small Business Institute/Small Business Development Centers.** Through the Small Business Institute (SBI), advanced business students from more than 450 colleges and universities provide in-depth, long-term counseling under faculty supervision to small businesses. Additional export counseling and assistance are offered through Small Business Development Centers (SBDC's) which are located within some colleges and universities. Students in these two programs provide technical help by developing an export marketing feasibility study and analysis for their client firms.

- **Call Contact Program.** A third facet of the SBA counseling service is the Call Contract Program that uses professional management and technical consultants. This program is employed where firms require highly sophisticated marketing information and production technology to identify and service overseas markets.

- **Export training.** SBA Field Offices co-sponsor export training programs with the Department of Commerce, other Federal agencies, and various private sector international-trade organizations. These programs are conducted by experienced international traders.

- **Financial assistance.** The SBA operates loan guarantee and direct loan programs to assist small business exporters. (See Chapter 11 for more information.)

- **Legal advice.** Through an arrangement with the Federal Bar Association (FBA), exporters may receive initial exporting legal assistance. Under this program, qualified attorneys from the International Law Council of the FBA, working through SBA Field Offices, provide free initial consultations to small companies on the legal aspects of exporting.

For information on any of the programs funded by SBA, contact the nearest SBA field office (see Appendix V for address and phone number).

Department of Agriculture

The U.S. Department of Agriculture's (USDA) export promotion efforts are centered in the Foreign Agricultural Service (FAS), but other USDA agencies offer services to the U.S. exporter of agricultural products. These include the Economic Research Service, the Office of Transportation, the Animal & Plant Health Inspection Service, the Food Safety and Inspection Service, and the Federal Grain Inspection Service. A wide variety of other valuable programs is offered, such as promotion of U.S. farm products in foreign markets, services of commodity and marketing specialists in Washington, DC, trade fair exhibits, publications and information services, and financing programs (brief information on USDA's financing programs is contained in Chapter 11). For more information on programs contact the Director of Export Programs Division, FAS, U.S. Department of Agriculture, Washington, DC. Telephone: (202) 447-6343.

State governments

State development agencies, Departments of Commerce, and other departments within State governments often provide valuable assistance to exporters within the State. State export development programs are growing rapidly. In many areas, county and city economic development agencies also have export assistance programs. The aid offered by these groups typically includes:

- **Export education**—helping the exporter analyze export potential and orienting the firm to export techniques and strategies. This help may take the form of group seminars or individual counseling sessions.

- **Marketing assistance**—identifying potential markets for U.S. products or services, including trade leads.

- **Market development**—helping select export strategies and obtain financing, counseling on packaging, shipping, etc.

- **Trade missions**—organizing trips abroad enabling exporters to call on potential foreign customers. (For more information on trade missions, see Chapter 7.)

- **Trade shows**—organizing and sponsoring exhibitions of State-produced goods and services in overseas markets.

Appendix V of this GUIDE lists the agencies in each State responsible for export assistance to local firms. Also included are the names of other government and private organizations, with their telephone numbers and addresses. The chart at the beginning of Appendix V gives a quick overview of the types of services currently available from each State development agency. Readers interested in the role played by State development agencies in promoting and supporting exports may also wish to contact the National Association of State Development Agencies (NASDA), 444 North Capitol Street, Washington, DC 20001. Telephone: (202) 624-5411.

To determine if a particular county or city has local export assistance programs, contact the appropriate economic development agency. Appendix V includes contact information for several major cities.

Commercial banks

More than 300 U.S. banks have international banking departments with specialists familiar with specific foreign countries and various types of commodities and transactions. These large banks, located in major U.S. cities, maintain correspondent relationships with smaller banks throughout the country. Larger banks also maintain correspondent relationships with banks in most foreign countries or operate their own overseas branches, providing a direct channel to foreign customers.

International banking specialists are generally well informed about export matters, even in areas that fall outside the usual limits of international banking. If they are unable to provide direct guidance or assistance, they may be able to refer inquirers to other specialists who can. Banks frequently provide consultation and guidance free of charge to their clients, since they derive income primarily from loans to the exporter and from fees for special services. Many banks also have publications available to help exporters. These materials often cover particular countries and their business practices and can be a valuable tool for initial familiarization with foreign industry.

The many services a commercial bank may perform for its clients include:

- Advice on export regulations.
- Exchange of currencies.
- Assistance in financing exports.
- Collection of foreign invoices, drafts, letters of credit, and other foreign receivables.
- Transfer of funds to other countries.
- Letters of introduction and letters of credit for travelers.
- Credit information on potential buyers overseas.
- Credit assistance to the exporter's foreign buyers.

Trading companies

Trading companies are of many different types, ranging from giant international companies, many foreign owned, to highly specialized, small operations. Export Management Companies (EMC's) and Export Trading Companies (ETC's) are similar types of trading companies that provide a multitude of services, such as performing market research, appointing overseas distributors or commission representatives, exhibiting a client's products at international trade shows, advertising, shipping,

and arranging documentation. In short, the trading company can take full responsibility for the export end of the business, relieving the manufacturer of all the details except filling orders. Trading companies may work simultaneously for a number of exporters, and they may buy and sell or work on the basis of a commission, salary, or retainer plus commission. Often, products of a trading company's clients are related, although the items usually are noncompetitive. The advantage of a trading company is that it can immediately make available marketing resources that would take years for a smaller firm to develop on its own. Many trading companies also finance sales and extend credit, facilitating prompt payment to the exporter. For more information on using EMC's and ETC's, see Chapter 4.

World trade clubs

Local or regional world trade clubs are composed of area business people who represent firms engaged in international trade and shipping, banks, forwarders, customs brokers, government agencies, and other service organizations involved in world trade. These clubs conduct educational programs on international trade and organize promotional events to stimulate interest in world trade.

By participating in a local association, a company can receive valuable and timely advice on world markets and opportunities from business people who are already knowledgeable on virtually any facet of international business. Another important advantage of membership in a local world trade club is the availability of benefits—such as services, discounts and contacts—in affiliated clubs from foreign countries.

Chambers of commerce and trade associations

Many local chambers of commerce and major trade associations in the United States provide sophisticated and extensive services for members interested in exporting. Such services include:

- Export seminars, workshops and roundtables geared to specific industry interests.
- Documenting (providing certificates of origin).
- Trade promotion, including overseas missions, mailings and event planning.
- Organization of U.S. pavilions in foreign trade shows.
- Contacts with foreign companies and distributors.
- Transportation routings and consolidating shipments.
- Hosting of visiting trade missions.
- International activities at their own domestic trade shows.

9

In addition, some industry associations can supply detailed information on market demand for products in selected countries and refer members to export management companies. Most trade associations play an active role in lobbying for U.S. trade policies beneficial to their industries.

Industry trade associations typically collect and maintain files on international trade news and trends affecting manufacturers. Often they publish articles and newsletters that include government research as soon as it is made available.

American chambers of commerce abroad

A valuable and reliable source of market information in any foreign country is the local American chamber of commerce. Secretaries of these organizations are knowledgeable about local trade opportunities, actual and potential competition, periods of maximum trade activity, and similar considerations.

American chambers of commerce abroad usually handle inquiries from any U.S. business. Detailed service, however, is ordinarily undertaken free of charge only for members of affiliated organizations. Some chambers have a set schedule of charges for services rendered to non-members. For contact information on American Chambers in major foreign markets, see Appendix VI.

International trade consultants and other advisors

International trade consultants can advise and assist a manufacturer on all aspects of foreign marketing. Trade consultants do not normally deal specifically with one product, although they may advise on product adaptation to a foreign market. They research domestic and foreign regulations and also assess commercial and political risk. They conduct foreign market research and establish contacts with foreign government agencies and other necessary resources, such as advertising companies, product service facilities, and local attorneys.

These consultants can locate and qualify foreign joint venture partners and conduct feasibility studies for the sale of manufacturing rights, the location and construction of manufacturing facilities, and the establishment of foreign branches. After sales agreements are completed, trade consultants can also ensure that follow-through is smooth and that any problems that arise are dealt with effectively.

Trade consultants usually specialize by subject matter and by global area or country. For example, firms may specialize in high technology exports to the Far East. Their consultants can advise on which agents or distributors are likely to be successful, what kinds of promotion are needed, who the competitors are, and how to deal with them. They are also knowledgeable about foreign government regulations, contract laws, and taxation. Some firms may be more specialized than others; for example, some may be thoroughly knowledgeable on legal aspects and taxation and less knowledgeable on marketing strategies.

Many large accounting firms, law firms, and specialized marketing firms provide international trade consulting services. When selecting a consulting firm, the exporter should pay particular attention to the experience and knowledge of the consultant who is in charge of its project. To find an appropriate firm, advice should be sought from other exporters and some of the other resources listed in this chapter, such as the US&FCS District Office or local chambers of commerce.

Consultants are of greatest value to a firm that knows exactly what it wants. For this reason, and because private consultants are expensive, it pays to take full advantage of publicly funded sources of advice before hiring a consultant.

Market research

3

Market research includes all methods that a company uses to determine which foreign markets have the best potential for its products. Results of this research inform the firm of:

- The largest markets for its product.
- The fastest growing markets.
- Market trends and outlook.
- Market conditions and practices.
- Competitive firms and products.

A firm may begin to export without conducting any market research if it receives unsolicited orders from abroad. While this type of selling is valuable, the firm may discover even more promising markets by conducting a systematic search. A firm opting to export indirectly (see Chapter 4) by using an export management company (EMC) may wish to select markets to enter before selecting the EMC, since many EMC's have strengths in specific markets but not in others.

Some of the questions that market research can answer are listed below.

Questions to guide market research

- Is there an overseas market for the firm's products or services?
- Are there specific foreign markets that look promising?
- What new markets are likely to open up or expand abroad?
- What is the size of the market and where is it heading?
- What are the major economic, political, legal, social, technological, and other environmental factors in the market?
- What are the demographic and cultural characteristics of the market, such as disposable income, occupation, age, sex, opinions, interests, activities, tastes, values, etc.?
- Who are present and potential customers abroad?
- What are their needs and desires?
- How would the product or service be used?
- What is the nature of competition in the foreign market?
- Who are the major direct and indirect competitors?
- How are competitive products distributed, promoted and sold?
- Are there any foreign government barriers or incentives?

Adapted from: Vinay Kothari, "Researching for Export/Marketing" in *Export Promotion*, M. Czinkota, Ed., Praeger Publishers, New York, NY 1983 pp. 154-176.

A firm may research a market by using either primary or secondary data resources. In conducting primary market research, a company collects data directly from the foreign marketplace through interviews, surveys, and other direct contact with representatives and potential buyers. Primary market research has the advantage of being tailored to the company's needs and provides answers to specific questions, but the collection of such data is time consuming and expensive.

In conducting secondary market research, a company collects data from compiled sources, such as trade statistics for a country or a product. Working with secondary sources is less expensive and helps the company to focus its marketing efforts. Although secondary data sources are critical to market research, they do have limitations. The most recent statistics for some countries may be over 2 years old. Product breakdowns may be too broad to be of much value to a company. Statistics on services are often unavailable. Finally, statistics may be distorted by incomplete data gathering techniques. Yet, even with these limitations, secondary research is a valuable and relatively easy first step for a company to take. It may be the only step needed if the company decides to export indirectly through an intermediary, since the other firm may have advanced research capabilities.

Methods of market research

Because of the expense of primary market research, most firms rely on secondary data sources. Secondary market research is conducted in three basic ways:

- The first is by keeping abreast of world events that influence the international marketplace, watching for announcement of specific projects, or simply visiting likely markets. For example, a thawing of political hostilities often leads to the opening of economic channels between countries.
- The second method is through analysis of trade and economic statistics. Trade statistics are generally compiled by product category (often by SIC code) and by country. These statistics provide the U.S. firm with information concerning shipments of its products over specified periods of time. Demographic and general economic statistics, such as population size and make-up, per capita income, and production levels by industry can be important indicators of the market potential for a company's products.

- The third method is to obtain the advice of experts. A company may accomplish this by:
  — Contacting trade specialists at the Department of Commerce and other government agencies.
  — Attending seminars, workshops, and international trade shows.
  — Hiring an international trade and marketing consultant.
  — Talking to successful exporters of similar products.
  — Contacting trade and industry association staff.

Gathering and evaluating secondary market research can be complex and tedious. However, there are several publications available that can help simplify the process. The following approach to market research refers to these publications and resources described later in this chapter.

A step-by-step approach to market research

The U.S. company may find the following approach useful:

Screen potential markets

Step 1. Obtain export statistics that indicate product exports to various countries. *Export Statistics Profiles (ESP)* from the Department of Commerce can assist. If ESP's are not available for a certain product, the firm should consult the *Custom Statistical Service* (Commerce), *Foreign Trade Report, FT 410* (Census), *Export Information System Data Reports* (Small Business Administration) or *Annual Worldwide Industry Reviews* (Commerce).

Step 2. Identify 5-10 large and fast growing markets for the firm's product. Look at these over time (the past 3-5 years). Has market growth been consistent year to year? Did import growth occur even during periods of economic recession? If not, did growth resume with economic recovery?

Step 3. Identify some smaller but fast-emerging markets that may provide ground floor opportunities. If the market is just beginning to open up, there may be fewer competitors than in established markets. Growth rates should be substantially higher in these countries to qualify as up-and-coming markets, given the lower starting point.

Step 4. Target three to five of the most statistically promising markets for further assessment. Consult with US&FCS District Offices, business associates, freight forwarders and others to help refine targeted markets.

Assess targeted markets

Step 1. Examine trends for company products, as well as trends regarding related products that could influence demand. Calculate overall consumption of the product and the amount accounted for by imports. *International Market Research - IMR, Country Market Surveys - CMS's, Country Trade Statistics - CTS, Export Statistics Profiles - ESP's, Annual Worldwide Industry Reviews - AWIR's,* (all Commerce) give economic backgrounds and market trends for each country. Demographic information (population, age, etc.) can be obtained from *World Population* (Census) and *Statistical Yearbook* (United Nations).

Step 2. Ascertain the sources of competition, including the extent of domestic industry production and the major foreign countries the firm is competing against in each targeted market. *IMR Studies* and *CMS's* (both from Commerce) can be helpful. Look at U.S. market share.

Step 3. Analyze factors affecting marketing and use of the product in each market, such as end-user sectors, channels of distribution, cultural idiosyncrasies, and business practices. Again, *IMR Studies* and *CMS's* are useful.

Step 4. Identify any foreign barriers (tariff or non-tariff) for the product being imported into the country (see Chapter 12 for an analysis of tariff and non-tariff barriers). Identify any U.S. barriers (such as export controls) affecting exports to the country. *IMR Studies* and *CMS* are useful.

Step 5. Identify any U.S. or foreign government incentives to promote exporting the product or service. Once again, *IMR Studies* and *CMS* are helpful.

Draw conclusions

After analyzing the data, the company may conclude that its marketing resources would be better used if applied to a few countries. In general, company efforts should be directed to fewer than 10 markets if the firm is new to exporting; one or two countries may be enough to start with. The company's internal resources should help determine its level of effort.

The following section describes the publications mentioned above and includes additional sources. Because there are many research sources, the firm may wish to seek advice from a US&FCS District Office (see Appendix V).

Sources of market research

There are many domestic, foreign, and international sources of information concerning foreign markets. Several of these sources are given here, and others may be found in the bibliography in Appendix VIII. Available information ranges from simple trade statistics to in-depth market surveys.

Trade statistics indicate total exports or imports by country and by product and allow an exporter to compare the size of the market for a product among various countries. Some statistics also reflect the U.S. share of the total country market in order to gauge the overall competitiveness of U.S. producers. By looking at statistics over several years, an exporter can determine which markets are growing and which are shrinking.

Market surveys provide a narrative description and assessment of particular markets along with relevant statistics. The reports are often based on original research conducted in the countries studied and may include specific information on both buyers and competitors.

The potential exporter may find many of the reports referred to below at a US&FCS District Office (see Appendix V) or at a business or university library. In addition, the Foreign Trade Reference Room in the U.S. Department of Commerce in Washington, DC, (Room 2233) offers extensive trade statistics.

The sources that follow are listed in three groups. The first group, Product/industry data resources, is useful when a U.S. firm wants to compare and select foreign markets for a specific product or industry. The second group, Country data resources, is useful when a company has tentatively selected one or more countries for its exports and wants more detailed information on its product's market or on economic and political conditions in the area. Actual trade leads and contacts may also be provided, as well as special market conditions, such as trade barriers. The third group, Worldwide background data, provides information on all countries concerning demographics, production, GNP, trade policy, political climate, consumer profiles, and trends.

Product/industry data resources

- **Export Statistics Profiles (ESP).** This publication analyzes exports for a single industry — product-by-product, country-by-country—over each of the last 5 years to date. Data are often rank-ordered by dollar value to identify quickly the leading products and industries. The basic element of the ESP consists of tables showing the sales of each product in the industry to each country, as well as competitive information, growth, and future trends. Each ESP also includes an Export Market Brief — a narrative analysis highlighting the industry's prospects, performance, and leading products. ESP's are currently available for 35 industries; the cost for each is $70. Contact the local US&FCS District Office or call (202) 377-2432.

- **Custom Statistical Service.** This service offers data on products not covered in one of the standard

ESP industries. In addition, this service allows the exporter to tailor data to meet his or her specific needs. Data are available in formats different from those contained in the standard ESP, such as quantity and unit value and percentages, as well as for imports of products. The cost ranges from $50 to over $1000. Contact the local US&FCS District Office or call (202) 377-2432.

- **Foreign Trade Report, FT 410.** The monthly FT 410 provides a statistical record of shipments of all merchandise from the United States to foreign countries, including both the quantity and dollar value of exports to each country during the month covered by the report. It also contains cumulative export statistics from the first of the calendar year. Report FT 410 (monthly and cumulative for U.S. Exports, Schedule E Commodity by Country) is available by subscription from the Superintendent of Documents, U.S. Government Printing Office, Washington, DC 20402, (202) 783-3238. The cost is $9.50 per single issue, $100 for a year's subscription. The reports may also be available at US&FCS District Offices and many large libraries.

- **International Market Research (IMR).** These reports are in-depth analyses for those who want a more complete picture for one industry in one country. A report includes information such as market size and outlook, end-user analysis, distribution channels, cultural characteristics, business customs and practices, competitive situation, trade barriers, and trade contacts. IMRs cost $50 to $200. Contact the local US&FCS District Office or call (202) 377-2432.

- **Country Market Surveys (CMS).** These surveys are 8- to 12-page summaries of IMR reports on industry themes. They highlight market size, trends, and prospects in an easy-to-read format. The CMS cost $10 for each country. Contact the local US&FCS District Office or call (202) 377-2432.

- **Competitive Assessments.** The U.S. Department of Commerce has published over 20 industry studies that examine the present and future international competitiveness of each industry. Industries examined range from solid wood products to fiber optics. Topics usually include industry performance, recent foreign competition (and foreign government assistance), U.S. Government assistance, trends, and an assessment of future international competitiveness. Prices for the reports are usually $4 - $6. Contact the local US&FCS District Office or the Office of Trade Information and Analysis, Industrial Analysis Division, Room 4881, U.S. Department of Commerce, Washington, DC 20230. Tel: (202) 377-4944.

- **Annual Worldwide Industry Reviews (AWIR).** This product is a combination of country-by-country market assessments, export trends, and 5-year statistical tables of U.S. exports for a single industry

13

integrated into a report of one to three volumes. They show an industry's performance for the most recent year in many countries. Each volume covers 9-20 countries. A single volume costs $200, two volumes within the same industry cost $350, and three volumes within the same industry, $500. Contact the local US&FCS District Office or call (202) 377-2432.

- **Product Market Profiles (PMP).** A PMP is a single product, multicountry report that includes trade contacts, specific trade leads, and statistical analysis. The cost is $300 to $500. Contact the local US&FCS District Office or call (202) 377-2432.

- **Comparison Shopping Service.** This service provides a custom-tailored export market research survey on a U.S. client firm's specific product in a single country. The survey covers key marketing factors in the target country, including overall marketability, names of competitors, comparative prices, entry and distribution channels, and names of potential sales representatives or licensees. The survey is conducted on-site by U.S. commercial officers. The service is available for standard off-the-shelf products (no custom or specialty items) in selected countries. The cost is $500 per country involved.

- **Market Share Reports.** This product provides basic data to evaluate overall trends in the size of markets for exporters. Also measures changes in the import demand for specific products and compares the competitive position of U.S. and foreign exporters. Commodity reports cost $6.50 each. Contact the National Technical Information Service, U.S. Department of Commerce, Box 1553, Springfield, VA 22161. Telephone: (202) 487-4630.

- **Export Information System (XIS) Data Reports.** Available from the U.S. Small Business Administration (SBA) for approximately 1700 product categories, the XIS Data Reports provide to a small business a list of the 25 largest importing markets for its product, the 10 best markets for U.S. exporters of that product, the trends within those markets and the major sources of foreign competition, based on Department of Commerce and United Nations data. There is no charge to small businesses for this service. For more information, the local SBA Field Office should be contacted.

- **FINDEX: The Directory of Market Research Reports, Studies and Surveys.** This publication contains over 10,000 listings of market research reports, studies, and surveys and costs $245. Contact FIND/SVP The Information Clearinghouse, 500 Fifth Avenue, New York, NY 10036. Telephone: (212) 354-2424.

Country Data Resources:

- **Country Market Profiles (CMP).** These are single country, multi-industry reports that include

relevant trade statistics, economic and market analysis, and trade contacts in a single report. The cost is $300 per country report. Contact the local US&FCS District Office or call (202) 377-2432.

- **Country Trade Statistics (CTS).** Each CTS gives details of all U.S. exports to a single country over the most recent 5 year period. They show the exporter which U.S. industries look best for export to a particular country. Each country report contains four key statistical tables showing the leading and fastest growing U.S. exports of about 200 product categories to the country. The cost is $25 for each country with discounts for multicountry orders. Contact the local US&FCS District Office or call (202) 377-2432.

- **Foreign Economic Trends (FET).** FET's present current business and economic developments and the latest economic indicators for more than 100 countries. FET's are prepared either annually or semiannually depending on the country. The price for an annual subscription is $66, single copies are $1.75 each. Contact the local US&FCS District Office or call (202) 377-2432.

- **International Market Information (IMI).** These special bulletins point out unique market situations and new opportunities to U.S. exporters in specific markets. IMI's cost $15 to $100. Contact the local US&FCS District Office or call (202) 377-2432.

- **Overseas Business Reports (OBR's).** The reports provide background statistics and information on specific countries useful to exporters. They present economic and commercial profiles, issue semiannual outlooks for U.S. trade, and publish selected statistical reports on the direction, volume, and nature of U.S. foreign trade with the country. An annual subscription is $44 and can be ordered by contacting the Superintendent of Documents, U.S. Government Printing Office, Washington, DC 20402. Telephone: (202) 783-3238.

- **Background Notes.** This series surveys a country's people, geography, economy, government, and foreign policy. Prepared by the Department of State, it includes important national economic and trade information, including major trading partners. Annual subscription is $34 and can be ordered by contacting the Superintendent of Documents, U.S. Government Printing Office, Washington, DC 20402. Telephone: (202) 783-3238.

- **U.S. Agency for International Development's Congressional Presentations.** These publications provide country-by-country data on nations to which the agency will provide funds in the coming year. The publications also provide detailed information on past funding activities in each individual country. In addition, the publications list projects and their locations that the agency desires to fund in the upcoming year (i.e. a hydro-electrical project in Egypt). Since these projects require U.S. goods and services, the **Congressional Presentations** can give U.S. exporters an opportunity to plan ahead by allowing an early look at potential projects (see Chapter 7 for more details on the Agency's programs). For ordering information, contact the U.S. Agency for International Development (AID), Department of State, Washington, DC 20523. Telephone: (703) 235-1840.

- **Trade and Development Program's Congressional Presentation.** This publication reports the dollar amount spent by the agency by industry in specific countries around the world for the past several years. (For a description of Trade and Development activities to stimulate U.S. exports, see Chapter 7.) For ordering information about Trade and Development's **Congressional Presentation,** contact Trade and Development Program, U.S. Department of State, Washington, DC 20523. Telephone: (703) 235-3663.

- **Exporters Encyclopedia.** An extensive handbook on exporting, this publication contains market information on over 220 world markets, which are individually covered. The cost is $365. Contact Dun's Marketing Services, Three Century Drive, Parsippany, NJ 07054. Telephone: (800) 526-0651 (toll free).

- **Doing Business in Foreign Countries.** A series on doing business in most foreign countries, these individual guides are often provided to clients or interested parties by some large or international accounting firms, banks, or other service firms. These publications provide information on specific countries and include demographic and cultural backgrounds, economic climates, restrictions and incentives to trade, duties, documentation requirements, tax structure, and other useful information.

Worldwide background data

- **Statistical Yearbook.** This international trade information on products is provided by the United Nations. Information on importing countries and, to help assess competition, exports by country are included. Paperback version costs $55, clothbound costs $65. Order by calling 800-521-8110 (toll free).

- **World Population.** The U.S. Bureau of the Census collects and analyzes worldwide demographic data that can assist exporters in identifying potential markets for their products. Information on each country—total population, fertility, mortality, urban population, growth rate, and life expectancy—is updated every 2 years. Also published are detailed demographic profiles (including analysis of labor force structure, infant mortality, etc.) of individual countries (price and availability varies). **World Population** is free. Contact the Center for International Research, Room 407, Scuderi Building, U.S. Bureau of the Census, Washington, DC 20233.

- **International Economic Indicators.** These are quarterly reports providing basic data (for years and quarters) on the economies of the United States and seven principal industrial countries. They include statistics on gross national product, industrial production, trade, prices, finance, and labor; they also measure changes in key competitive indicators. The reports can provide an overall view of international trends or a basis for more detailed analyses of the economic situation. Annual subscription is available for $13 through: ITA Publications Sales Branch, Room 1617D, U.S. Department of Commerce, Washington, DC 20230. A single issue costs $4.

- **International Financial Statistics.** This is a monthly publication produced by the International Monetary Fund. It presents statistics on exchange rates, money and banking, production, government finance, interest rates, and other subjects. The subscription rate for 12 monthly issues, including a yearbook issue and two supplemental series with expanded coverage is $100. The single issue cost is $10. Available from the International Monetary Fund, Publications Unit, 700 19th Street, NW., Washington, DC 20431. Telephone: (202) 473-7430.

- **World Bank Atlas.** Published by the World Bank, this publication presents population, gross domestic product, and average growth rates for every country. The price is $2.50 and is available from World Bank Publications, P.O. Box 37525, Washington, DC 20013.

Department of Commerce

The U.S. Department of Commerce provides information on markets through seminars and personal counseling in local U.S. and Foreign Commercial Service (US&FCS) District Offices (see Appendix V). In addition, several offices of the Department of Commerce in Washington, DC offer specific market information to the U.S. company. These include:

US&FCS Foreign Operations

The US&FCS Foreign Operations staff supports and represents U.S. trade interests abroad, particularly in export expansion. Approximately 175 US&FCS officers currently maintain offices in 66 countries. US&FCS officers develop country marketing strategies and can readily assist a business in its market research efforts. Regional Coordinators for the US&FCS can be contacted by calling:

- Africa, Near East and South Asia: (202) 377-1599
- East Asia and Pacific: (202) 377-3922
- Europe: (202) 377-2736
- Western Hemisphere: (202) 377-2736

Export Counseling Center and Market Research Division

These US&FCS offices provide U.S. firms with assistance in market research efforts. The Export Counseling Center provides counseling on market research (among many other services) for a company's products and services overseas. The Export Counseling Center can be reached at (202) 377-3181. Many of the research reports described in this chapter are planned and prepared by the Office of Product Development and Distribution, Market Research Division, (202) 377-5037.

Product/service sector counseling

Trade and industry specialists within the Department of Commerce specialize in particular products or services and can provide information on potential markets, as well as other assistance. Specialists in the following areas are available:

- Aerospace: (202) 377-8228
- Automotive and Consumer Goods: (202) 377-5783
- Basic Industries: (202) 377-0614
- Capital Goods and International Construction: (202) 377-5455
- Science and Electronics: (202) 377-4466
- Services: (202) 377-3575
- Textiles and Apparel: (202) 377-2043

Each of these sectors has within it specialists for particular industries. The offices of these specialists are listed in Appendix IV.

Country counseling

Specific country counseling is available to a U.S. company through the Country Desk Officers within the Department of Commerce. There is at least one individual assigned to each country in the world, available to give advice on markets and related topics for that country. Country Desk Specialists are listed in Appendix IV.

Small Business Administration

Although known primarily for financial assistance, the Small Business Administration (SBA) also provides market related information to the U.S. business community. For more information on SBA counseling, the firm should contact its local SBA field office (see Appendix V).

Department of Agriculture

The Department of Agriculture's Foreign Agricultural Service (FAS) administers several programs to assist the U.S. firm in its research efforts. Agricultural Attaches, Agricultural Overseas Trade Offices, and Commodity and Marketing Specialists can all assist the exporter in researching markets for agricultural products. Contact FAS Media and Public Affairs Branch, U.S. Department of Agriculture, Room 5918-South, Washington, DC 20250, (202) 447-7937.

Associations and consultants

Many associations can provide advice on markets for the company's research efforts through publications or through direct advice by an international expert. Some consulting firms also provide market research assistance. Consultants may have expertise in a specific market (Japan, for example), or in specific industries (e.g., computer marketing). Before the U.S. company selects a consultant to perform research, it should examine samples of the consultant's work, and if possible, obtain specific recommendations from previous clients.

Methods of exporting and channels of distribution

4

As described in Chapter 1, the most common methods of exporting are indirect selling and direct selling. In indirect selling, a second U.S. firm acts as a sales intermediary and normally assumes responsibility for finding overseas buyers and shipping products. In direct selling, the original U.S. firm deals directly with a foreign firm.

There are several factors to consider when deciding whether to market indirectly or directly, including:

- The size of the firm;
- The nature of its products;
- Previous export experience and expertise; and
- Business conditions in the selected overseas markets.

The paramount consideration in determining whether to market indirectly or directly is the level of resources a company is willing to devote to the international marketing effort.

Distribution considerations

- Which channels of distribution should the firm use to market its products abroad?
- Where should the firm produce its products and how should it distribute them in the foreign market?
- What types of agents, brokers, wholesalers, dealers, distributors, retailers, etc., should the firm use?
- What are the characteristics and capabilities of the available intermediaries?
- Should the assistance of an EMC (export management company) be acquired?

Indirect exporting

The principal advantage of indirect marketing for a smaller U.S. company is that it provides a way to penetrate foreign markets without getting involved in the complexities and risks of exporting. There are several kinds of intermediary firms that provide a range of export services. Each type of firm offers distinct advantages for the U.S. company.

Commission agents

Commission or buying agents are "finders" for foreign firms that want to purchase U.S. products. They seek to obtain the desired items at the lowest possible price and are paid a commission by their foreign clients. In some cases, they may be foreign government agencies or quasi-governmental firms empowered to locate and purchase desired goods. Foreign government purchasing missions are one example.

Export management companies

An export management company (EMC) acts as the export department for one or several manufacturers of noncompetitive products. It solicits and transacts business in the names of the manufacturers it represents or in its own name for a commission, salary, or retainer plus commission. Some EMC's provide immediate payment for the manufacturer's products by either arranging financing or directly purchasing products for resale. Typically, only larger EMC's can afford to purchase or finance exports.

There are over 2,000 EMC's in the United States, the majority of which are small. Due to their size limitations, EMC's usually specialize either by product, by foreign market, or both. Because of their specialization, the best EMC's know their products and the markets they serve very well and usually have well-established networks of foreign distributors already in place. This immediate access to foreign markets is one of the principal reasons for using an EMC, since establishing a productive relationship with a foreign representative may be a costly and lengthy process.

One disadvantage in using an EMC is that a manufacturer may lose control over foreign sales. Most manufacturers are properly concerned that their product and company image be well maintained in foreign markets. An important way for a company to retain sufficient control in such an arrangement is to carefully select an EMC that can meet the company's needs and maintain close communications with it. For example, a company may ask for regular reports on efforts to market its products and may require approval of certain types of efforts, such as advertising programs or service arrangements. If a company wants to maintain this type of relationship with an EMC, it should negotiate points of concern before entering an agreement, since not all EMC's are willing to comply with the company's concerns.

A further description of services rendered to exporters by EMC's (and suggestions for choosing an appropriate firm) is available through the U.S. Department of Commerce's pamphlet, The *EMC— Your Export Department.* (Publications Distribution, Room 1617D, U.S. Department of Commerce, Washington, DC 20230). Also, the Association of Export Management Companies in New York can be contacted for a list of EMC's in different regions (see Appendix VII.) *The Directory of Leading U.S. Export Management Companies* is available from Bergano Book Company, P.O. Box 190, Fairfield, CT. 06430. $37.50.

Export trading companies

An export trading company (ETC) is an organization designed to facilitate the export of U.S. goods and services. It can be either a trade intermediary, providing export related services to producers, or an organization set up by producers themselves. An ETC is similar to an export management company. Traditionally, however, EMC's do not take title to goods being exported and typically provide only export facilitation services. An ETC is generally understood to be an organization that provides a broader range of services than an EMC, though there may be little practical distinction.

The goals of the Export Trading Company Act, passed in 1982, are to stimulate U.S. exports by: 1) promoting and encouraging the formation of export trading companies, 2) expanding the options available for export financing by permitting bank holding companies to invest in export trading companies and reducing restrictions on trade finance provided by financial institutions, and 3) reducing uncertainty regarding the application of U.S. antitrust law to export operations. This Act allows banks, for the first time in recent history, to make equity investments in those commercial ventures qualifying as export trading companies. In addition, for the first time, the EximBank is allowed to make working capital guarantees to U.S. exporters. Through the Office of Export Trading Company Affairs (OETCA) within the International Trade Administration, the Department of Commerce promotes the formation of export trading companies, administers the antitrust certification process, and issues Certificates of Review.

OETCA informs the business community of the benefits of ETC's through conferences, presentations before trade associations and civic organizations, and publications. The major publication covering ETC's is the *Export Trading Company Guidebook,* which provides examples of model ETC's. OETCA provides specific assistance to businesses seeking to take advantage of the Act.

OETCA has also established the Contact Facilitation Service (CFS) to provide an information clearinghouse for producers of U.S. goods and services and for organizations that provide trade facilitation services. A CFS directory is updated and published annually. The directory provides users with the names and addresses of banks, ETC's, manufacturing firms, and service organizations as well as the export products or the export related services that these firms supply.

The Certificates of Review are issued by the Secretary of Commerce with the concurrence of the Department of Justice. Any U.S. corporation or partnership, any resident individual, and State or local entity may apply for a Certificate of Review. A certificate can be issued to an applicant if it is determined that the proposed "export trade activities and methods of operation" will not result in a substantial lessening of domestic competition or restraint of trade within the U.S. For the conduct covered by the certificate, its holder (and other individuals or firms named as members) is given immunity from government suits under U.S. Federal and State antitrust laws. In private party actions, liability is reduced from treble to single damages, greatly reducing the probability of nuisance suits. The Certificate of Review program provides exporters with an antitrust "insurance policy" intended to foster joint activities where economies of scale and risk diversification can be achieved. The Act also amends the Sherman and FTC Acts to clarify the jurisdictional reach of these statutes to export trade. Both acts now apply to export trade only if there is a "direct substantial and reasonably foreseeable" effect on domestic commerce or the export commerce of a U.S. competitor.

Firms and individuals interested in obtaining a copy of either the *Export Trading Company Guidebook* or the *Contact Facilitation Service Directory,* or who are interested in additional information, should contact the Office of Export Trading Company Affairs, Room 5618, U.S. Department of Commerce, Washington, DC 20230. Telephone: (202) 377-5131.

Export agents, merchants or remarketers

Export agents, merchants, or remarketers purchase products directly from the manufacturer, packing and marking the products according to their own specifications. They then sell overseas through their contacts, in their own names, and assume all risks for accounts.

In transactions with export agents, merchants, or remarketers, a U.S. firm relinquishes control over the marketing promotion of its product, which could have an adverse effect on future sales efforts abroad. For example, the product could be underpriced or incorrectly positioned in the market or, after sales, service could be neglected.

Piggyback marketing

Piggyback marketing is an arrangement in which one manufacturer or service firm distributes another's product or service. The most common piggybacking situation is when a U.S. company has a contract with an overseas buyer to provide a wide range of products or services. Often, this company does not produce all of the products it is under contract to provide, and it turns to other U.S. companies to provide the remaining products. The original U.S. producer piggybacks its products to the international marketplace, generally without incurring the marketing and distribution costs associated with exporting. Successful arrangements usually require that the product lines be complementary and appealing to the same customers.

State-controlled trading companies

Some socialist countries have State trading monopolies that control all foreign trade. Worldwide changes in foreign policy, however, can have a profound impact on international trade with these countries. Because of this, they may become important markets in the future. For the time being, however, export opportunities to most socialist countries are found primarily for such items as raw materials, agricultural machinery, and manufacturing equipment, rather than high technology products, consumer or household goods. This is due to the shortage of foreign exchange and the emphasis on self-sufficiency, as well as national security concerns.

Direct exporting

The advantages of direct exporting for a U.S. company include more control over the export process, potentially higher profits, and a closer relationship to the overseas buyer and marketplace. These advantages do not come easily, however, since the U.S. company needs to devote more time, personnel, and other corporate resources than are needed with indirect exporting.

When a company chooses to export directly to foreign markets, bypassing the use of EMC's or other intermediaries in the United States, it usually makes internal organizational changes to support more complex functions. A direct exporter normally selects the markets it wishes to penetrate, chooses the best channels of distribution for each market, and then makes specific foreign business connections in order to sell its product. The rest of this Chapter discusses these aspects of direct exporting in more detail.

Organizing for exporting

A company new to exporting generally treats its export sales no differently from domestic sales, using existing personnel and organizational structures. As international sales and inquiries increase, however, the company may separate the management of its exports from that of its domestic sales.

The advantages of separating international from domestic business include the centralization of specialized skills needed to deal with the international marketplace. Another advantage is a focused marketing effort, one that is more likely to lead to increased international sales. A possible disadvantage of such a separation is the less efficient use of corporate resources due to segmentation.

When a company separates international from domestic business, it may do so at different levels within the organization. For example, when a company first begins to export, it may create an export department with a full or part-time manager who reports to the head of domestic sales and marketing. At later stages a company may choose to increase the autonomy of the export department to the point of creating an international division that reports directly to the president.

Larger companies at advanced stages of exporting may choose to retain the international division or to organize along product or geographic lines. If a company has distinct product lines, it may choose to create an international department within each product division. A company with products that have common end-users may choose to organize geographically; for example, it may form a division for Europe, another for the Far East, etc.

The above examples of organizing a separate international structure within a company generally apply once international sales become significant or within a large company with substantial financial resources. A small company's initial needs may be satisfied by a single export manager who has responsibility for the full range of international activities.

Regardless of how a company organizes for exporting, it should insure that the organization facilitates the marketer's job. Successful marketing skills can help the firm overcome the handicap of operating in an unfamiliar market. Experience has shown that a company's success in foreign markets depends less on the unique attributes of its products than on its marketing methods.

Once a company has been organized to handle exporting, the proper channel of distribution needs to be selected in each market. These channels include agents, distributors, retailers and end-users.

Sales representatives or agents

Overseas, a sales representative is the equivalent of a manufacturer's representative here in the United States. The representative uses the company's product literature and samples to present the product to potential buyers. The sales representative usually works on a commission basis, assumes no risk or responsibility, and is under contract for a definite period of time (renewable by mutual agreement). The contract defines territory, terms of sale, method of compensation, and other details. The sales representative may operate on either an exclusive or nonexclusive basis.

Distributors

The foreign distributor is a merchant who purchases merchandise from a U.S. exporter (often at substantial discount) and resells it at a profit. The foreign distributor generally provides support and service for the product, relieving the U.S. company of these responsibilities. The distributor usually carries an inventory of products, a sufficient supply of spare parts, and maintains adequate facilities and personnel for normal servicing operations. The distributor normally carries noncompetitive but complementary products.

The payment terms and length of association between the U.S. company and the foreign distributor is established by contract. Some U.S. companies prefer to begin with a relatively short trial period and then extend the contract if the relationship proves satisfactory to both parties.

Foreign retailers

A company may also sell directly to a foreign retailer, although in such transactions, products are generally limited to consumer lines. This method relies mainly on traveling sales representatives who directly contact foreign retailers, though results may be accomplished by mailing catalogs, brochures, or other literature. While the direct mail approach can eliminate commissions and traveling expenses, a firm that uses it may find that its products are not receiving proper consideration.

Direct sales to end-users

A U.S. business may sell its products or services directly to end-users in foreign countries. These buyers can be foreign governments, institutions such as hospitals, banks, schools, or businesses. Buyers can be identified at trade shows, through international publications, or through U.S. Government contact programs, such as the Department of Commerce's Export Mailing List Service. Chapter 7 details these and other buyer contact activities and programs.

The U.S. company should be aware that if a product is sold in such a direct fashion, the exporter is responsible for shipping, payment collection, and product servicing, unless other arrangements are made. If the cost of providing these services is not built into the export price, a company could end up making far less than originally intended.

Locating foreign representatives and buyers

A company that chooses to use foreign representatives may meet them during overseas business trips or at domestic and international trade shows. There are other methods that are effective and can be employed without leaving the United States. The availability of good secondary sources of information does not imply that travel is not necessary; however, a company can save time by first doing homework in the United States. These methods include use of US&FCS' contact program,

banks and service organizations, and publications. For more information on these methods, see Chapter 7.

Contacting and evaluating foreign representatives

Once the U.S. company has identified a number of potential agents or distributors in the selected market, it should write directly to each. Just as the U.S. firm is seeking information on the foreign representative, the representative is interested in corporate and product information on the U.S. firm. Therefore, the firm should provide full information on its history, resources, personnel, the product line, previous export activity, and all other pertinent matters. The prospective representative may want more information than the company normally provides to a casual buyer. The firm may wish to include a photograph or two of plant facilities and products. More information on correspondence with foreign firms is located in Chapter 9.

A U.S. firm should investigate potential representatives carefully before entering into an agreement. To evaluate the qualifications of potential overseas agents and distributors, the U.S. firm needs to know the following information:

- Current status and history of the firm, including the background on the group's principal officers.

- Personnel and other resources (salespeople, warehouse and service facilities, etc.).

- Sales territory that the representative covers.

- Methods of introducing new products into their sales territory.

- Names and addresses of U.S. firms that the agent or distributor currently represents.

- Data on whether the representative can meet special requirements of the U.S. company.

A U.S. company may obtain much of this information from business associates who currently work with foreign representatives. In addition, the company may wish to obtain at least two supporting business and credit reports to insure that the distributor or agent is reputable. By using a second credit report from another source, the U.S. firm may gain new or more complete information. Reports are available from commercial firms and from the U.S. Department of Commerce's World Traders Data Reports (WTDR) program.

A WTDR is a background report prepared on a specific foreign firm by the US&FCS commercial officers overseas. WTDR's give such information as the type of organization, year established, relative size, number of employees, general reputation, territory covered, language preferred, product lines handled, principal owners, financial references, and trade references. Each also contains a general narrative report by the U.S. Commercial Officer conducting the investigation concerning the reliability of the foreign firm. Reports are not available for all countries. A fee is charged per report. Request forms and further information on this service are available from any US&FCS District Office.

Commercial firms and banks are also sources of credit information on overseas representatives. They can provide information directly or from their correspondent banks or branches overseas. Directories of international businesses may also provide credit information on foreign firms.

If the U.S. company has the information necessary, it may wish to contact a few of the foreign firm's U.S. clients to obtain an evaluation of the representative's character, reliability, efficiency, and past performance. It is important for the U.S. firm to learn about other product lines that the foreign firm represents to protect itself against possible conflicts of interest.

Once the company has established correspondence with foreign representatives, it may wish to travel to the foreign country to observe the size, condition and location of offices and warehouses. In addition, the U.S. company should meet the sales force and try to assess their strength in the marketplace. If travel to each distributor or agent is difficult, the company may decide to meet with them at trade shows, both in the U.S. and worldwide.

Negotiating an agreement with a foreign representative

When the U.S. company has found a prospective representative that meets its requirements, the next step is to negotiate a foreign sales agreement. US&FCS District Offices can provide counseling to firms planning to negotiate foreign sales agreements with representatives and distributors.

The potential representative is interested in the company's pricing structure and profit potential. Representatives are also concerned with the terms of payment, product regulation, competitors and their market shares, the amount of support provided by the U.S. firm (sales aids, promotional material, advertising, etc.), training for sales and service staff, and the company's ability to deliver on schedule.

The agreement may contain provisions that the foreign representative:

1. Not have business dealings with competitive firms (this provision may cause problems in some European countries, and may also cause problems under U.S. antitrust laws);

2. Not reveal any confidential information in a way that would prove injurious, detrimental, or competitive to the U.S. firm;

3. Not enter into agreements binding to the U.S. firm; and

4. Refer all inquiries received from outside the designated sales territory to the U.S. firm for appropriate action.

To ensure a conscientious sales effort from the foreign representative, the agreement should include a requirement that the foreign representative apply the utmost skill and ability to the sale of the product for the compensation named in the contract. It may be appropriate to include performance requirements regarding a minimum sales volume and an expected rate of increase.

The U.S. company should seek to avoid provisions that could be contrary to U.S. antitrust laws. The new Export Trading Company Act (mentioned earlier in this chapter) provides a means to obtain antitrust protection when two or more companies combine for exporting. In addition, the U.S. firm should obtain legal advice when preparing and entering into any foreign agreement. The exporter should be aware of U.S. and foreign laws that govern such contracts. In some countries national laws give extraordinary protection to the representative at the expense of the exporter and may make termination of the contract difficult or costly.

Export product preparation

5

The selection and preparation of a firm's product for export requires not only knowledge of the product, but also knowledge of the unique characteristics of each market being targeted. The market research conducted (Chapter 3) and the contacts made with foreign representatives (Chapter 4) should give the U.S. company an idea of what products can be sold where. Before the sale can occur, however, the company may need to modify a particular product in order to satisfy buyer tastes or needs in foreign markets.

If the company manufactures more than one product or offers many models of a single product, it should choose the one best suited to the targeted market. Ideally, the firm chooses one or two products that fit the market without major design or engineering modifications. This is possible when the U.S. company—

- Deals with international customers with the same demographic characteristics or with the same specifications for manufactured goods,
- Supplies parts for U.S. goods that are exported to foreign countries without modifications,
- Produces a unique product that is sold based on its status or foreign appeal, or
- Produces a product that has few or no distinguishing features and the product is sold almost exclusively on a commodity or price basis.

Product preparation considerations

- What foreign needs does the product satisfy?
- Should the firm modify its domestic market product and sell it abroad? Should it develop a new product for the foreign market?
- What product should the firm offer abroad?
- What specific features—design, color, size, packaging, brand, warranty, etc.—should the product have?
- What specific services are necessary abroad at the presale and postsale stages?
- Are the firm's service/repair facilities adequate?

Product adaptation

For a U.S. company to successfully enter a foreign market, its product may have to be modified to conform to government regulations, geographic and climatic conditions, buyer preferences, or standard of living. The company may also need to modify its product to facilitate shipment or to compensate for possible differences in engineering or design standards.

Foreign government product regulations are common in international trade, and all indications point to the expansion of such regulations in the future. These regulations can take the form of high tarriffs or of non-tarriff barriers, such as regulations on product specifications. Governments impose these regulations to—

- Protect domestic industries from foreign competition,
- Protect the health of the country's citizens,
- Force importers to comply with environmental controls,
- Insure that importers meet local requirements in electrical or measurement systems,
- Restrict the flow of goods originating in or having components from certain countries, and
- Protect the country's citizens from cultural influences deemed inappropriate.

Where particularly burdensome or discriminatory barriers are imposed by a foreign government, a U.S. company may be able to get help from the U.S. Government to press for their removal. The firm should contact a U.S. and Foreign Commercial Service District Office or the U.S. Trade Representative in Washington, DC for further information (see Appendix IV).

It is often necessary for a company to adapt its product to account for geographic and climatic conditions, as well as availability of resources. Factors such as topography, humidity, and energy costs can affect the performance of a product or even define its use. The cost of petroleum products along with a country's infrastructure, for example, may indicate the demand for a company's energy consuming products.

Buyer preferences in a foreign market may also lead a U.S. manufacturer to modify the product. Local customs, such as religion or the use of leisure time, often determine whether a product will sell in a market. The sensory impact of a product, such as taste or visual impact, may also be a critical factor. The Japanese desire for beautiful packaging, for example, has led many U.S. companies to redesign cartons and packages specifically for this market.

A country's standard of living can also determine whether a company needs to modify a product. The level of income, the level of education, and the availability of energy are all factors that help predict the acceptance of a product in a foreign market. If a country's standard of living is lower than that of the United States, a manufacturer may find a market for less sophisticated product models that have become obsolete in the United States. Certain high technology products are inappropriate in some countries, not only because of their cost, but also because of their function. For example, a computerized industrial washing machine might replace workers in a country where employment is a high priority. In addition, these products may need a level of servicing unavailable in some countries.

Market potential must be of sufficient size for a company to justify the direct and indirect costs involved in product adaptation. The firm should assess the costs to be incurred and the increased revenues expected from adaptation, though these things may be difficult to determine. The decision to adapt a product is based in part on the degree of commitment to the specific foreign market, since a firm with short-term goals may have a different perspective from a firm with longer-term goals.

Engineering and redesign

In addition to adaptations related to cultural and consumer preference, the exporter should be aware that even fundamental aspects of its products may require change. For example, many foreign countries have different electrical standards from those in the United States. It is not unusual to find phases, cycles, or voltages (both in home and commercial use) that would damage or impair the operating efficiency of equipment designed for use in the United States. These electrical standards sometimes vary even within a given country. Knowing this, the manufacturer can determine whether it is necessary to substitute a special motor or arrange for a different drive ratio to achieve the desired operating RPM.

Many kinds of equipment must be engineered in the metric system for integration with other pieces of equipment or for compliance with the standards of a given country. A report prepared for the Department of Commerce concludes:

> "Traditional business planning considerations such as price, quality, financing, service, and delivery overwhelm considerations of metric. However, industries such as construction and engineering services and lumber and wood products are finding metric to be an important detail in selling to foreign markets." (J.F. Coates, Inc., *The Role of Metric in U.S. Exports*, March 19, 1984, p. 15.)

Since freight charges are usually assessed by weight or volume (whichever provides the greater revenue for the carrier), a company should give some consideration to shipping an item unassembled to reduce delivery costs. This also facilitates shipment on narrow roads or movement through doorways and elevators.

Branding, labeling and packaging

Consumers are concerned with both the product itself and the product's supplementary features, such as packaging, warranties, and service.

Branding and labeling of products in foreign markets raise new considerations for the U.S. company:

- Are international brand names important to promote and distinguish a product? Conversely, should local brands or private labels be employed to heighten local interest?

- Are the colors used on labels and packages offensive or attractive to the foreign buyer? In some countries, certain colors are associated with death, national flags, or other cultural factors.

- Can labels be produced in official or customary languages, if required by law or practice?

- Does information on product content and country of origin have to be provided?

- Are weights and measures stated in the local unit?

- Must each item be labelled individually?

- Are local tastes and knowledge considered? A dry cereal box picturing a U.S. athlete may not be as attractive to consumers as the picture of a local sports hero.

A company may find that building international recognition for a brand is expensive. Protection for brand names varies from one country to another, and in some developing countries, barriers to the use of foreign brands or trademarks may exist. In other countries, piracy of a company's brand names and counterfeiting of its products are widespread. In order for a company to protect its products and brand names, it must comply with local laws on patents, copyrights and trademarks. A U.S. firm may find it useful to obtain the advice of local lawyers and consultants where appropriate.

Installation

Another element of product preparation that a company should consider is the ease of installation of that product overseas. If technicians or engineers are needed overseas to assist in installation, the company should minimize their time in the field if possible. To achieve this, the company may wish to pre-assemble or pre-test the product before shipping.

Disassembly of a product for shipment and re-assembly abroad may be considered by the company.

23

This can save the firm shipping costs, but it may add to delay in payment if the sale is contingent on an assembled product. Even if sending trained personnel is not required, the company should be careful to give training manuals, installation instructions, parts lists, etc., that have been translated into local languages.

Warranties

The company should include a warranty on the product, since the buyer expects a specific level of performance and a guarantee that it will be achieved. Levels of expectation for a warranty vary from country to country depending on the country's level of development, competitive practices, the activism of consumer groups, local standards of production quality, and other similar factors.

A company may use warranties for advertising purposes to distinguish its product from its competition. Strong warranties may be required to break into a new market, especially if the company is an unknown supplier. In some cases, warranties may be instrumental in making the sale and may be a major element of negotiation. In other cases, however, warranties similar to those in the United States are not expected. By providing an unnecessary warranty, the company may raise the product's cost beyond that of its competitors.

Servicing

Of special concern to foreign consumers is the service the U.S. company provides for its product. Service after the sale is critical for some products; if the company's service plans or capabilities are inadequate, future sales may be inhibited. If servicing the product is a major factor in the sale, the buyer may wish to confirm the existence of spare parts, service technicians, or local distributors. More details on after sale service can be found in Chapter 15.

6

The export of services

Why are services important?

Service industries span a wide variety of enterprises running from hamburgers to high-technology. The service sector accounts for about 70 percent of the U.S. Gross National Product and employment. In 1984, the service sector accounted for nearly 85 percent of the growth in total non-farm employment. Gains in service jobs were estimated to average 170,000 more jobs per month during the third quarter of 1984.

Internationally, a similar change has taken place. Trade in services constitutes between 20-25 percent of overall world trade today. In some countries, such as Panama and the Netherlands, services account for 40 percent or more of total merchandise trade. The world market for services has grown over the past decade at an annual rate of about 16 percent, compared to a rate of about 7 percent for merchandise trade.

The income generated and the jobs created through the sale of services abroad are just as important to the U.S. economy as income and jobs resulting from the production and exportation of goods. Given the shift toward services, both domestically and internationally, and the substantial competitive advantage of the United States in the services field, those who have services to offer can become major participants in world trade.

Typical service exports

The service sector accounts for a great share of the U.S. economy although some services are not easily exported. While it would be very difficult to export most personal services, such as the service performed by a waiter in a restaurant, by contrast, most business services can be exported—especially those highly innovative, specialized, or technologically advanced services that are efficiently performed in the United States. Sectors with particularly high export potential include:

Construction, design, and engineering.—The vast experience and technological leadership of the U.S. construction industry, as well as special skills in operations, maintenance, and management, frequently give U.S. firms a competitive edge in international projects. Some U.S. firms with expertise in specialized fields, such as electric power utilities, also export related construction, design, and engineering services, such as power plant design services.

Banking and financial services.—U.S. financial institutions are very competitive internationally, particularly when offering account management, credit card operations, collection management, and other services they have pioneered.

Insurance services.—U.S. insurers offer valuable services ranging from underwriting and risk evaluation to insurance operations and management contracts in the international marketplace.

Legal and accounting services.—Firms in this field typically aid other U.S. firms operating abroad through their international legal and accounting activities. They also use their experience to serve foreign firms in their business operations.

Computer and data services.—The U.S. computer services and data industries lead the world in marketing new technologies, enjoying a competitive advantage in computer operations, data manipulation, and data transmission.

Teaching services.—The vast U.S. educational sector offers substantial new services for foreign purchasers, particularly in areas such as management motivation and the teaching of operational, managerial, and theoretical issues.

Management consulting services.—Organizations and business enterprises all over the world look to the United States in the field of management. U.S. management consulting firms as well as other U.S. firms that are willing to sell their particular management skills find great potential overseas for export of their services.

Exporting services versus exporting products

There are many obvious differences between services and products. Consequently, there are important features which differentiate exporting services from exporting products:

* Services are less tangible than products, providing little in terms of samples that can be seen by the potential foreign buyer. This makes communicating a service offer much more difficult than communicating a product offer. For example, brochures or catalogues explaining services often must show a "proxy" for the service. A construction company, for instance, can show a picture of a construction site, but this picture will not fully communicate the actual performance of the service as much as will a picture of

the finished building. Much more attention must be paid to translating the intangibility of a service into a tangible and saleable offer.

- The intangibility of services also makes financing more difficult. Frequently, even financial institutions with international experience are less willing to provide financial support for service exports than for product exports, because the value of services is more difficult to monitor. Customer complaints and difficulties in receiving payments can also appear more troublesome to assess.

- Services are often more time-dependent than products. Quite frequently, a service can be offered only at a specific time, and as time passes, the service, if not used, perishes. For example, to offer data transmission through special telephone lines may require providing an open telephone line. If this line is not heavily used, the cost of maintaining it may not be covered.

- Selling services is also more personal than selling products, since it quite often requires direct involvement with the customer. This, in turn, demands greater cultural sensitivity when providing services, since a buffer of indirect communication and interaction does not exist.

- Services are much more difficult to standardize than products. Frequently, service activities must be tailored to the specific needs of the buyer. This need for adaptation often necessitates direct participation and cooperation in the service delivery by the service client.

Demand for certain services can derive from product exports. Many of our merchandise exports would not take place if they were not supported by service activities such as banking, insurance, and transportation. Services can be crucial in stimulating product export and are a critical factor in maintaining such exports. However, in such cases, services follow products rather than taking the lead over them.

Marketing services abroad

Since service exports are often delivered in the support of product exports, a sensible approach for some beginning exporters is to follow the path of relevant product exports. For years, many large accounting and banking firms have exported by following their major multinational clients abroad and continuing to assist them in their international activities. Smaller service exporters which cooperate closely with manufacturing firms can also determine where these manufacturing firms are operating internationally and aim to provide service support for these manufacturers abroad.

For service providers whose activities are independent from products, a different strategy is needed. These individuals and firms should search for market situations abroad which are similar to the domestic market.

Many opportunities derive from an understanding of the process and stage of development of relevant trade activities abroad. Just as U.S. society has undergone change, foreign societies are subject to changing economic trends. If, for example, new transportation services are opened up in a country, an expert in the area of containerization may offer services to improve the efficiency of the new system.

Leads for service activities can also be gathered by keeping informed about international projects sponsored by organizations such as the World Bank, the Caribbean Development Bank, the Inter-American Development Bank, the United Nations, and the World Health Organization. Very frequently, such projects are in need of service support.

Government support for service exports

In recognition of the increasing importance of service exports, the U.S. Department of Commerce has assigned the Office of Service Industries with responsibility for analyzing and promoting services trade. The Office of Service Industries provides information on opportunities and operations of services abroad. The phone number for the Office of Service Industries is (202) 377-3575. For questions on specific industry sectors, contact the following divisions: Information Industries Division (202) 377-4781; Transportation, Tourism and Marketing Division (202) 377-4581; Finance and Management Industries Division (202) 377-0339.

Through the Worldwide Services Program (WSP), the Department of Commerce provides the same overseas publicity in *Commercial News USA* magazine for U.S. service firms as the New Product Information Service (NPIS) and International Market Search (IMS) do for manufacturers (see Chapter 7). A brief description of the service with the firm's name and address is listed under the appropriate category. Interested overseas parties are instructed to contact listed firms directly. Application forms are available through US&FCS District Offices. A modest fee is charged for this service, which distributes the listed information to almost 200,000 overseas agents, distributors, government officials, etc.

Both the U.S. Agency for International Development (AID) and the U.S. Trade and Development Program (TDP) offer opportunities for U.S. service firms. For a more complete description of their activities, please see Chapter 7.

The Export-Import Bank (Eximbank) of the United States has introduced a new program to assist U.S. design, engineering, and architectural firms with foreign contracts. For information on this program, contact the Bank's Engineering Division (202) 566-8802.

Making contacts

7

After a company has identified its most promising markets and devised strategies to enter those markets, the next step is to actually locate a buyer. This may be the end-user of a company's product or service and may result in a relatively simple transaction between the U.S. firm and the buyer. However, in many cases, U.S. exporters need an in-country presence through an agent or distributor in order to reach the eventual buyer. Alternatively, the firm may identify customers through attendance at trade shows, trade missions, direct mail campaigns and advertising.

Regardless of the method chosen for making contacts and developing sales leads, the exporter faces many questions, such as:

- Who specifically are potential buyers?

- What trade shows are the most effective?

- Which marketing techniques are most successful?

This chapter attempts to give U.S. exporters the means to answer these questions. The marketing techniques described are by no means exhaustive. However, the chapter describes sources of assistance in locating buyers, evaluating trade missions and shows, and conducting other programs designed to make contacts.

Department of Commerce

Contact programs

The U.S. and Foreign Commercial Service (US&FCS) can readily assist the exporter in identifying and qualifying direct leads for potential buyers, agents, joint venture partners, and licensees from both private and public sources. Along with its various product, country and program experts, the US&FCS has an extensive network of commercial officers stationed in nearly every country.

Listed below are services and publications available through the US&FCS. Exporters should contact the nearest US&FCS District Office (see Appendix V) for more information or contact Export Promotion Services, US&FCS, U.S. Department of Commerce, P.O. Box 14702, Washington, DC 20044.

Export Mailing List Service (EMLS)

This service provides mailing lists of prospective overseas customers from the Commerce Department's automated worldwide file of foreign firms. An EML identifies manufacturers, agents, retailers, service firms, government agencies, and other one-to-one contacts. The information on this list includes name and address, cable and telephone numbers, name and title of a key official, product/service interests, year established, and additional data. EML information is available in two forms:

- *Export Mailing Lists* are on-line, custom retrievals based on the market criteria specified. Output is available on either mailing labels, printouts or computer tape. An EML costs $35 and up, depending on the scope of the search.

- *Trade Lists* are directories listing companies in a single country across all product sectors or companies in a single industry across all countries. Trade Lists cost $12 to $40 each depending on print date.

Trade Opportunities Program (TOP)

This service provides timely sales leads from overseas firms seeking to buy or represent U.S. products and services. U.S. commercial officers worldwide gather leads through local channels. Lead details, such as specifications, quantities, end-use, delivery and bid deadlines, are telexed daily to the computer center in Washington, DC, and then sent directly to subscribers. Trade opportunity information is available in two forms:

- *TOP Notice* searches the TOP computer daily and automatically sends subscribers only the leads for those products and services previously specified. The TOP Notice Service costs $25 to set up a subscriber's interest profile, and $37.50, prepaid, for each block of 50 leads.

- *TOP Bulletin* is a weekly publication of all the leads received the previous week for all products from all countries. A year's subscription costs $175 (see sample).

Agent/Distributor Service (A/DS)

The Agent/Distributor Service (A/DS) is used to locate foreign import agents and distributors. An A/DS provides a custom search overseas for interested and qualified foreign representatives on behalf of a U.S. exporter. Officers abroad conduct the search and prepare a report identifying up to six foreign prospects that have examined the U.S. firm's product literature and have expressed interest in representing the U.S. firm's products.

The U.S. company is given the names and addresses of the foreign firms, names and titles of persons to contact, telephone numbers, cable addresses and telex numbers, and brief comments about the agent or distributor and their stated interest in the proposal. A fee is charged for this service.

A/DS application forms may be obtained from US&FCS District Offices. Trade specialists at these offices can help in the preparation of applications and can provide guidance if there are any factors barring the desired relationship.

Commercial News USA

Commercial News USA is a monthly magazine published by the US&FCS to promote U.S. products and services to overseas markets. Three contact programs support *Commercial News USA:*

- *New Product Information Service (NPIS)*. NPIS is designed to help U.S. manufacturers publicize new products in foreign markets while at the same time testing market interest. New U.S. products available for export are described in issues of *Commercial News USA,* along with a picture of the product and the manufacturer's address. Descriptions of some new products are also chosen by Commerce to be broadcast by the Voice of America (VOA) as part of this program. VOA transmits new product information on a daily basis in up to 40 languages.

- *International Market Search (IMS)*. Several times a year, *Commercial News USA* devotes an entire issue to the technology, products and services of a single industry. This information is also used for VOA broadcasts.

- *Worldwide Services Program (WSP)*. This program provides the same overseas exposure in *Commercial News USA* for U.S. service firms as NPIS and IMS do for manufacturers.

The export information in *Commercial News USA* is disseminated through 240 U.S. embassies and consular posts around the world to a potential audience of approximately 200,000 overseas business readers. These posts, located in 96 countries, distribute *Commercial News USA* directly to more than 80,000 business and government addressees, and many of these posts reprint selected product and service descriptions in commercial newsletters that are tailored in content and language to the individual country. The posts distribute these newsletters to potential buyers and agents in the local business community, to American chambers of commerce abroad, and other multipliers. Foreign embassies in the U.S. also receive copies. The magazine is distributed at international trade fairs in which the Department of Commerce sponsors a U.S. pavilion.

Interested firms should contact the nearest US&FCS District Office for information on *Commercial News USA* and its supporting programs, which are open to participation by U.S. companies at low cost.

Trade show programs

Some products, because of their very nature, are difficult to sell unless the potential buyer has an opportunity to examine them in person. Sales letters and printed literature can be helpful, but they are certainly no substitute for an actual presentation of products in the export market. Two ways for a company to actually present its products to an overseas market are through participation in trade fairs and trade missions overseas.

In today's international market, trade fairs are "shop windows" where thousands of firms from many countries display their wares. They are marketplaces where buyer and seller can meet with mutual convenience. Some fairs, especially those in Europe, have a history that goes back centuries.

Attendance at trade fairs involves a great deal of planning. The potential exhibitor must take into account the following logistical considerations:

- Choosing the proper fair out of the hundreds that are held every year.

- Obtaining space at the fair, along with design and construction of the exhibit.

- Shipment of products to the show, along with unpacking and set-up.

- Providing proper hospitality (refreshments, etc.), along with maintenance of the exhibit.

- Breakdown, packing and return of samples and goods.

There are many excellent international trade fairs, both privately run and government sponsored. A trade magazine or association can generally provide information on major shows. Because of the many considerations facing the exhibitor, a company may wish to attend a U.S. Department of Commerce Certified International Trade Fair, Foreign Buyer Show, or a Commerce-organized U.S. pavilion overseas.

Certified Trade Fair Program

The Department of Commerce Certified Trade Fair Program is designed to encourage private organizations to recruit U.S. group participation in trade fairs overseas. In order to receive certification, the organization must demonstrate that:

1. The fair is a leading international trade event for an industry; and

2. The fair organizer is capable of recruiting a minimum of 20 U.S. exhibitors and assisting these exhibitors with freight forwarding, customs clearance, exhibit design and set-up, public relations, and overall show promotion. They must agree to assist new-to-export exhibitors as well as small businesses interested in exporting.

In addition to the services the organizer provides, U.S. exhibitors have the U.S. Department of Commerce facilities and services available to them. In addition to monitoring and promoting the U.S. group exhibit at the fair, the Department of Commerce can:

- Assign a Washington contact person to coordinate Commerce assistance.

- Operate the Business Information Office, which can provide meeting space, translators, hospitality and assistance from US&FCS personnel to U.S. exhibitors and foreign customers.

- Help in contacting buyers, agents and distributors, along with other business leds and marketing assistance.

- Authorize use of Certification logo and provide a press release on certification of the event.

Foreign Buyer Program

The U.S. Department of Commerce encourages foreign buyers to attend selected U.S. trade shows. The U.S. and Foreign Commercial Service (US&FCS) selects leading U.S. trade shows in industries with high export potential. U.S. firms are assisted in fullfilling their international business objectives through their participation in selected U.S. trade shows where they can meet foreign buyers, agents/distributors, potential licensees or joint ventures.

The US&FCS works closely with U.S. companies exhibiting at these shows by helping U.S. firms match their products, marketing objectives, and georgraphic targets with the needs of the international business visitors. Each show selected for the Foreign Buyer Program receives special promotion through U.S. embassy and regional commercial newsletters, *Commercial News USA, Business America,* foreign trade association and chambers of Commerce journals, and trade journals overseas.

Through the 48 US&FCS District Offices, International Trade Specialists are ready to take exhibiting U.S. firms through the exporting process and provide counseling to them prior to the trade show. Additionally, an International Trade Specialist is available at each show to provide "on-the-spot" export counseling. The Foreign Buyer Program is also an excellent means for experienced exporters to penetrate new markets.

For additional information contact U.S. Department of Commerce, U.S. & Foreign Commercial Service, Export Promotion Services, Room 2118, Washington, DC 20230. For an application and additional information contact The Marketing Development Division on 202-377-0871.

A U.S. Department of Commerce-organized U.S. pavilion in an overseas trade fair is completely recruited and managed by the US&FCS in a foreign market, providing all of the above mentioned services. These trade fairs open many market opportunities for U.S. firms, especially in newly industrialized and developing countries. The Department of Commerce develops and operates U.S. exhibitions in foreign markets where U.S.-based show organizers do not operate exhibitions.

Further information on the Department of Commerce's overseas trade promotion facilities and the various overseas events discussed in this chapter may be obtained by contacting the Office of Marketing Programs, Room 2114, Export Promotion Services, US&FCS, U.S. Department of Commerce, Washington, DC 20230. Telephone: (202) 377-4231.

Trade mission programs

Trade missions are planned visits to potential buyers or clients overseas. Missions can be undertaken by individual firms or as part of an organized group. Like trade shows, trade missions require careful planning and attention to scheduling. Because much of the planning and coordination is done for participants, a firm may wish to participate in a U.S. Department of Commerce-sponsored mission.

Commerce-sponsored trade missions are carefully organized and planned to achieve maximum results in expanding exports of U.S.-produced goods and services. They are usually composed of fewer than 12 but more than 5 U.S. business executives. Markets to be visited and products to be promoted are carefully selected based on relevant market research and on consultations with US&FCS officers abroad. The primary objectives of Commerce-sponsored trade missions are to introduce U.S. firms to appropriate foreign buyers and to establish agencies and representation, joint ventures and licensing agreements.

Three types of trade missions have been developed to help U.S. exporters penetrate overseas markets:

- *U.S. Specialized Trade Missions.* U.S. Specialized Trade Missions are planned, organized, and led by U.S. Department of Commerce personnel. Commerce carefully selects a product line and an itinerary that appear to offer the best potential for export sales, provides detailed marketing information, and arranges advance programming and publicity. Commercial officers make hour-by-hour individual appointments tailored to the specific needs of each participating firm, inviting key foreign government officials in purchasing and policy-making positions to meet with the mission. Mission members pay their own expenses and a share of the operating costs of the mission.

- *State & Industry-Organized Government-Approved (S&IOGA) Trade Missions.* S&IOGA Trade Missions are planned and organized by State development agencies, trade associations, chambers of commerce, and other export-oriented groups. To qualify for U.S. Government sponsorship, organizers of this type of trade mission must agree to follow Commerce criteria in planning and recruiting the mission. The Commerce Department offers guidance and assistance from the planning stages to the completion of the mission and coordinates the support of all relevant offices and the assistance of the US&FCS officers in each city on the mission's itinerary. The overseas operations of S&IOGA trade missions are substantially the same as those of specialized missions.

Mission members pay their own travel and hotel expenses and the organizers are responsible for all overseas costs incurred on the mission's behalf.

- *U.S. Seminar Missions.* Like trade missions, seminar missions promote the sale of U.S. goods and services abroad and help to establish agents and other foreign representation for U.S. exporters. Unlike specialized trade missions, they are especially designed to facilitate the sale of particularly sophisticated products and technology and concentrate on concepts and systems. A "U.S. Seminar Team" consisting of representatives of a high-technology industry give presentations and lead discussions on technological subjects. The team also addresses pertinent developmental or industrial problems of the host country. This is followed by individual private, sales-oriented appointments that are scheduled by the US&FCS posts.

For more information on the above trade mission services, contact the Office of Marketing Programs, Room 2116, Export Promotion Services, US&FCS, U.S. Department of Commerce, Washington, DC 20230, Telephone: (202) 377-4231.

Other promotion activities

Export Development Offices

The US&FCS operates Export Development Offices (EDO's) in seven cities overseas to provide a variety of programs and services to U.S. exporters. Staffed by US&FCS Officers, the EDO's are the principal U.S. export promotion facilities overseas.

The primary role played by the EDO (in conjunction with the US&FCS in the local U.S. embassy or consulate) is threefold:

1. It conducts or assists in market research within the county, helping to identify specific marketing opportunities and to determine which products have the greatest sales potential.

2. It conducts export promotion events in its region that have been organized on the basis of market research findings.

3. It helps to organize participation of specific U.S. exporters in these events.

Located worldwide in Tokyo, Sydney, Seoul, Milan, London, Mexico City, and Sao Paulo, these offices organize and coordinate a range of export promotion programs, including on-site trade shows, U.S. pavilions in international trade fairs, solo U.S. exhibitions, trade seminars, trade missions, catalog and video/catalog exhibitions, and special promotions. Each EDO performs these functions only in the country in which it is located.

When not being used to stage trade exhibitions, EDO's with exhibit and conference facilities frequently are made available to individual firms or associations. Facilities can be used for sales promo-

tions, seminars, sales meetings, and the like. EDO's and some commercial offices overseas also provide use of limited office space for a nominal fee for traveling U.S. business representatives, as well as local telephone use, a market briefing, use of audio visual equipment, and assistance in making appointments.

For the current address of the Export Development Office in a particular country, please contact the commercial officer at the U.S. embassy in that country.

Catalog exhibitions

U.S. firms may test product interest in foreign markets, develop sales leads, and locate agents or distributors through catalog exhibitions sponsored by the US&FCS of the Department of Commerce and in some instances, in conjunction with the Department of State's U.S. Foreign Service Posts. These exhibitions feature displays of a large number of U.S. product catalogs, sales brochures, and other graphic sales aids at U.S. embassies and consulates or in conjunction with trade shows. The Department of Commerce supports each catalog exhibition by selecting a U.S. industry expert to assist the exhibition. Commercial staff forward to participants sales leads and a visitors list of those foreign buyers attending the event.

Video/catalog exhibitions

Video/catalog exhibitions are video tape presentations prerecorded in sound and color and distributed to selected posts for display. These tapes take the place of live product demonstrations, enabling the exhibitor's products to be explained, demonstrated, and sold more economically. The major advantage of the video/catalog exhibition over a conventional catalog exhibition is that it offers the foreign buyer a chance to see U.S. products in actual use. This program is particularly well suited for use in developing markets. Post commercial staff supports each exhibition and assists the U.S. industry expert selected by US&FCS to answer foreign buyers inquires. For more information on this and the catalog exhibitions program, U.S. firms should contact a local US&FCS District Office or the Office of Marketing Programs, Room 2117, Export Promotion Services, U.S. Department of Commerce, Washington, DC 20230. Telephone: (202) 377-3973.

Major projects program

This program is designed to help U.S. firms win contracts for planning, engineering, and construction of large foreign infrastructure and industrial systems projects, including equipment and turnkey installations. Assistance is provided when requested by a U.S. embassy, a prospective foreign client, or a U.S. firm, either to encourage U.S. companies to bid on a particular project or to help them pursue overseas contracts.

Speed and flexibility in developing a strategy for each case are essential elements in the assistance given U.S. firms. As circumstances warrant, the Office of International Major Projects mobilizes and coordinates appropriate support from other U.S. Government agencies, including Foreign Service posts abroad. For further information, contact: Office of International Major Projects, Room 2007, Trade Development, International Trade Administration, U.S. Department of Commerce, Washington, DC 20230. Telephone: (202) 377-5225.

Department of Agriculture

Foreign Agricultural Service

Through a network of counselors, attaches, trade officers, commodity analysts and marketing specialists, the U.S. Department of Agriculture's Foreign Agricultural Service (FAS) can help arrange contacts overseas and provide promotional assistance.

The following is a listing of the programs and services offered:

Commodity and Marketing Programs (CMP)

The CMP area of FAS handles inquiries for specific commodity related information. Commodity Programs consist of six divisions:

1. Dairy, Livestock and Poultry Division, (202) 447-8031

2. Grain and Feed Division, (202) 447-6219

3. Horticulture and Tropical Products Division, (202) 447-6590

4. Oilseeds and Products Division, (202) 447-7037

5. Tobacco, Cotton and Seed Division, (202) 382-9516

6. Forest Products Division, (202) 382-8138.

Each division provides analysis (consumption, trade, stocks, etc.), support, and marketing information.

Export Programs Division (EPD)

The Export Programs Division is responsible for administering the market development initiative for FAS. The Program Operations Branch (202-477-3031) serves to expand overseas markets for U.S. agricultural and food commodities and products through trade shows and trade groups. Through its sales team program, FAS arranges visits with foreign buyers in overseas markets.

Trade specialists in EPD solicit participation and manage Stateside services while FAS foreign offices manage the overseas needs for participants in agriculture and food product trade events in foreign countries. These events are USDA/FAS sponsored pavilions at large international shows or promotion events for U.S. products only, sponsored and managed by FAS foreign offices.

The Label Clearance Program helps exporters of potential branded products to evaluate the acceptability of their labels and products in specific foreign markets. EPD charges $25 per label per country for this service and provides it to all participants in USDA/FAS sponsored trade shows.

FAS Sales Teams

Through its sales team program, FAS arranges personal visits with foreign buyers. FAS selects a market with good export potential and invites five or six U.S. firms handling food products with sales possibilities in that market to participate in a coordinated sales mission. FAS makes all the arrangements, including preparation and printing of a sales team brochure, rental of sales room facilities, and scheduling appointments with potential buyers.

Export Incentive Program (EIP)

Through its Export Incentive Program, FAS assists U.S. firms in promoting their products overseas by reimbursing firms for a portion of their export promotion expenditures.

Value-Added Promotion Program (VAPP)

In addition to the above incentive programs, FAS operates the Value-Added Promotion Program (VAPP) through regional cooperator groups. The program is designed to assist processors, packers, manufacturers, distributors, export agents, wholesalers, export trading companies, or other firms promoting their products in specific export markets.

Agricultural Information and Marketing Services (AIMS)

AIMS functions as a liaison between U.S. companies and foreign buyers seeking U.S. food and agricultural products. U.S. companies subscribing to AIMS services receive marketing, trade, and economic information gathered by agricultural counselors, attaches, and trade officers at U.S. embassies and consulates. The material available includes:

- *Trade Leads* is information from foreign importers currently seeking agricultural products from U.S. suppliers and is available daily from AIMS. Over 500 leads about agricultural sales opportunities are processed each month.

- *Product Publicity* is a 100 word description of new or new-to-export agricultural products that can be distributed to 35,000 importers worldwide through the monthly newsletter "Contacts for U.S. Farm Products."

- *Foreign Contacts* are worldwide lists of foreign importers who normally handle specific agricultural products. This listing is available from the AIMS foreign contacts data base.

- *International Marketing Profiles (IMPs)* present detailed statistical information on agricultural trade activity. Two series of automated marketing research reports, one examining agricultural trade activity in selected countries and the other examining markets for specified product groups, give timely information on leading foreign markets and export products, import preferences for U.S. products, and principal competitors around the world. A list of market contacts is also included.

- *Buyer Alert Program* forwards specific information about the products U.S. suppliers want to sell to foreign importers using the Buyer Alert service in their countries. The service is an export marketing tool targeted at helping U.S. suppliers introduce their products to the world marketplace by using high-speed telecommunications links.

Contact: AIMS, Foreign Agricultural Service, Room 4645 South Building, U.S. Department of Agriculture, Washington, DC 20250. Telephone: (202) 447-7103.

Agency for International Development

The Agency for International Development (AID) is the agency that administers most of the foreign economic assistance programs for the Federal government. AID offers U.S. exporters opportunities to compete in the sales of goods or services supplied to foreign countries under loans and grants made by AID. U.S. exporters can benefit from two AID programs—the Commodity Import Programs (CIP) and Project Procurements. In both of these programs, AID recipient countries purchase the commodities directly through U.S. suppliers, either through competitive bid or negotiated procurements.

Commodity Import Programs

The CIP provides loans or grants assistance to certain countries to finance the procurement of basic products, not exclusively agricultural commodities but other products as well. These products are purchased by both public and private sector entities.

CIP opportunities offered under competitive bid are announced in the *AID-Financed Export Opportunities* publication. In addition, negotiated procurements offered by the public sector are announced in the *AID Procurement Information Bulletin* publication. Both these publications are free and available through the AID Office of Business Relations, Agency for International Development, Washington, DC 20323.

Project Procurements

AID finances large-scale projects (irrigation, health networks, etc.) where commodities are needed. Called Project Procurements, these opportunities are all public sector projects and are reported in the above mentioned publications.

Service firms can also find opportunities under Project Procurements announced in the *"Commerce Business Daily,"* which identifies buyers of services. The U.S. Department of Commerce produces this publication and makes it available through the Superintendent of Documents, Government Printing Office, Washington, DC 20402. This publication identifies procurement opportunities throughout the U.S. Government and costs $160/year for first class mailing and $81 for second class mailing.

Trade and Development Program

The Trade and Development Program (TDP) is an agency of the U.S. Government that primarily funds feasibility studies for both public and private sector projects in developing countries. TDP finances studies in five principal sectors:

- Large scale energy generation and conservation.
- Infrastructure.
- Mineral development.
- Agribusiness.
- Basic industrial facilities.

A major purpose of TDP funding is to help U.S. engineering and planning firms win major contracts in foreign countries. By encouraging the use of U.S. firms in planning and design of a capital project, TDP participation increases the likelihood that U.S. goods, technology, and services will be procured during project implementation. Becoming familiar with recently funded or pending TDP projects is a good way for U.S. service firms and manufacturers to learn of export opportunities.

For further information on TDP activities, U.S. firms should contact Trade and Development Program, Department of State, Washington, DC 20523. Telephone: (703) 235-3663.

State and local government assistance

Most States can provide an array of services to the exporter. Many of these States maintain international offices in major markets, with the most common locations being in northern Europe and Japan. They can provide assistance in making contacts in foreign markets, providing such services as:

- Specific trade leads with foreign buyers.
- Assistance for trade missions, such as itinerary planning, appointment scheduling, travel and accommodations.
- Promotional service for goods or services.
- Help in qualifying potential buyers, agents or distributors.

In addition, some international offices of State development organizations help organize and promote foreign buyer missions to the U.S. These buyers visit the State to buy U.S. goods and can be an effective way to export with little effort.

Increasingly, many cities and counties are providing these same services. Appendix V lists contacts at both State and city level.

Business and service organization contacts

Contacts made through business colleagues and associations can often prove invaluable to the U.S. exporter. A colleague with first hand experience in an international market may give a personal recommendation for an agent, distributor, or potential buyer. Conversely, the recommendation against the use of a representative for credit or reliability reasons may save the firm from a great deal of problems. Attendance at export seminars and industry trade shows are excellent methods of networking with business people who have international experience. In addition, trade associations can provide a valuable source of contacts with individuals who may wish to share their experience of identifying and selling to buyers and representatives in foreign markets.

Banks can be another source of assistance in locating overseas representation. The international departments, branches, or correspondent banks of U.S. banks may assist in the location of reputable firms qualified and willing to represent U.S. exporters. In addition, freight forwarders, freight carriers, airlines, port authorities, and American chambers of commerce maintain offices throughout the world. These service firms often have contacts with qualified representatives and can make recommendations to the U.S. firm. Foreign embassy and consulate commercial offices may also be able to provide directories and assistance.

Promotion in publications and other media

A large and varied assortment of magazines covering international markets is available to exporters through U.S. publishers. These range from spec-ialized international magazines relating to individual industries such as construction, beverages, and textiles, to worldwide industrial magazines covering many industries. Many consumer publications produced by U.S.-based publishers are also available. Several of these are produced in foreign language editions and also offer "regional buys" for specific export markets of the world. In addition, several business directories in the U.S. list foreign representatives geographically or by industry specialization.

Publishers frequently supply potential exporters with helpful market information, make specific recommendations for selling in the markets they cover, help advertisers locate sales representation, and render other services to aid the international advertiser. A complete list of these international publications may be found in the International Section of *The Business Publication,* a book published by Standard Rate and Data Service, 5201 Old Orchard Road, Skokie, Illinois 60077. Many of these directories are available at libraries, US&FCS District Offices, or in the Department of Commerce's Reference Room, Room 7046, Washington, DC. State departments of commerce, appropriate trade associations, business libraries, and major universities may also be tapped for these various publications.

Television, radio, and specially produced motion pictures may also be used by a U.S. business for promoting products or services, depending on the country. In areas where programs may be seen and heard in public places, television and radio promotions offer one of the few means of bringing an advertising message to great numbers of people. In many countries, particularly in Latin American, various forms of outdoor advertising (billboards, posters, electric signs, streetcar, and bus cards) are widely used to reach the mass audience.

Because of the specialized knowledge required to advertise and promote successfully in foreign markets, U.S. firms may find useful the services of a U.S. advertising agency with offices or correspondents abroad. Some U.S. agencies handle nothing but foreign advertising, and some marketing consultants specialize in the problems peculiar to selling in foreign markets. The International Advertising Association, Inc., 475 Fifth Avenue, New York, New York 10017, can provide names of domestic agencies that handle overseas accounts.

Business travel abroad

8

Business travel abroad can locate and cultivate new customers and improve relationships and communication with current foreign representatives and associates. As in domestic business, there is nothing like a face-to-face meeting with a client or customer.

The following suggestions can assist U.S. companies in preparing for a trip. By keeping in mind that even little things (such as forgetting to check foreign holiday schedules or neglecting to arrange for translator services) can cost time, opportunity, and money, a firm can get maximum value from its time spent abroad.

Planning the itinerary

A well-planned itinerary enables a traveler to make the best possible use of time abroad. Although travel time is expensive, care must be taken not to overload the schedule. Two or three definite appointments, confirmed well in advance and spaced comfortably throughout one day, are more productive and enjoyable than a crowded agenda that forces the businessperson to rush from one meeting to the next before business is really concluded.

The following travel tips should be kept in mind:

The travel plans should reflect what is hoped to be accomplished. The traveler should give some thought to the trip's goals and their relative priorities.

- The traveler should accomplish as much as possible before the trip begins by obtaining names of possible contacts, arranging appointments, checking transportation schedules, etc. The most important meetings should be confirmed before leaving the United States.

- As a general rule, the businessperson should keep the schedule flexible enough to allow for both unexpected problems (such as transportation delays) and unexpected opportunities. For instance, accepting an unscheduled luncheon invitation from a prospective client should not make it necessary for the U.S. visitor to miss the next scheduled meeting.

- The traveler should check the normal work days and business hours in the countries to be visited. In many Middle Eastern regions, for instance, the work week typically runs from Saturday to Thursday. In many countries, lunch hours—or siestas—of 2, 3, even 4 hours are customary.

- Along the same lines, take into account foreign holidays. Commerce's *Business America* magazine annually publishes a list of holidays observed in countries around the world. A free reprint of this useful schedule, entitled *"World Commercial Holidays,"* can be obtained by contacting the local U.S. and Foreign Commercial Service (US&FCS) District Office.

- The U.S. businessperson should be aware that travel from one country to another may be restricted. For example, a passport containing an Israeli visa may disallow the traveler from entering certain countries in the Mideast.

Other preparations

Frequently, a travel agent can arrange for transportation and hotel reservations quickly and efficiently. The agent can also help plan the itinerary, obtain the best travel rates, explain which countries require visas, advise on hotels (rates, locations, etc.), and provide other valuable services. Since the agent's fees are paid by the hotels, airlines, and others carriers, this assistance and expertise may cost nothing.

The U.S. traveler should obtain the necessary travel documents 2 or 3 months before departure, especially if visas are needed. The travel agent can help make the arrangements. A valid U.S. passport is required for all travel outside the United States and Canada. If traveling on an old passport, the U.S. citizen should make sure that it remains valid for the entire duration of the trip.

Passports may be obtained through certain local post offices and U.S. District Courts. Application must be made in person, and a separate passport is needed for each family member who will be traveling. A passport costs $40. Additional information can be obtained by contacting the nearest local passport office, or by calling the Passport Office in Washington, DC. Telephone: (202) 783-8200.

Visas, required by many countries, cannot be obtained through the U.S. Passport Office. They are provided for a small fee by the foreign country's embassy or consulate in the United States. In order to obtain a visa, the traveler must have a current U.S. passport. In addition, many countries require a recent photo in order to issue visas. The traveler should allow several weeks to obtain visas, especially if traveling to Communist or developing nations (a list of embassies and consulates in the United States is provided in Appendix IV). Some countries that do not require visas for tourist travel do require them for business travel. Visa requirements may change from time to time.

Requirements for vaccinations differ from country to country. A travel agent or airline can advise the traveler on various requirements. In some cases, vaccinations against typhus, typhoid, and other diseases are advisable though they may not be required.

Business preparations for international travel

Before leaving the United States, the traveler should be prepared to deal with any language differences encountered by learning whether individuals expected to be met are comfortable speaking English. If not, plans should be made for translation. Business language is generally more technical than the conversational speech with which many travelers are familiar—and mistakes can be costly.

In some countries, exchanging business cards at any first meeting is considered a basic part of good business manners. As a matter of courtesy, it is best to carry business cards printed both in English and in the language of the country being visited. Some international airlines arrange this service.

The following travel checklist covers a number of considerations that apply equally to business travelers and those traveling for pleasure. A travel agent or various travel publications can help take them into account.

- Seasonal weather conditions in the countries being visited.

- Healthcare (what to eat abroad, special medical problems, prescription drugs, etc.).

- Electrical current (a transformer or plug adapter may be needed to use electrical appliances).

- Money (exchanging currency, using credit cards and travelers' checks, etc.).

- Transportation and communication abroad.

- Tipping (who is tipped and how much is appropriate).

- U.S. Customs regulations on what can be brought home.

Assistance from U.S. embassies and consulates

Economic and commercial officers in U.S. embassies and consulates abroad can provide assistance to U.S. exporters, both through in-depth briefings and by arranging introductions to appropriate firms, individuals, or foreign government officials. Because of the value and low cost of these services, it is recommended that the exporter visit the U.S. embassy soon after arriving in a foreign country. When planning a trip, business travelers can discuss their needs and the services available at particular embassies with US&FCS district office staff. It is also advisable to write directly to the U.S. embassy or consulate in the countries to be visited at least 2 weeks before leaving the United States and to address any communication to the Commercial Section. The U.S. business traveler should identify his or her business affiliation and complete address, and indicate the objective of the trip and the type of assistance required from the post. Also, a description of the firm and the extent of its international experience would be helpful to the post. Addresses of U.S. embassies and consulates are provided in *Key Officers of Foreign Service Posts,* a publication available from the Superintendent of Documents, U.S. Government Printing Office, Washington, DC 20402. Telephone: (202) 783-3238. The cost for this publication is $10 for 1 year and includes 3 updates.

Export Development Offices and some commercial offices operated by the US&FCS can provide for a nominal fee "an office away from the office" for U.S. exporters who travel abroad and need a well-equiped base of operations for a limited time. EDO's can provide office space for up to 5 days at various foreign locations (see Appendix VI for a list of EDO's). Also included are local telephone service, use of audiovisual equipment, a market briefing, a list of key business prospects, and assistance in making initial appointments. Help is also available in obtaining secretarial and interpreter services (at the U.S. company's expense). Information on these services may be obtained from a local US&FCS District Office (see Appendix V). The many other functions of EDO's are detailed in Chapter 7.

Carnets

Foreign customs regulations vary widely from place to place, and the traveler is wise to learn in advance those that apply to each country to be visited. Allowances for cigarettes, liquor, currency, and certain other items must be taken into account, or they can be impounded at national borders. Business travelers who plan to carry product samples with them should be alert to import duties they may be required to pay. In some specified countries, duties and extensive customs procedures on sample products may be avoided by obtaining an "ATA Carnet."

The United States is a member of the ATA Carnet System, which permits U.S. commercial and professional travelers to take commercial samples, tools of the trade, advertising material, cinematographic, audio-visual, medical, scientific, or other professional equipment into member countries for temporary periods of time without paying customs duties and taxes or posting a bond at the border of each country to be visited.

The following countries currently participate in the ATA Carnet System:

Australia, Austria, Belgium, Bulgaria, Canada*, Cyprus, Czechoslovakia, Denmark, Finland, France, Gibralter, Greece, Hong Kong, Hungary, Iceland, Ireland, Israel, Italy, Ivory Coast, Japan, Mauritius, The Netherlands, New Zealand, Norway, Poland, Portugal, Romania, Senegal, Singapore, Sri Lanka *, South Africa, South Korea, Spain, Sweden, Switzerland, Turkey, United Kingdom, United States, West Germany, and Yugoslavia

* Certain professional equipment not accepted.

Since other countries are frequently added to the Carnet system, the traveler should contact the U.S. Council of the International Business (at the address given below) if the country to be visited is not included in this list. Applications for Carnets should also be made to the same organization.

A fee is charged for the Carnet, depending on the value of the goods to be covered. A bond, letter of credit, or bank guaranty of 40 percent of the value of the goods is also required to cover duties and taxes that would be due if goods imported into a foreign country by Carnet were not reexported and the duties were not paid by the Carnet holder. The Carnets generally are valid for 12 months.

The address of the U.S. Council of the International Business is 1212 Avenue of the Americas, New York, New York 10036. Telephone: (212) 354-4480. Council offices are also located in Schaunburgh, Illinois; Los Angeles, California; and San Francisco, California. Further information on the ATA Carnet System can be found in "Carnet: Move Goods Duty-free Through Customs," a free and informative brochure published by the Council.

Cultural factors

Business executives who hope to profit from their travel should learn about the history, culture, and customs of the countries to be visited. Flexibility and cultural adaptation should be the guiding principles when traveling abroad on business. Business manners and methods, religious customs, dietary practices, humor, acceptable dress, all vary widely from country to country. It is important to acquire through reading or training a basic knowledge of the business culture, management attitudes, business methods, and consumer habits of the country being visited. This does not mean that the traveler must "go native" when conducting business abroad. It does mean that the traveler should be sensitive to the customs and business procedures of the country being visited.

Generally, these customs and procedures fall into one of three categories. First, there are certain cultural customs and expectations that should be adhered to in order to conduct business. For example, in the Middle East, engaging in small talk before engaging in business is standard practice. In addition, there are cultural customs that exist from which a foreigner may be excused. For example, not eating certain foods is often acceptable if the refusal is gracious. Third, there may be cultural exclusives that are customs that a foreigner should not attempt to adopt. For example, most religious or political activities should be avoided.

Making the sale

Selling overseas

9

Many successful exporters first started selling internationally by responding to an inquiry from a foreign firm. Thousands of U.S. firms receive such requests annually, but most firms do not become successful exporters. What separates the successful exporter from the unsuccessful exporter? There is no single answer, but often the firm that becomes successful knows how to respond to inquiries, can "separate the wheat from the chaff," recognizes the business practices involved in international selling, and takes time to build a relationship with the client. Although this may seem to be a large number of factors, they are all related and flow out of one another.

Responding to inquiries

Most, but not all, foreign letters of inquiry are in English. If an inquiry in a foreign language is received, a firm may look to certain service providers (such as banks, or freight forwarders) for assistance in translation. Most large cities have commercial translators who translate for a fee. Many colleges and universities also provide translation services.

If the inquiry received is like most, it asks for product specification, information and price. Some of the inquiries are from foreign firms that want information on purchasing a product for internal use, while others (distributors and agents) want to sell the product in their market. A few firms may know a product well enough and want to place an order. Most inquiries want delivery schedules, shipping costs, terms, and in some cases, exclusivity arrangements.

Regardless of the inquiry, a firm should establish a policy to deal with it and others, such as the following:

- Reply to all correspondents except to those who obviously will not turn into customers. Do not disregard the inquiry merely because it contains grammatical or typographical errors. These may result from the writer knowing English only as a second language. Similarly, if the printing quality of the stationery does not meet standards ordinarily expected, keep in mind that printing standards in the correspondent's country may be different. Despite first impressions, the inquiry may be from a reputable, well established firm.

- Reply promptly, completely, and clearly. The correspondent naturally wants to know something about the U.S. firm before doing business with it. The letter should introduce the firm

sufficiently and establish it as a reliable supplier. The reply should provide a short but adequate introduction to the firm, including bank references and other sources that confirm reliability. The firm's policy on exports should be stated in the initial letter. This should include cost, terms, delivery, etc.

- Enclose information on the firm's goods or services.

- Send reply airmail. Surface mail can take weeks or even months, whereas airmail usually takes only days. If a foreign firm's letter shows both a street address and post office box, write to the P.O. Box. Mail delivery in some countries may be unreliable, thus many firms prefer to have mail sent to their post office box.

- Set up a file for foreign letters. They may turn into definite prospects as export business grows. If the firm has a middleman handling exports, he may use the file.

Sometimes, a firm requests a more formal price quotation, called a "pro forma invoice." This is a quotation, but in an invoice format. It is rarely used in domestic business, but is frequently used in international trade. A foreign firm may ask for a pro forma because it wants to find out, in detail, what it has to spend to buy a product. For more details on pro forma invoices, see Chapter 10.

Separating the wheat from the chaff

How can a firm tell if an overseas inquiry is legitimate and from an established source?

A U.S. company can obtain more information about a foreign firm making an inquiry by checking with the following sources of information about foreign firms:

- *A good business library.* There are several publications that list and qualify international firms, including Jane's *Major Companies of Europe,* Dun & Bradstreet's *Principal International Business,* and *Europe's 5,000 Largest Companies.*

- *International banks.* Bankers have access to vast amounts of information on foreign firms and are usually very willing to assist corporate customers.

- *Foreign embassies in Washington, DC or consulates in other major cities.* The commercial (business) sections of most foreign embassies have directories of firms located in their countries.

- *U.S. Department of Commerce.* The U.S. Department of Commerce can obtain information on international firms through its *World Traders Data Reports (WTDR's)*. WTDR's are available for a fee through any local US&FCS District Office. See Chapter 4 for a more complete description of WTDR's.

Business practices in international selling

Awareness of accepted business practices is necessary for successful international selling. As cultures vary, there is no single code in which to conduct business. Certain business practices, however, transcend cultural differences. Businesspersons should, for example:

- Answer requests promptly and clearly.

- Keep promises made. A good way to lose customers is to break promises. The biggest complaint from foreign importers about U.S. suppliers is a failure to ship as promised. A first order is particularly important as it shapes a customer's image of a firm as a dependable or undependable supplier.

- Be polite, courteous, and friendly. It is important however, to avoid undue familiarity or slang. Some overseas firms feel that the usual brief U.S. business letter is lacking in courtesy.

- Personally sign all letters. Form letters are not satisfactory.

When traveling to a new market, it is important that the traveller learn as much about the culture as possible in order to avoid an embarrassing situation. For example, when in Mexico, it is customary to inquire about a colleague's wife and family, whereas in many Middle Eastern countries, it is taboo. Patting a U.S. colleague on the back for congratulations is a common practice. In Japan, however, this behavior would be discourteous. Clothes, expressions, posture and actions are all important considerations when dealing internationally.

Other important considerations are religious and national holidays. Trying to conduct business on July 4th in the United States would be difficult, if not impossible. Likewise, different dates have special significance in various countries. Some countries have long (by U.S. standards) holidays, making business difficult. For example, the month of fasting before the 5 day Ramadan religious festival in Saudi Arabia makes doing business difficult. For information on various commercial and religious holidays, refer to Chapter 8.

Numerous seminars, film series, books and publications exist to help the overseas traveller learn about other cultures. If a business colleague has returned from abroad or has expertise in a particular market, try to obtain cultural information from him or her. A little research and observance in cultural behavior can go a long way in international commerce. Likewise, a lack of sensitivity to another's customs can stop a deal in its tracks. Foreign government consulates in U.S. cities offer a wealth of information on business customs and norms for their countries (see Appendix VI).

Building a working relationship

Once a relationship has been established with an overseas customer, agent, or distributor, it is important that the exporter work on building and maintaining that relationship. Again, common courtesy should dictate business activity, and by following the points outlined in this chapter, a United States firm can present itself well. Beyond these points, the exporter should keep in mind that a foreign contact should be treated and serviced like domestic contacts. For example, the U.S. company should keep customers and contacts notified of all changes, including price, personnel, address, and phone numbers.

Because of distance, a contact can age quickly and cease to be of use unless communication is maintained. For many companies, this means monthly or quarterly visits to the customers or distributors. This level of service, although not absolutely necessary, ensures that both the company and product maintain high visibility in the marketplace. This may well mean the difference between limited sales or expanded international trade and profit.

Pricing, quotations, and terms

10

Proper pricing, complete and accurate quotations, and choice of terms for the sale are all critical elements in selling a product or service internationally. Of the three, pricing is the most problematic, even for the experienced exporter.

Pricing considerations for the U.S. exporter

- At what price should the firm sell its product in the foreign market?

- Does the foreign price reflect the product's quality?

- Is the price competitive?

- Should the firm pursue market penetration or market-skimming pricing objectives abroad?

- What type of discount (trade, cash, quantity) and allowances (advertising, trade-off) should the firm offer its foreign customers?

- Should prices differ with market segment?

- What should the firm do about product line pricing?

- What pricing options are available if our costs increase or decrease? Is the demand in the foreign market elastic or inelastic?

- How are prices going to be viewed by the foreign government—reasonable, exploitative?

As in the domestic market, the price at which a product or service is sold directly determines a firm's revenues. It is essential that a firm's market research include an evaluation of all of the variables that may affect the price range for the product or service. If a firm's price is too high, the product or service will not sell. If the price is too low, export activities may not be sufficiently profitable or may create a net loss.

The traditional components for determining proper pricing are costs, market demand, and competition. These categories are the same for domestic and foreign sales and must be evaluated in view of the firm's objective in entering the foreign market. An analysis of each component from an export perspective may result in export prices that are different from domestic prices.

Foreign market objectives

An important aspect of a company's pricing analysis involves determining market objectives. Is the company attempting to penetrate a new market?

Looking for long term market growth? Looking for an outlet for surplus production or outmoded products? For example, many firms view the foreign market as a secondary market and consequently have lower expectations regarding market share and sales volume. Pricing decisions are naturally affected by this view.

Firms also may have to tailor their marketing and pricing objectives for particular foreign markets. For example, marketing objectives for sales to a developing nation where per capita income may be one-tenth of that of the United States will by necessity be different than the objectives for Europe or Japan.

Costs

The computation of the actual cost of producing a product and bringing it to market or providing a service is the core element in determining whether exporting is financially viable. Many new exporters calculate their export price by the cost-plus method alone. In the cost-plus method of calculation, the exporter starts with the domestic manufacturing cost and adds administration, R & D, overhead, freight forwarding, distributor margins, customs charges and profit.

The net effect of this pricing approach may be that the export price escalates into an uncompetitive range. For example:

	Domestic Sale	Export Sale
Factory Price	$ 7.50	$ 7.50
Domestic Freight	.70	.70
	8.20	8.20
Export Documentation		.50
		8.70
Ocean Freight & Insurance		1.20
		9.90
Import Duty (12 percent of landed cost)		1.19
		11.09
Wholesaler Markup (15 percent)	1.23	
	9.43	
Importer/Distributor Markup (22 percent)		2.44
		13.53
Retail Markup 50 percent	4.72	6.77
	14.15	20.30
Final Consumer Price	$14.15	$20.30

Here it clearly can be seen that if an export product has the same Ex Factory price as the domestic product, its final consumer price will be considerably higher.

The most realistic method of pricing is what is termed "marginal cost" pricing. This method considers the direct, out-of-pocket expenses of producing and selling products for export as a floor beneath which prices cannot be set without incurring a loss. For example, export products may have to be modified for the export market to accommodate different sizes, electrical systems, labels, etc. Changes of this nature may increase costs. On the other hand, the export product may be a stripped-down version of the domestic product, thus lowering costs. Or, if additional products can be produced without increasing fixed costs, the incremental cost of producing additional products for export should be lower than the earlier average production costs for the domestic market.

In addition to production costs, overhead, and R & D, other costs should be allocated to domestic and export products in proportion to the benefit derived from those expenditures. Additional costs often associated with export sales include:

- Market research and credit checks.
- Business travel.
- International postage, cable, and telephone rates.
- Translation costs.
- Commissions, training charges, and other costs involving foreign representatives.
- Consultants and freight forwarders.
- Product modification and special packaging.

Once the actual cost of the export product has been calculated, the exporter should then formulate an approximate consumer price for the foreign market.

Market demand

As in the domestic market, demand in the foreign market is a key to setting prices. What will the market bear for a specific product or service?

For most consumer goods, per capita income is a good gauge of a market's ability to pay. Per capita income for most of the industrialized nations is comparable to that of the United States. For the rest of the world, it is much lower. Some products may create such a strong demand—certain chic goods like "Levis" for example—that even low per capita income will not affect their selling price. However, in most lower per capita income markets, product simplification to reduce selling price may be an answer. The firm must also keep in mind that currency valuations alter the affordability of goods. Thus pricing should accommodate wild fluctuations in currency and the relative strength of

the dollar if possible. The firm should also consider who the customers will be when pricing. For example, if the firm's main customers in a developing country are expatriates or the upperclass, they may be able to set a high price for a product even if the average per capita income is low.

Competition

In the domestic market, few companies are free to set prices without carefully evaluating their competitors' pricing policies. This is also true in exporting and further complicated by the need to evaluate the competition's prices in each export market the exporter intends to enter.

Where a particular foreign market is being serviced by many competitors, the exporter may have little choice but to match the going price, or even go below it, to establish a market share. If the exporter's product or service is new to a particular foreign market it may be actually possible to set a higher price than normally charged domestically.

Pricing summary

- Determine objective in foreign market.
- Compute actual cost of export product.
- Compute final consumer price.
- Evaluate market demand and competition.
- Consider product modification to reduce export price.

Quotations and ''pro forma'' invoices

Many export transactions, particularly first time export transactions, begin with the receipt of an inquiry from abroad, followed by a request for a quotation or a "pro forma" invoice.

A quotation basically describes the product, states a price for that product at a specified delivery point, sets the time of shipment, and specifies the terms of payment. Since the foreign buyer may not be familiar with the product, its description in an overseas quotation usually must be more detailed than in a domestic quotation. The description should include:

1. Buyer's name and address.

2. Buyer's reference number and date of inquiry.

3. Listing of requested products and brief description.

4. Price of each item (advisable to quote in U.S. dollars in order to reduce foreign exchange risk and indicate whether items are new or used).

5. Gross and net shipping weight (in metric where appropriate).

6. Total cubic volume and dimensions (in metric where appropriate) packed for export.

7. Trade discount, if applicable.

8. Delivery point.

9. Terms of payment.

10. Insurance and shipping costs.

11. Validity period for quotation.

12. Total charges to be paid by customer.

13. Estimated shipping date to factory or U.S. port (it is preferable to give U.S. port).

14. Estimate date of shipment arrival.

Often, a seller is requested to submit a pro forma invoice with or instead of a quotation. These invoices are not for payment purposes but are essentially quotations in an invoice format. In addition to the items listed above, a pro forma invoice should include a statement certifying that the pro forma invoice is true and correct and a statement describing the country of origin of the goods. Also, the invoice should be conspicuously marked "pro forma invoice". They are only models that the buyer uses when applying for an import license or arranging for funds. In fact, it is good business practice to include a pro forma invoice with any international quotation, whether it has been requested or not (See the following sample).

When preparing final collection invoices at the time of shipment, it is advisable to check with the Department of Commerce or some other reliable source for special invoicing requirements that may prevail in the country of destination.

IMPORTANT: Price quotations should state *explicitly* that they are subject to change without notice. If a specific price is agreed upon or guaranteed by the exporter, the precise period during which the offer remains valid should be specified.

Med-Tech International
1511 K Street, N.W.
Washington, DC 20005

Phone: (202) 393-7690

PRO FORMA INVOICE

Telex: 350421 TRANSNA WSH

Date: Jan. 12, 1985

To: Gomez Y. Cartagena
Aptdo. Postal 77
Bogota, Colombia
We hereby quote as follows

Your Reference: Ltr., Jan. 6, 1985

Our Reference: Col. 85-14

Terms of Sale: Letter of Credit

Quantity	Model	Description	Unit	Net	Extension
3	2-50	Separators in accordance with attached specs.	$14,750.00		$44,250.00
3	14-40	First-stage Filter Assemblies per attached specifications	$ 1,200.00		$ 3,600.00
3	custom	Drive Units—30 hp each (for operation on 3-phase 440 v., 50 cy. current) complete with remote controls	$ 3,235.00		$12,705.00

TOTAL FOB Washington, DC Domestic packed $60,555.00
Export processing, packaging, prepaid inland freight to Dulles .... $ 3,115.00
International airport & forwarder's handling charges
        FAS Dulles Airport Virginia $63,670.00
Estimated air freight and insurance .... $ 2,960.00
        Est. CIF Buenaventura, Colombia $66,630.00

Estimated Gross Weight 9,360 lbs.	**Estimated Cube 520 cu. ft.**
Export Packed 4,212 kg.	**Export Packed 15.6 cu. meters**

PLEASE NOTE
1) All prices quoted herein are U.S. Dollars.
2) Prices quoted herein for merchandise only are valid for 60 days from this date.
3) Any changes in shipping costs or insurance rates are for account of the Buyer.
4) We estimate Ex-Factory shipment approximately 60 days from receipt here of purchase order and letter of credit.

Terms of sale

In any sales agreement, it is very important that a common understanding exist regarding the delivery terms. The terms in international business transactions often sound similar to those used in domestic business, but frequently have very different meanings.

Confusion over terms of sale can result in a lost sale or a loss on a sale. For this reason, the exporter must know the terms before preparing a quotation or a pro forma invoice. A complete list of important terms and their definitions is contained in "Incoterms 1980," a booklet issued by ICC Publishing Corporation, Inc., 801 Second Avenue, Suite 1204, New York, New York 10017. The cost is $6 plus postage, handling, and sales tax if applicable. "A Guide to Incoterms" is also available from ICC for $10. This companion publication to "Incoterms" uses illustrations and commentary to explain how buyer and seller divide risks and obligations—and therefore the costs—in specific kinds of international trade transactions.

The following are a few of the more common terms used in international trade.

- **C.I.F. (Cost, Insurance, Freight)** to named overseas port of import. Under this term, the seller quotes a price for the goods, including insurance, all transportation, and miscellaneous charges to the point of debarkation from vessel or aircraft.

- **C. and F. (Cost and Freight)** to named overseas port of import. Under this term, the seller quotes a price for the goods that includes the cost of transportation to the named point of debarkation. The cost of insurance is left to the buyer's account.

- **F.A.S. (Free Alongside a Ship at named U.S. port of export).** Under this term, the seller quotes a price for goods that includes charges for delivery of the goods alongside a vessel at the port. The seller handles the cost of unloading and wharfage; loading, ocean transportation, and insurance are left to the buyer.

- **F.O.B. (Free On Board).** Under this term, the seller quotes a price for goods that includes the cost of loading them into transport vessels at a named point.

- **F.O.B. (named inland point of origin).** The price quoted applies only at a designated inland shipping point. The seller is responsible for loading goods into the transport vessel, the buyer for all subsequent expenses.

- **F.O.B. (named port of exportation).** The quoted price includes the cost of transporting the goods to the named point.

- **F.O.B. VESSEL (named port of export).** The seller quotes a price covering all expenses up to, and including, delivery of goods upon an overseas vessel provided by or for the buyer.

- **EX (named point of origin);** e.g., EX FACTORY, EX WAREHOUSE, etc. Under this term, the price quoted applies only at the point of origin, and the seller agrees to place the goods at the disposal of the buyer at the specified place on the date or within the period fixed. All other charges are for the account of the buyer.

When quoting a price, the exporter should make it meaningful to the prospective buyer. A price for industrial machinery quoted "F.O.B. Saginaw, Michigan, not export packed" would be meaningless to most prospective foreign buyers. Such buyers would have difficulty determining the total costs and, accordingly, would be hesitant to place an order.

The exporter should quote C.I.F. whenever possible. It shows the foreign buyer what it costs to get the product to a port in or near the desired country.

If assistance is needed in figuring the C.I.F. price, an international freight forwarder (see Chapter 13) can provide help to U.S. firms. The exporter should furnish to the freight forwarder a description of the product to be exported with its weight and cubic measurement when packed; the freight forwarder can then compute the C.I.F. price. There is usually no charge for this service.

If at all possible, the exporter should quote the price in U.S. dollars. This eliminates the risk of possible exchange rate fluctuations and the problems of currency conversion. (As a courtesy, the exporter may also wish to include a second pro forma invoice in the foreign currency of the buyer.)

A simple misunderstanding regarding delivery terms may prevent an exporter from meeting contractual obligations or make the exporter responsible for shipping costs he or she sought to avoid. It is important to understand and use delivery terms correctly.

Financing the sale

11

Exporters naturally want to get paid as quickly as possible and importers usually prefer delaying payment at least until they have received and resold the goods. Because of the intense competition for export markets, being able to offer good payment terms is often necessary to make a sale. Exporters should be aware of the many financing options open to them in order to choose the one that is most favorable for both the buyer and the seller. The primary options are briefly described in this chapter.

Major considerations in financing

The following are some of the most important factors to consider when making decisions about financing.

- **The need for financing to make the sale**

  In some cases, favorable terms make a product more competitive. If the competition offers better terms and has a similar product, a sale can be lost. In other cases, the exporter may need financing in order to produce the goods that have been ordered or to finance other aspects of a sale, including promotion and selling expenses, engineering modifications, shipping costs, etc.

- **The cost of different methods of financing**

  Interest rates and fees vary. The total cost and its effect on price and profit should be well understood.

- **The length of time that financing is required**

  Costs increase with length of terms. Different methods of financing are available for different lengths of time (short, medium, and long-term).

- **The risk involved**

  Some methods of financing may reduce the risk to the exporter, such as financing through letters of credit or various forms of risk insurance. In any case, the creditworthiness of the buyer is a factor either in direct risk to the exporter or in possible higher cost for interest or insurance. Several methods can be used to check a potential buyer's credit. (See Chapter 14.) The US&FCS District Office or a bank can provide more information on these methods.

- **The company's own financial resources**

  The company may be able to extend credit without seeking outside financing, or the company may have sufficient financial strength to establish a commercial line of credit. If neither of these is possible or desirable, other options exist.

Commercial banks

A logical first step in choosing financing is to approach a local commercial bank for advice. If a company finds that its bank does not have an international department, then a good bank can be recommended by several sources:

- The US&FCS District Office.
- Eximbank or The Small Business Administration.
- The company's current bank.
- The company's freight forwarder.
- An experienced exporter referred by the local District Export Council or World Trade Club.

Most of these sources can also discuss financing needs and make helpful suggestions.

If a company is new to exporting or is a small or medium-sized business, it is important to select a bank that not only has an international department, but that also is sincerely interested in serving businesses of similar type or size. Of the many thousands of banks in the United States, several hundred have international departments, about half of which find it profitable to serve small- or medium-size exporters.

When selecting a bank, the exporter should ask the following questions:

- How big is the bank's international department?
- Does it have foreign branches or correspondent banks? Where are they located?
- What are charges for confirming a letter of credit, processing drafts, and collecting payment?
- Can the bank provide buyer credit reports? Free or at what cost?
- Does it have experience with U.S. and State government financing programs that support small business export transactions? If not, is it willing to participate in these programs?
- What other services can it provide (trade leads, etc.)?

Types of bank financing

The same type of commercial loans that finance domestic activities—including loans for working capital and revolving lines of credit—are available to finance export sales until payment is received. However, most banks do not usually extend credit solely on the basis of an order; thus these loans can tie up assets that must be used as collateral and can use up limited credit lines that may be needed for other transactions.

In many cases, Federal and State small business export finance programs can help reduce the need for collateral and extend the amount of credit available. There are also ways to avoid normal commercial loans altogether by requesting banker's acceptance financing.

If an export transaction is paid by using letters of credit or trade drafts (see Chapter 14 on methods of payment), banker's acceptance financing can be used to provide immediate payment to the exporter. This follows even though the letter of credit or draft calls for payment from the buyer up to 180 days in the future.

When a letter of credit or draft is formally approved for payment (through endorsement by a bank or by the buyer), it is called an "acceptance." This document can either be kept by the exporter until the stated terms of credit have expired and then be presented for payment, or it can usually be sold immediately to a U.S. bank at a discount. In the case of an irrevocable letter of credit, payment is guaranteed by a foreign bank, and the U.S. bank will not require collateral or other proof of ability to pay from the exporter. With a trade draft, such proof may be required since the bank must come to the exporter for repayment if the buyer defaults.

The advantages of banker's acceptance financing, especially when a letter of credit is used, are the following:

- The exporter receives immediate payment in contrast to commercial loans where the cost of goods is financed but profit is not realized until payment is received.

- Less of the exporter's capital and credit line is tied up in financing (none if a letter of credit is used).

- The total interest charges and fees are usually lower—thus costs are lower for both buyer and seller.

As with any type of export financing, it should be noted that finance charges for banker's acceptances may be passed through to the buyer as part of the terms of sale (made clear in the quotation and invoice as part of the price or an added charge). For more information on this type of financing, contact one of the sources of advice listed earlier in this chapter.

Federal Government export financing programs

A bank with a good international department experienced with government export finance programs can often advise an exporter on the different programs available. Most of the programs described below—including State programs—are intended to work through a commercial bank. Banks that participate in these programs are the agents that apply on the exporter's behalf for program benefits. The exporter need not become an expert, yet knowing the existence of these financing opportunities can be quite valuable.

Even if a bank that is currently being used by an exporter has had no experience with government export financing programs, this bank may still be used if it is willing to follow program guidelines. If assistance is needed in locating a bank that uses any of these programs, contact the appropriate Federal or State agency. The descriptions below provide a basic overview. More information can be had from the government agency listed, from banks, and also from the Department of Commerce publication *A Guide to Financing Exports*, available from US&FCS District Offices. The Department of Commerce operates no financing programs but can help exporters choose among programs that exist: Contact a local US&FCS District Office or the Office of Trade Finance, International Trade Administration, in Washington, DC. Telephone: (202) 377-3277.

Export-Import Bank

The Export-Import Bank (Eximbank) of the United States offers direct loans for large projects and equipment sales that usually require long-term financing; it guarantees loans made by cooperating U.S. and foreign commercial banks to U.S. exporters and to foreign buyers of U.S. products and services; and, through a private insurance association, the Foreign Credit Insurance Association (FCIA), it provides insurance to U.S. exporters enabling them to extend credit to their overseas buyers.

In all cases, Eximbank must find a "reasonable assurance of repayment" as a precondition of participating in the transaction. However, because the bank offers loan guarantees and credit insurance, a major effect of using Eximbank programs is to reduce the amount of collateral required to finance a loan and to generally make financing more available than would be the case without its support.

Among Eximbank's array of loan, guarantee, and insurance programs are four that are especially helpful to small companies and those that are new to exporting.

1. **Working Capital Guarantee Program.**—This program can guarantee loans for working capital needed before actual sales. The loan is made by

a commercial lender to a U.S. exporter; however, Eximbank guarantees repayment of 90 percent of the principal. Thus, the lender retains only a 10 percent risk on the loan.

The purpose of the loan must be for a specific export-related activity, such as inventory purchases or the development of export marketing programs that may include foreign marketing trips, trade fair participation, and other promotional activities. The term of the loan generally ranges from one month to one year, but may be of longer duration if required.

Security for the loan must have a value of at least 110 percent of the outstanding balance (in contrast to 150 percent to 200 percent that would be required without Eximbank's guarantee). The total cost for the loan is similar to the cost of regular commercial loans.

2. **Export Credit Insurance.**—Credit insurance is available through FCIA to cover 100 percent of losses for political reasons (war, expropriation, currency inconvertibility, etc.) and up to 95 percent of commercial losses (nonpayment by the buyer due to insolvency or default). Having such insurance can encourage the exporter to extend credit or more favorable terms to foreign buyers and thus to be more competitive. Credit insurance also encourages commercial banks to extend credit on the basis of covered accounts receivables. About 200 banks in the United States have purchased Master Policies from FCIA that can insure all of their loans to U.S. exporters. Banks charge a nominal fee, roughly 1 percent of the amount insured. In 1984, Eximbank and FCIA started a new program to allow organizations other than banks to purchase "Umbrella Policies" to cover their clients. Thus, this type of coverage is available from organizations such as export trading companies, freight forwarders, and local economic development agencies.

Policies can also be purchased by a single exporter. A special New-to-Export policy is offered with greater coverage than for policies available to more experienced exporters. This introductory policy is available for companies that had export sales of less than $750,000 a year in the last 2 years and that have not previously used Eximbank or FCIA programs.

FCIA policies offer considerable protection, but they do not make exporting completely risk-free. The exporter is expected to exercise good credit judgment and to assume a portion of the commercial risks. Furthermore, even though credit insurance can cover a majority of the risk, the exporter must also consider the administrative time to file a claim and the resulting delay of payment if a buyer defaults.

3. **Commercial Bank Guarantees.**—Eximbank offers guarantees against non-payment of foreign purchasers on medium-term (181 days to 5 years) export loans by U.S. commercial banks. Loans may be used to finance capital and quasi-capital goods and services. A minimum 15 percent cash payment must be made by the foreign buyer. Eximbank's guarantee covers 100 percent of political risk and up to 90 percent of commercial risk. Coverage is currently available for approximately 140 countries.

4. **Small Business Credit Program.**—In addition to the risks that the foreign buyer will not repay an export loan, a commercial bank providing export financing faces the risk that its cost of money will rise before the loan is repaid. For this reason, banks generally prefer to extend floating rate loans. Foreign purchasers, however, are frequently unwilling to accept fluctuating interest rate risk in addition to the foreign exchange risk they bear on foreign currency loans. Eximbank's small business credit program enables U.S. banks to offer medium-term fixed rate export loans to finance sales of small U.S. companies' products and services with interest rates fixed at the lowest rates permitted under the export credit guidelines followed by all members of the Organization for Economic Cooperation and Development (OECD). The OECD rates are reviewed every 6 months and adjusted as necessary to reflect changes in prevailing interest rates.

The Small Business Credit Program covers loans made to finance capital and quasi-capital goods and services of U.S. small business exporters. Exporters must meet Small Business Administration "small business" definitions in order to qualify; however, a similar program is available for larger firms if there is evidence that the Eximbank-covered loan is needed to match foreign competition. Eximbank requires that the purchaser make a minimum 15 percent cash payment. The bank loan covers up to 85 percent of the export contract, on terms ranging from over 1 year to 5 years. At the time of commitment, the interest rate is fixed according to the classification of the country to which the export is shipped.

Eximbank and FCIA also provide other credit programs for medium and long-term financing. Long-term financing (5 years and longer) is generally for export of capital equipment and large-scale installations. This financing takes the form either of a direct credit to an overseas buyer or a financial guarantee assuring repayment of a private bank credit. Eximbank often blends these two forms of support into a single financing package. The chart below gives a brief guide to the use of different programs. In the chart, exports are divided into three categories, and for each category there are two or more program options.

EXIMBANK/FCIA
Program Selection Chart

Exports	Appropriate Programs
Short-Term (up to 180 days)	
Consumables	Export Credit Insurance
Small manufactured items	Working Capital
Spare Parts	Guarantee
Raw Materials	
Medium-Term (181 days to 5 years)	
Mining and refining equipment	Export Credit Insurance
	Commercial Bank
Construction equipment	Guarantees
Agricultural equipment	Small Business Credit
General aviation aircraft	Program
General aviation aircraft	Medium-Term Credit
Planning/feasibility studies	Working Capital
	Guarantee
Long-Term (5 years and longer)	
Power plants	Direct Loans
LPG & gas producing plants	Financial Guarantees
Other major projects	
Commercial jet aircraft or locomotives	
Other heavy capital goods	

For more information on these programs, contact a cooperating bank or one of the other advisors suggested in this guide. Eximbank also provides a toll-free hotline telephone service to advise and assist small businesses interested in exporting: (800) 424-5201.

Small Business Administration

The Small Business Administration (SBA) provides several financial assistance programs to U.S. exporters, some of which are similar to Eximbank's programs. Under a recent agreement between the two agencies, they can now join their resources to make more credit available to a single borrower— up to $1,000,000 per borrower. Applications are made by a U.S. exporter through a commercial bank that submits the application to an SBA field office for processing.

Under SBA's Export Revolving Line of Credit Loan program (ERLC), any number of withdrawals and repayments can be made as long as the dollar limit of the line is not exceeded and disbursements are made within the stated maturity period (not over 18 months). Proceeds can be used only to finance labor and materials needed for manufacturing, to purchase inventory to meet an export order, and to penetrate or develop foreign markets. Examples of eligible expenses for developing foreign markets include: Professional export marketing advice or services, foreign business travel, and trade show participation.

Under the ERLC program, funds may not be used to pay existing obligations or to purchase fixed assets; however, SBA has "regular" business loan guarantee and direct loan programs that can finance these activities. Thus, if an exporter needs to increase or modify production capacity to supply new foreign markets (or for any other purpose) SBA financing can also assist.

SBA generally defines a small business as one that is independently owned and operated and is not dominant in its field. To be eligible for SBA loans and other assistance, a business must meet a size standard set by the Agency. In addition, an applicant must normally have been in business (not necessarily in exporting) for at least 12 full months before filing an application. However, this requirement may be waived if the company's management has had sufficient experience in other companies.

Since the SBA's financial assistance programs are restricted to providing loans and loan guarantees to firms located in the United States—its possessions and territories—the agency is unable to provide financial assistance for the establishment of overseas joint ventures. In addition, by law, the agency cannot make a loan if a business is able to obtain funds from a bank or other private financial institution.

For more specific information on the SBA's financial assistance programs, policies, and requirements, contact the nearest SBA field office.

Overseas Private Investment Corporation

Through the Overseas Private Investment Corporation (OPIC), the Federal Government facilitates U.S. private investments in less developed nations. OPIC is an independent, financially self-supporting corporation, fully owned by the U.S. Government with offices in Washington, DC.

In addition to financing insurance programs for investors in foreign projects, OPIC offers specialized insurance and financing services for U.S. service contractors and exporters operating in developing countries.

Many developing countries require foreign firms to post bid, performance or advance payment guaranties in the form of standby letters of credit when bidding on or performing overseas contracts. OPIC's political risk insurance for contractors and exporters protects against the arbitrary or unfair drawing of such letters of credit.

In addition, contractors and exporters may also obtain insurance against the risks of currency inconvertibility; confiscation of tangible assets and bank accounts; war, revolution, insurrection and civil strife; and losses sustained when a government owner fails to settle a dispute in accordance with the provisions of the underlying contract.

For more information on any of these programs, a toll-free telephone number may be used: (800) 424-6742 (653-2800 if calling from within the Washington, DC, metropolitan area).

Private Export Funding Corporation

The Private Export Funding Corporation (PEFCO) is a private corporation owned by 62 investors, mostly commercial banks. PEFCO makes medium and long-term loans to borrowers in foreign countries for the purchase of U.S. goods and services. All of its loans must be covered by an unconditional guarantee of Eximbank for principal and interest. PEFCO's funds may be used to supplement the financing of U.S. exports available through commercial banks or Eximbank. PEFCO generally does not make loans of less then $1 million; there is no maximum loan amount.

Before contacting PEFCO, the potential borrower (a foreign buyer) or the U.S. exporter should obtain an indication from Eximbank that its board will issue a Financial Guarantee for part of the required financing. Exporters or foreign buyers with no experience in using Eximbank or PEFCO funding should first approach an experienced commercial bank; the bank will then determine whether a PEFCO loan would be a reasonable supplement to the funds provided by other sources.

Department of Agriculture

The Foreign Agricultural Service (FAS) of the U.S. Department of Agriculture provides financial support for U.S. agricultural exports through the Food for Peace program and the Commodity Credit Corporation. Under the Food for Peace program, Title I of the Agricultural Trade Development and Assistance Act of 1954 (Public Law 480, as amended) authorizes U.S. Government financing of sales of U.S. agricultural commodities to friendly countries on concessional credit terms. Sales are made by private business firms usually by bids. FAS administers agreements under this program. Among those commodities that have recently been included under this program are: Wheat, corn, grain sorghum, rice, vegetable oil, wheat flour, dry edible beans, blended/fortified foods, and cotton.

Through the Commodity Credit Corporation (CCC), FAS provides U.S. exporters with short-term, commercial export financing support under two programs: The Export Credit Guarantee Program and the Blended Credit Program.

Firms may obtain additional information on these financial programs by contacting: General Sales Manager, Export Credits, Foreign Agricultural Service, 14th Street and Independence Ave., S.W., Washington, DC 20250. Telephone: (202) 447-3224.

State and local export finance programs

As of January 1, 1985, 15 State governments have authority to operate export financing programs. In addition, about 30 other States are currently exploring such mechanisms. Some of these programs allow a State development agency to act as a delivery agent for Eximbank programs. Other programs include State funded loan guarantee programs.

The Illinois program, one of the most comprehensive, authorizes both pre-shipment and post-shipment assistance in the form of loans to lenders and loan guarantees to exporters and their banks. The program is aimed at small and medium-sized businesses and requires that exports contain 25 percent value added in-State. Several State programs, including Illinois', have established mechanisms for direct involvement of private sector representatives in the design and operation of the program. This feature is intended to ensure that the program is responsive to business needs and is easy to use.

Exporters should contact the State's economic development agency for more information (see Appendix V for address and phone number).

Export trading companies and export management companies

Many export trading companies (ETC's) and export management companies (EMC's) can help finance export sales in addition to acting as export representatives. However, this is true mainly for larger companies. Large ETC's may of course be able to purchase goods for export on-the-spot and thus eliminate the need for financing and other risks. When this is not the case, trading companies in a few instances may provide short-term financing themselves, but more significantly, they are also offering established contacts to make it easier for their exporter clients to obtain credit and credit insurance. Moreover, several trading companies are large enough to arrange countertrade transactions, in which trading and financing would be inseparable (see Chapter 14 for more information on countertrade).

Other private sources

Factoring

Certain companies, known as "factoring houses" or simply "factors" purchase export receivables (i.e., the invoices to foreign buyers) for a somewhat discounted price, perhaps 2 to 4 percent less than their face value. The actual amount of the discount depends on the factoring house, the kind of products involved, the customer, and the country. Factors offer two important advantages: 1) Immediate payment is received for the exported goods, freeing cash that could otherwise be tied up for months, and 2) the burden of collection is eliminated.

Arrangements with factoring houses are made either with or without "recourse." Arrangements "with recourse" leave the exporter liable for repaying the factor if the foreign buyer defaults or other problems prevent payment within a reasonable period. Arrangements "without recourse" free the exporter from this responsibility. Naturally, factors that accept export receivables "without recourse" generally require a large discount.

Confirming

Designed to help exporters and importers expand their markets, improve cash flow, and create greater profit leverage, "confirming" is a financial service in which an independent company confirms an export order in the vendor's own country and makes payment for the goods in the currency of that country. This service can pay for and finance on terms the following items: The goods themselves, transportation (ocean or air), inland transportation at both ends, forwarding fees, customs brokerage fees, duties, etc. For the U.S. exporter, this means that the entire export transaction, from factory to end-user, can be fully coordinated and paid for with terms. Though common in Europe, confirming is still in its infancy in the United States.

Export regulations, customs benefits, and tax incentives

12

This chapter covers a wide range of regulations, procedures, and practices that fall into one of three categories: 1) Regulations that exporters must follow to comply with U.S. law; 2) procedures that exporters should follow to ensure a successful export transaction; and 3) programs and certain tax procedures that open new markets or provide financial benefits to exporters.

Export regulations

Although a basic part of exporting, export licensing is one of the most widely misunderstood aspects of government regulation of exporting. At first glance, the export licensing procedure may appear complex, but in most cases, it is a rather straight-forward process. Exporters should remember, however, that violations of *The Export Administration Regulations* carry both civil and criminal penalties, so if in doubt, U.S. Department of Commerce officials or qualified professional consultants should be consulted for assistance in complying with export regulations.

The Export Administration Regulations are available by subscription from the Superintendent of Documents, U.S. Government Printing Office, Washington, DC 20402. Subscription forms may be obtained from the nearest US&FCS District Office, or from the Office of Export Administration, Operations Division, Room 2091, U.S. Department of Commerce, Washington DC 20230. Telephone: (202) 377-4266.

Export License

For reasons of national security, foreign policy, or short supply of certain domestic products, the U.S. controls the export of all goods and technology through the granting of two types of export licenses: General Licenses and Validated Licenses. Licenses are given for *transactions*, not for individuals or companies. Except for U.S. territories and possessions and, in most cases, Canada, all items exported require an export license. Several agencies of the U.S. Government are involved in the export license procedure.

General License

A General License is a broad grant of authority by the Goverment to all exporters for certain categories of products. Individual exporters do not need to apply for General Licenses.

Validated License

In brief, a Validated License is a specific grant of authority from the Goverment to particular exporter to export a particular product. The Licenses are granted on a case-by-case basis for either a single tranaction or for a specified period of time. An exporter must apply for a Validated Export License.

How to determine which license to use

The first step in complying with the export licensing regulations is to determine whether a product requires a General or a Validated License. (See chart) The determination of which license is needed is based on what is being exported and where it is going.

Basically, this determination involves a three-step procedure:

1. What is the destination of the product? A firm must check the schedule of "Country Groups" contained in the *Export Administration Regulations* (15 CFR Part 370, Suppl. No. 1) to see which "Country Group" the export destination falls under.

2. What is being exported? The firm must check the "Commodity Control List" (15 CFR Section 399.1 Suppl. No. 1) to see whether the product requires a Validated License for shipment to the "Country Groups" identified in the preceeding step.

3. Finally, the firm must determine whether any "special restrictions" apply to the export transaction. 15 CFR Parts 376, 378, 385, and other provisions of the *Export Administration Regulations* may impose additional export restrictions, e.g. certain country-specfic foreign policy controls.

In order to avoid any possible confusion, the exporter is advised to seek assistance in determining the proper license. The best source is the Department of Commerce's Exporter Assistance Division, which can be contacted either by telephone or in writing: Exporter Assistnce Division, Room 1099D, U.S. Department of Commerce, Washington, DC 20230. Telephone: (202) 377-4811. Or, the exporter may check with the local US&FCS District Office. An exporter can also request a preliminary, written advisory opinion from the Department of Commerce. In order to save time, however, the firm might also consider using the

51

services of a consulting or law firm to obtain the export license, particularly for the first few transactions.

Shipments under a General License

If, after reviewing *The Export Administration Regulations* or after consultation with the Department of Commerce, it is determined that a Validated License is not required, an exporter may ship its product under a General License.

A General License, as mentioned above, does not require a specific application. If exporting under a General License, the exporter must determine whether a "Destination Control Statement" is required. Destination Control Statements are discussed below.

Finally, if the shipment is valued at $500 or more, or requires a validated export license, the exporter must complete a Shipper's Export Declaration (SED). The SED is used by Customs to indicate the type of export license being used and to keep track of what is exported. They are also used by the Bureau of Census to compile statistics on U.S. trade patterns.

Shipments under a Validated License

If a Validated License is required, the U.S. exporter must prepare and submit Form ITA-622P "Application for a Validated Export License". The applicant must be certain to follow the instructions on the back of the form carefully. A cover letter that explains the domestic use of the product should be included, stating how the product will be used by the foreign purchaser. Technical manuals and specification sheets should also be included, along with a statement indicating whether the product can be altered for other uses.

The exporter should also attach to the application a stamped self-addressed post card with the following form typed on the back of the postcard:

Date Received: _____

Case No: _____

This card is completed by the Department of Commerce and mailed back to the applicant so that, in the event of a delay or any other problem with the application, the exporter can easily refer to the application number.

If the application is approved, the actual Validated License is mailed to the applicant. The license contains an export license number that must be inserted on the Shipper's Export Declaration (SED). Unlike goods exported under a General License, all goods exported under a Validated License must have a SED.

The final steps in complying with the Validated License procedure involve post-export activities. First, the exporter must record on the back of the license all shipments made under the license. Second, the U.S. firm must return the licenses to the Department of Commerce after the license has been used or after it has expired. It is advisable that the exporter keep copies of all documents related to the export transaction.

How to avoid delays in receiving a Validated License

There are three errors commonly made by exporters in filling out license applications that account for most delays in processing applications:

1. Failure to sign the application.

2. Inadequate response to Section 9b of the application. Section 9b "Description of Commodity or Technical Data" calls for a description of the item(s) that is to be exported. The applicant must be specific. The applicant is encouraged to attach additional material to fully explain the product.

3. Inadequate response to Section 12 of the application. Section 12 asks to describe the specific end-use of the products or technical data. Again, the applicant must be specific. A vague response, or "Unknown" may likely result in a rejection of the application.

If an exporter is in doubt about the need for a Validated License, he may still apply for one. If a Validated License is not required, the applicant will be so notified (the application will be "Returned Without Action"). This notification may be useful should the exporter have any problems with customs clearance of the products.

In an emergency situation, the Department of Commerce may consider processing a Validated License application on an expedited basis, but this procedure cannot be used as a substitute for the timely filing of an application.

Additional documentation

In addition to filing an application for a Validated License, certain applications must be accompanied by documents supplied by the prospective purchaser or the government of the country of destination. By reviewing *The Export Administration Regulations*, the exporter can determine whether any supporting documents are required.

The most common supporting documents are the International Import Certificate and the Statement of Ultimate Consignee and Purchaser. The International Import Certificate (Form ITA-645P/ATF-4522/DSP-53) is a statement issued by the government of the country of destination that certifies that the exported products will be disposed of responsibly in the designated country. It is the responsibility of the exporter to obtain the certificate and submit it with the Validated License application.

The Statement of Ultimate Consignee and Purchaser (ITA Form-629P) is a written assurance that the foreign purchaser of the goods will not resell or dispose of goods in a manner contrary to the export license under which the goods were originally exported. The exporter must send the statement to the foreign purchaser for completion. The exporter then files this form along with the export license application.

In addition to obtaining the appropriate export license, U.S. exporters should be careful to meet all other international trade regulations established by specific legislation or other authority of the U.S. Government. The import regulations of foreign countries must, of course, also be taken into account. The exporter should also keep in mind that even if help is received with the license and documentation from others, such as banks, freight forwarders or consultants, it remains the responsibility of the exporter to ensure that all statements are true and accurate.

Antidiversion, Antiboycott, and Antitrust Requirements

Antidiversion Clause

To help ensure that U.S. exports go only to legally authorized destinations, the U.S. Government requires a "destination control statement" on shipping documents. Under this requirement, the commercial invoice and bill of lading (or air waybill) for nearly all commercial shipments leaving the United States must display a statement notifying the carrier and all foreign parties (the ultimate and intermediate consignees and purchaser) that the U.S. material has been licensed for export only to certain destinations and may not be diverted contrary to U.S. law. Exceptions to the use of the destination control statement are shipments intended for consumption in Canada and shipments being made under certain General Licenses. Advice on the appropriate statement to be used can be provided by the Department of Commerce, the US&FCS District Office, an attorney or freight forwarder.

Antiboycott Regulations

The United States has an established policy of opposing restrictive trade practices or boycotts fostered or imposed by foreign countries against other countries friendly to the United States. This policy is implemented through the Antiboycott provisions of the Export Administration Act enforced by the Department of Commerce and, under various regulations, enforced by the Treasury Department.

In general, these laws prohibit "United States persons" from participating in foreign boycotts or taking actions that further or support such boycotts. The Antiboycott regulations carry out this general purpose by:

- Prohibiting U.S. persons from refusing to do business with blacklisted firms and boycotted friendly countries pursuant to foreign boycott demands.

- Prohibiting U.S. persons from discriminating against other U.S. persons on the basis of race, religion, sex, or national origin in order to comply with a foreign boycott.

- Prohibiting U.S. persons from furnishing information about their business relationships with friendly foreign countries or blacklisted companies in response to boycott requirements.

- Providing for public disclosure of requests to comply with foreign boycotts.

- Requiring U.S. persons who receive requests to comply with foreign boycotts to disclose publicly whether they have complied with such requests.

- Ensuring that the antiboycott provisions of the Export Administration Act apply to all U.S. persons, including intermediaries in the export process, as well as foreign subsidiaries that are "controlled in fact" by U.S. companies.

The Department of Commerce's Office of Antiboycott Compliance (OAC) administers the program through ongoing investigations of corporate activities. The OAC operates an automated boycott reporting system to provide statistical and enforcement data to Congress and to the public, issuing interpretations of the regulations for the affected public and offering nonbinding informal guidance to the private sector on specific compliance concerns. U.S. firms with questions about complying with antiboycott regulations should call OAC at (202) 377-2381 or write the Office of Antiboycott Compliance, Room 3886, International Trade Administration, U.S. Department of Commerce, Washington, DC 20230.

Antitrust Laws

The U.S. antitrust laws reflect this Nation's commitment to an economy based on competition. They are intended to foster the efficient allocation of resources by providing consumers with goods and services at the lowest price that efficient business operations can profitably offer. Various foreign countries, including the European Economic Community (Common Market), Canada, the United Kingdom, Federal Republic of Germany, Japan and Australia, also have their own antitrust laws that must be complied with by U.S. firms when exporting to such nations.

The U.S. antitrust statutes do not provide a checklist of specific requirements, but instead set forth broad principles that are applied to the specific facts and circumstances of a business transaction. Under the U.S. antitrust laws, some types of trade restraints, known as *per se* violations, are regarded as conclusively illegal. *Per se* violations include price fixing agreements and conspiracies, divisions of markets by competitors, and certain group boycotts and tying arrangements.

Most restraints of trade in the United States are judged under a second legal standard known as the "rule of reason." The rule of reason requires a showing that: (1) Certain acts occurred; and (2) such acts had an anticompetitive effect. Under the rule of reason, a variety of factors are considered, including business justification, impact upon prices and output in the market, barriers to entry and market shares of the parties.

In the case of exports by U.S. firms, there are special limitations on the application of the *per se* and rule of reason tests by U.S. courts. Under Title IV of the Export Trading Company Act (also known as the Foreign Trade Antitrust Improvements Act), there must be a "direct, substantial and reasonably foreseeable" effect on the domestic or import commerce of the United States or on the export commerce of a U.S. person before an activity may be challenged under the Sherman or Federal Trade Commission Acts (two of the primary Federal antitrust statutes). This provision clarifies the particular circumstances under which the overseas activities of U.S. exporters may be challenged under these two antitrust statutes. Under Title III of the Export Trading Company Act (discussed in Chapter 4), the U.S. Department of Commerce, with the concurrence of the U.S. Department of Justice, can issue an export trade certificate of review that provides certain exemptions from the Federal and State antitrust laws.

While the great majority of international business transactions do not pose antitrust problems, antitrust issues may be raised in various types of transactions. These include, but are not necessarily limited to: Overseas distribution arrangements; overseas joint ventures for research, manufacturing, construction and distribution; patent, trademark, copyright, and know-how licenses; mergers and acquisitions involving foreign firms; and raw material procurement agreements and concessions. The sections of this *Guide* on Technology Licensing, Joint Ventures and Wholly-Owned Branch and Subsidiary Operations discuss in greater detail the potential U.S. and foreign antitrust problems posed by such transactions (See Chapter 16). Where potential antitrust issues are raised, it is advisable to obtain the advice and assistance of qualified antitrust counsel.

For particular transactions that pose difficult antitrust issues, and for which an export trade certificate of review is not desired, the Antitrust Division of the U.S. Department of Justice can be asked to state its enforcement views in a Business Review letter. The Business Review procedure is initiated by writing a letter to the Antitrust Division describing the particular business transaction that is contemplated and requesting the Department's views on the antitrust legality of the transaction.

Certain aspects of the Federal antitrust laws and the Antitrust Division's enforcement policies are explored in two useful sets of guidelines published by the Justice Department. These are the *Antitrust Guide for International Operations* (1977), *Antitrust Guide Concerning Research Joint Ventures* (1980), and Foreign Corrupt Practices Act (FCPA).

The Foreign Corrupt Practices Act of 1977 (FCPA) makes (among other things) certain payments, offers of payments, and gifts to foreign officials, foreign political parties, or foreign political candidates illegal if made corruptly for the purpose of obtaining, retaining, or directing business to any person. It also establishes record keeping and internal accounting control requirements for all publicly held corporations, whether or not these corporations are engaged in international business. The U.S. Department of Justice and the Securities and Exchange Commission (SEC) share responsibility for enforcing this law.

The "FCPA Review Procedure" was established by the Department of Justice to help reduce uncertainties within the U.S. business community about the antibribery provisions of the Act. Under this procedure—similar to the Business Review Procedure available for antitrust considerations—a business can submit to the Justice Department details of a proposed international transaction and request a determination of Justice's enforcement intentions if the transaction were to proceed. Justice's Criminal Division has expressed its intention to respond to the request within 30 days after receiving all the information it considers relevant to the proposed transaction. The FCPA Review Procedure applies only to possible bribery violations falling within the jurisdiction of the Department of Justice and not the violations of other sections of the law that fall under the jurisdiction of the SEC. However, the SEC, as a matter of policy, has decided to acquiesce in the bribery determinations made by the Department of Justice under its FCPA Review Procedure. The SEC makes its own determinations regarding violations of the accounting and other sections of law under its jurisdiction.

FDA & EPA restrictions

In addition to the various export regulations already discussed, a limited number of exporters are also affected by rules and regulations enforced by the Food and Drug Administration (FDA) and the Environmental Protection Agency (EPA).

FDA

The FDA enforces U.S. laws intended to assure the consumer that foods are pure and wholesome, that drugs and devices are safe and effective, and that cosmetics are safe. The FDA has promulgated a wide range of regulations to enforce these goals. Exporters of products covered by the FDA's regulations are affected as follows:

- If the item is intended for export only, meets the specifications of the foreign purchaser, is not in conflict with the laws of the country to which it is to be shipped, and is properly labeled, it is exempt from the adulteration and misbranding provisions of the Act (See 801(d)). This exemption does not apply to "new drugs" or "new animal drugs" that have not been approved as safe and effective, and certain devices.

- If the exporter thinks the export product may be covered by the FDA, it is important to contact the nearest FDA field office or the Public Health Service, Food and Drug Administration, 5600 Fishers Lane, Rockville, MD 20857.

EPA

EPA's involvement in exports is restricted to the export of hazardous waste. Although the EPA has no authority to control the export of hazardous waste, it has established an export notification system in recognition of the potential environmental, health, and foreign policy problems that may arise from such exports.

Under the Resource Conservation and Recovery Act (RCRA), generators of waste who wish to export waste considered hazardous are required to notify EPA before shipment of a given hazardous waste to a given foreign consignee. EPA then notifies the government of the foreign consignee. Export cannot occur until receipt of written approval by the foreign government.

An exporter of hazardous waste or similar material should contact the EPA before shipping. Contact the Office of International Activities, U.S. Environmental Protection Agency, Washington, DC 20460.

Import regulations of foreign governments

Import documentation requirements and other regulations imposed by foreign governments vary from country to country, and it is vital that the exporter be aware of the regulations that apply to his or her own operations and transactions. Many governments, for instance, require consular invoices, certificates of inspection, health certification, and various other documents. For a more complete description of foreign government import regulations, refer to Chapter 13.

Customs benefits for exporters

Drawback of custom duties

"Drawback" is a form of tax relief in which a custom duty, lawfully collected, is refunded or remitted wholly or in part because of the particular use made of the commodity on which the duty was collected. U.S. firms that import materials or components that they process or assemble for re-export may obtain drawback refunds of all duties paid on the imported merchandise, less one percent covering Customs costs. This practice encourages U.S. exporters by permitting them to compete in foreign markets without the handicap of including in their sales prices the duties paid on imported components.

The Tariff & Trade Act of 1984 was signed into law on October 30, 1984. The Act revises and expands drawbacks. At the time of this printing, regulations implementing the Act have not yet been promulgated. Under existing regulations several types of drawback have been authorized, but only three are of interest to most manufacturers.

1. If articles manufactured in the United States with the use of imported merchandise are exported, then the duties paid on the imported merchandise that was used may be refunded as drawback (less 1 percent).

2. If both imported merchandise and domestic merchandise of the same kind and quality are used to manufacture articles, some of which are exported, then duties which were paid on the imported merchandise are refundable as drawback, whether or not that merchandise was used in the exported articles.

3. If articles of foreign origin imported for consumption after December 28, 1980, are exported from the United States or are destroyed under the supervision of U.S. Customs within 3 years of the date of importation, in the same condition as when imported and without being "used" in the United States, then duties that were paid on the imported merchandise (less 1 percent) are refundable as drawback. Incidental operations on the merchandise (such as testing, cleaning, repacking, or inspection) are not considered to be "uses" of the article.

To obtain drawback, the U.S. firm must file a proposal with a Regional Commissioner of Customs (for the first type of drawback) or with the Drawback and Bonds Branch, Customs Headquarters, at the address below (for other types of drawback). These offices may also provide a model drawback proposal for the U.S. company.

It is necessary for drawback claimants to establish that the articles on which drawback is being claimed were exported within 5 years after importation of the merchandise in question. Once the request for drawback is approved, the proposal and approval together constitute the manufacturer's drawback rate. For more information contact: Drawback and Bonds Branch, Room 2414, U.S. Customs Headquarters, 1301 Constitution Avenue, N.W., Washington, DC 20229. Telephone: (202) 566-5856.

U.S. foreign trade zones

Exporters should also consider the customs privileges of U.S. foreign trade zones. These are domestic U.S. sites that are considered outside U.S. customs territory and are available for activities that might otherwise be carried on overseas for customs reasons. For export operations, the zones provide accelerated export status for purposes of excise tax rebates and customs drawback. For import and re-export activities, no duties or Federal excise taxes are charged on foreign goods moved into zones unless and until the goods, or products made from them, are moved into customs territory. This means that the use of zones can be profitable for operations involving foreign dutiable materials and components being assembled or produced here for re-export. Also, no quota restrictions ordinarily apply.

There are now 112 approved foreign trade zones in port communities throughout the United States. These facilities are available for operations involving storage, repacking, inspection, exhibition, assembly, manufacturing, and other processing. In addition, applications are pending for 15 new zones and more than 30 new subzones or expansions.

About 1500 business firms used foreign trade zones in fiscal year 1983. The value of merchandise moved to and from the zones during that year exceeded $10 billion.

Information about the zones is available from each zone manager, from the nearest US&FCS District Office, or from the Executive Secretary, Foreign Trade Zones Board, Room 1529, International Trade Administration, U.S. Department of Commerce, Washington, DC 20230. A listing of Foreign Trade Zones by State can be found in Appendix VII.

Foreign free port and free trade zones

To encourage and facilitate international trade, more than 300 free ports, free trade zones, and similar customs-privileged facilities are now in operation in some 75 foreign countries, usually in or near seaports or airports. Many U.S. manufacturers and their distributors use free ports or free trade zones for receipt of shipments of goods that are then reshipped in smaller lots to customers throughout the surrounding areas. Information about free trade zones, free ports, and similar facilities abroad may be obtained from the Office of Service Industries, Room 1124, International Trade Administration, U.S. Department of Commerce, Washington, DC 20230. Telephone: (202) 377-3575.

Bonded warehouses

Bonded warehouses can also be found in many locations. Here, goods can be warehoused without duties being assessed. Once goods are released, they are subject to duties.

Foreign Sales Corporation

President Reagan signed the Foreign Sales Corporation Act into law on July 18, 1984. It largely replaces the **Domestic International Sales Corporation (DISC)** tax incentive for exports. Effective for tax years beginning after Dec. 31, 1984, provisions of the export tax incentive are part of the Tax Reform Act of 1984. They add sections 921 through 927 to the Internal Revenue Code and amend the DISC provisions currently in sections 991 through 997 and sections 291 (a) (4) of the tax code. This new tax incentive for U.S. exports was designed to accommodate claims by our trading partners in the councils of the General Agreement on Tariffs and Trade (GATT) that the DISC was an illegal tax subsidy for exports.

A Foreign Sales Corporation (FSC) can obtain a corporate tax exemption from 15 percent to 32 percent of the earnings generated by the sale or lease of export property (50 percent U.S. content and other limitations) and services related and subsidary to the export of such property. The only pure services that qualify are architectural and engineering services for foreign construction projects and export management services for unrelated FSC's.

FSC's can be formed by manufacturers, nonmanufacturers, and export groups. A FSC can function as a principal, buying and selling for its own account, or as a commission agent. It can be related to a manufacturing parent or can be an independent merchant or broker.

An FSC must be incorporated and have its main office in a qualified foreign country or U.S. possession, defined as the U.S. Virgin Islands, American Samoa, Guam or the Northern Marianas. The FSC has to have at least one director who is not a U.S. resident and keep one set of its books of account (including copies of invoices) at its main offshore office. It must also file an election to become an FSC with the Internal Revenue Service.

The portion of the FSC income exempt from U.S. corporate taxation is 32 percent (30 percent for corporate-held FSCs), if it buys from independent suppliers or uses the section 482 "arms length" pricing rules with related suppliers. However, special administrative pricing rules are available, if the FSC is supplied by a related entity.

The first administrative pricing rule allows FSC's to share the profit from the export transaction on the basis of 23 percent allocated to the FSC and 77 percent allocated to the related supplier. If the FSC then conducts the required minimum of activity outside the U.S. customs territory, 16/23 of its 23 percent of combined profits is exempt from U.S. corporate taxation and 7/23 is not, i.e., 16 percent of the combined income is tax exempt.

The second alternative for FSC's, particularly those with low profit margin exports purchased from related suppliers, is for the FSC to take as its share of combined income 1.83 percent of gross receipts, not to exceed 46 percent of combined income, of which 1.27 percent of gross receipts, not to exceed 32 percent of combined income, is income exempt from U.S. corporate taxation—provided it conducts the required minimum of "offshore" activity. For both administrative pricing rules the portion of exempt income is reduced by 1/17 for corporate held FSC's.

The administrative pricing rules can be used to determine the amount of commissions available to a commission agent FSC. However, under either of the administrative pricing rules, the commission agent or buy-sell FSC is required to perform by itself, or by contract, all of the following activities (to the extent they are performed at all), with respect to the export transaction in question: (1) Solicit, negotiate and make the contract of sale; (2) provide advertising and sales promotion; (3) process customer orders and arrange for delivery; (4) provide for transportation; (5) assemble and transmit final invoices and receive payment; and (6) assume the credit risk. For FSC's generating more than $5 million in export sales to obtain the corporate tax exemption, some, but far from all, of these activities are required to be performed, either directly or by contract, outside the U.S. customs territory.

The FSC Act also allows a U.S. exporter to set up an Interest-charge DISC instead of a FSC and get a 94 percent deferral benefit on up to $10 million of its exports, provided the DISC shareholders pay a yearly interest charge on the deferred taxes accumulated after December 31, 1984. However, this interest charge is deductible.

Temporary regulations on the transition from a DISC to a Foreign Sales Corporation or Interest-charge DISC were issued by the Internal Revenue Service in the *Federal Register* of October 12, 1984. In addition, on December 12, 1984, the IRS issued temporary regulations on the FSC foreign management and foreign economic processes requirements, and on the FSC general rules and other requirements.

FSC's can be a valuable tool to increase export profits. For more information, U.S. companies may contact either the Office of Trade Finance— telephone: (202) 377-4471; or the Office of General Counsel—telephone: (202) 377-1328 at the Department of Commerce; or contact a local office of the Internal Revenue Service.

Commerce assistance related to the Multilateral Trade Negotiations

On April 12, 1979, the United States and many of its major trading partners reached agreement in Geneva on most aspects of the Multilateral Trade Negotiations (MTN) package, a process that began in 1973. The agreements produced by these far-reaching negotiations—most of which went into effect on January 1, 1980,—should liberalize world trade over the next decade. In addition to large tariff reductions over the next eight years, agreement was reached on several nontariff trade barrier (NTB's) codes that have a significant impact on international trade. Separate agreements or "Codes" were prepared covering the following NTB's:

- Subsidies and countervailing measures that prejudice imports.

- Antidumping duties used to counter predatory pricing.

- Discriminatory government procurement.

- Technical barriers to trade (standards).

- Uniform and equitable customs valuation for duty purposes.

- Import licensing (simplification) and harmonization of procedures.

- Trade in civil aircraft (both tariff and nontariff issues).

- The international trading framework.

In addition, several codes deal specifically with trade in agriculture.

One important benefit stemming from the MTN is an agreement opening many foreign government procurement orders to international bidding. Commerce's Trade Opportunities Program (TOP) has been designated the primary clearing point for tenders generated under this MTN Government Procurement Agreement (see Chapter 7). Details on specific procurement actions are sent to TOP by U.S. embassies and consulates in the countries covered by the MTN. These tenders are mailed within days, directly to TOP subscribers who have indicated their interest in receiving them. Brief summaries of the leads also appear in the *TOP Bulletin* and in *Commerce Business Daily*.

US&FCS District Offices can provide further information on the different MTN Codes and their potential impact on a company's future in international trade. Commerce has also published a series of pamphlets covering codes that are of special interest to U.S. exporters. These include codes on industrial tariffs, government procurement, customs valuation, product standards, import licensing procedures, and trade in civil aircraft. Copies of these pamphlets may be obtained from: Trade Advisory Center, Room 1001, International Trade Administration, U.S. Department of Commerce, Washington, DC 20230.

Patent, trademark, copyright, and trade secret considerations

The United States provides a wide range of protection for "intellectual property," i.e., patents, trademarks, service marks, copyrights and trade secrets. Many businesses, particularly "high tech" firms, the publishing industry, chemical and pharmaceutical firms, the recording industry, and computer software companies depend heavily on the protection afforded their creative products and processes.

In the United States, there are four major forms of intellectual property protection. A U.S. patent confers on its owner the exclusive right for 17 years from the date the patent is granted to manufacture, use, and sell the patented product or process within the United States. A trademark or service mark registered with the U.S. Patent and Trademark Office remains in force for twenty years from the date of registration and may be renewed for successive periods of 20 years unless previously cancelled or surrendered.

A work created (fixed in tangible form for the first time) in the United States on or after January 1, 1978, is automatically protected by a U.S. copyright from the moment of its creation. Such a copyright, as a general rule, has a term that endures for the author's life, plus an additional 50 years after the author's death. In the case of works made for hire and for anonymous and pseudonymous works (unless the author's identity is revealed in records of the Copyright Office of the Library of Congress), the duration of the copyright is 75 years from publication or 100 years from creation, whichever is shorter. Other more detailed provisions of the Copyright Act of 1976 govern the term of works created before January 1, 1978.

Trade secrets are protected by State unfair competition and contract law. Unlike a U.S. patent, a trade secret does not entitle its owner to a government-sanctioned monopoly of the discovered technology for a particular length of time. Nevertheless, trade secrets can be a very valuable and marketable form of technology. Trade secrets are typically protected by confidentiality agreements between a firm and its employees and by trade secret licensing agreement provisions that prohibit disclosures of the trade secret by the licensee or its employees.

Under various international treaties, U.S. patent and trademark applicants and U.S. copyright owners may obtain protection for their intellectual property in many other countries. Under the Paris Convention for the Protection of Industrial Property, a person or company who has applied for a patent or trademark in the United States will be granted a right of priority over all other applicants for the same invention or trademark in the other member countries, provided that the foreign application is filed within 12 months, in the case of utility patents, or 6 months, in the case of trademarks and design patents, after the U.S. application is filed. A later treaty, the Patent Cooperation Treaty, created a patent priority period of 18 months in signatory countries. The Patent Cooperation Treaty also established a standardized application format and centralized filing procedures that facilitate the filing of multiple patent applications for the same invention in the various member countries. Under the Universal Copyright Convention, works by U.S. authors, whether first published here or abroad, are entitled to copyright protection in all member countries.

Foreign countries vary greatly in the protection they give to intellectual property. Some countries have no patent system, while many third world countries that require approval of licensing agreement royalties attach little value to trade secrets and other forms of know-how. Even advanced industrialized countries grant a variety of terms for patents, trademarks, service marks and copyrights.

It is also important to recognize that a number of countries are parties to only some, or even none, of the treaties discussed above. Therefore, would-be U.S. exporters should carefully evaluate the intellectual property laws of their potential foreign markets, as well as applicable multilateral and bilateral treaties. U.S. firms generally should give serious consideration to obtaining patents, trademarks, service marks or copyrights (or at least filing the necessary applications) in their future foreign markets before they enter into technology licensing agreements, form international joint ventures, or establish overseas branches or subsidiaries.

In summary, U.S. exporters with intellectual property concerns should:

1. Obtain protection under all applicable U.S. laws for their inventions, trademarks, or copyrights.

2. Research the intellectual property laws of countries where they may conduct business. Consult with the US&FCS about particular countries.

3. Consider the use of "black box agreements" that can, where permitted under foreign law, provide some protection for partial disclosures of trade secrets while licensing or joint venture agreements are being considered.

4. Secure the services of competent local counsel to file appropriate patent, trademark, or copyright applications within priority periods.

5. Report any piracy or counterfeiting immediately to the International Trade Administration or the U.S. Customs Service.

FORM **ITA-629P**
(REV. 6-84)

U.S. DEPARTMENT OF COMMERCE
INTERNATIONAL TRADE ADMINISTRATION

STATEMENT BY ULTIMATE CONSIGNEE AND PURCHASER

GENERAL INSTRUCTIONS – This form must be submitted by the impor-ter (ultimate consignee shown in Item 1) and by the overseas buyer or purchaser, to the U.S. exporter or seller with whom the order for the com-modities described in Item 3 is placed. This completed statement will be submitted in support of one or more export license applications to the U.S. Department of Commerce. **All items on this form must be completed.** Where the information required is unknown or the item does not apply, write in the appropriate words "UNKNOWN" or "NOT APPLICABLE." If more space is needed, attach an additional copy of this form or sheet of paper signed as in Item 8. Submit form within 180 days from latest date in Item 8. Information furnished herewith is subject to the provisions of Section 12(c) of the Export Administration Act of 1979, 50 USC app. 2411(c), and its unauthorized disclosure is prohibited by law.

1. | **Ultimate consignee name and address**

Name

Street and number

City and Country

Reference *(if desired)*

2. | **Request** *(Check one)*

a. ☐ We request that this statement be considered a part of the application for export license filed by

_____
U.S. exporter or U.S. person with whom we have placed our order (order party)
for export to us of the commodities described in item 3.

b. ☐ We request that this statement be considered a part of every application for export license filed by

_____
U.S. exporter or U.S. person with whom we have placed or may place our order (order party)
for export to us of the type of commodities described in this statement, during the period ending June 30 of the

second year after the signing of this form, or on _____

3. | **Commodities**

We have placed or may place orders with the person or firm named in Item 2 for the commodities indicated below:

COMMODITY DESCRIPTION	(Fill in only if 2a is checked)	
	QUANTITY	VALUE

Sample

4. | **Disposition or use of commodities by ultimate consignee named in Item 1** *(Check and complete the appropriate box(es))*

We certify that the commodity(ies) listed in Item 3:

a. ☐ Will be used by us (as capital equipment) in the form in which received in a manufacturing process in the country named in Item 1 and will not be reexported or incorporated into an end product.

b. ☐ Will be processed or incorporated by us into the following product(s) _____
(Specify)

to be manufactured in the country named in Item 1 for distribution in _____
(Name

_____
of country or countries)

c. ☐ Will be resold by us in the form in which received in the country named in Item 1 for use or consumption therein.

The specific end-use by my customer will be _____
(Specify, if known)

d. ☐ Will be reexported by us in the form in which received to _____
(Name of country(ies))

e. ☐ Other *(Describe fully)* _____

NOTE: If Item (d) is checked, acceptance of this form by the Office of Export Administration as a supporting document for license app-lications shall not be construed as an authorization to reexport the commodities to which the form applies unless specific approval has been obtained from the Office of Export Administration for such reexport.

(Reproduction of this form is permissible, providing that content, format, size and color of paper are the same)

Please continue form and sign certification on reverse side.

USCOMM-DC 84-21766

Part C

After the sale

Documentation, shipping, and logistics

13

When preparing to ship a product overseas, the exporter needs to be aware of packing, labeling, documentation and insurance requirements. Because the goods are being shipped by unknown carriers to distant customers, the new exporter must be sure to follow all shipping requirements to help ensure that the merchandise:

- Is packed correctly so that it arrives in good condition;

- Is labeled correctly to ensure the goods are handled properly and arrive on time and at the right place;

- Is documented correctly to meet U.S. and foreign government requirements, as well as meeting proper collection standards; and

- Is insured against damage, loss, or pilferage.

Because of the variety of considerations involved in the physical export process, most new, as well as experienced exporters, rely on the services of an international freight forwarder to perform these services.

Freight forwarders

The international freight forwarder acts as an agent for the exporter in moving cargo to the overseas destination. These agents are familiar with the import rules and regulations of foreign countries, methods of shipping, U.S. Government export regulations, and with the documents connected with foreign trade.

Freight forwarders can assist with an order from the start by advising the exporter of the freight costs, port charges, consular fees, cost of special documentation, and insurance costs, as well as their handling fees—all of which help in the preparation of a price quotation. They may also recommend the type of packing that should be considered to help protect the merchandise in transit and can arrange to have the merchandise packed at the port or to have it containerized. The cost for their services is a legitimate export cost that should be figured into the price charged to the customer.

When the order is ready to ship, freight forwarders should be able to review the letter of credit, commercial invoices, packing list, etc., to ensure that everything is in order. If desired, they can also reserve the necessary space on board an ocean vessel.

If the cargo arrives at the port of export and the exporter has not already done so, freight forwarders may make the necessary arrangements with custom brokers to ensure that the goods comply with customs export documentation regulations. In addition, they may have the goods delivered to the carrier in time for loading aboard the selected vessel. They may also prepare the bill of lading and any special documentation that may be required. After shipment, they forward all documents directly to the customer or to the paying bank if desired.

Packing

In packing an item for export, the shipper should be aware of the demands that exporting puts on a package. There are four problems that must be kept in mind when designing an export shipping crate: Breakage, weight, moisture, and pilferage.

Besides the normal handling encountered in domestic transportation, an export order moving by ocean freight may be loaded aboard vessels by a sling, in a net, by conveyor, chute or other method, putting added strain on the package. In the ship's hold, goods may be stacked on top of each other or come into violent contact with other goods during the course of the voyage. Overseas, handling facilities may not be as sophisticated as in the United States, and the cargo may be dragged, pushed, rolled, or dropped during unloading, while moving through customs, or in transit to the final destination.

Moisture is a constant problem since cargo is subject to condensation even in the hold of a ship equipped with air conditioning and humidity control. The cargo may also be unloaded in the rain and some foreign ports do not have covered storage facilities. In addition, unless the cargo is adequately protected, theft and pilferage are constant threats.

Since proper packing is essential in exporting, often the buyer specifies packing requirements. If not, be sure the goods are prepared with the following considerations in mind:

- Pack in strong containers, adequately sealed and filled.

- To provide proper bracing in the container, regardless of size, making sure that the weight is evenly distributed.

- Goods should be packed on pallets if possible, to insure greater ease in handling.

- Packages and packing filler should be made of moisture resistant material.

- Avoid mention of contents or brand name on package to avoid pilferage. In addition, strapping, seals, and shrink wrapping are effective means to deter theft.

One increasingly popular method of shipment is the use of containers obtained from carriers or private leasing concerns. Varying in size, material, and construction, these can accommodate most cargo but are best suited for standard package sizes and shapes. Some containers are no more than semi-truck trailers lifted off their wheels and placed on a vessel at the port of export. These are then transferred to another set of wheels at the port of import for movement to an inland destination.

Normally, shipments by air do not require as heavy packing as ocean shipments, but must still be adequately protected, especially for highly pilferable items. In many instances, standard domestic packing is acceptable, especially if the product is durable in nature and there is no concern for display packaging. In other instances, high test (at least 250 pounds per square inch) cardboard or tri-wall construction boxes are adequate.

In the case of both ocean and air shipments, freight forwarders and carriers can advise on the best packaging. Marine insurance companies are also available for consultation. It is recommended that, if the firm is not equipped to package for export, it use a professional firm to perform this task.

Finally, since transportation costs are determined by volume and weight, special reinforced and lightweight packing materials have been devised for exporting. Care in packing goods to minimize volume and weight while giving strength may well save money for the U.S. exporter.

Labeling

Specific markings and labels are used on export shipping cartons and containers for several purposes, including:

- To meet shipping regulations;

- To assure proper handling;

- To conceal the identity of the contents; and

- To help receivers identify shipments.

The overseas buyer usually specifies export marks that should appear on the cargo for easy identification by receivers. Below is a list of markings that exporters need to include on cartons to be shipped:

- Shipper's mark;

- Country of origin (U.S.A.);

- Weight marking (in pounds and in kilograms);

- Number of package and size of case (in inches and centimeters);

- Handling marks (international pictorial symbols);

- Cautionary markings, such as "This Side Up," or "Use No Hooks" (in English and in the language of the country of destination);

- Port of entry; and

- Labels for hazardous materials (universal symbols adapted by the Inter-Governmental Maritime Consultative Organization).

Legibility is extremely important in order to avoid misunderstandings and delays in shipping. Letters are generally stenciled onto packages and containers in waterproof ink. Markings should appear on three faces of the container, preferably on the side, and/or ends and top. Old markings must be completely removed.

In addition to port marks, customer identification code and indication of origin, the marks should include the package number, gross and net weights, and dimensions. If the exporter is shipping more than one package, he or she should be sure to mark the number of packages in the shipment. The exporter should also include any special handling instructions on the package. It is a good idea to repeat these instructions in the language of the country of destination. Standard international shipping and handling symbols should also be used.

Exporters may find that customs regulations regarding freight labeling are strictly enforced; for example, most countries require that the country of origin be clearly labeled on each imported package. Most freight forwarders and export packing specialists can supply necessary information regarding specific regulations.

Documentation

When faced with the amount of documentation needed for exporting, some exporters think the shipment will sink under red tape before it leaves port. Before trying to handle all the documentation itself, a firm should seriously consider using a freight forwarder, a specialist in handling such documentation. Below is a list of documents that are commonly used in exporting. The documents actually used depends on both U.S. Government requirements and those requirements imposed by the importing country.

- **Commercial invoice.** As in a domestic transaction, the commercial invoice is a bill for the goods from the buyer to the seller. A commercial invoice should include basic information about the transaction, including a description of the goods, address of shipper and seller, delivery and payment terms, etc. The buyer needs the invoice to prove ownership and to arrange payment. Some governments use the commercial invoice to assess customs duties.

- **Bill of lading.** Bills of lading are contracts between the owner of the goods and the carrier (as in the case for domestic shipments). There are two types. "Straight" bills of lading are non-negotiable. Negotiable or "shipper's order" bills of lading can be bought, sold or traded while goods are in transit and are used for letter of credit transactions. The customer usually needs the original or a copy as proof of ownership to take possession of the goods.

- **Consular invoice.** Certain nations require a "consular invoice" which is used to control and identify goods. The invoice must be purchased from the consulate of the country to which the goods are being shipped and usually must be prepared in the language of that country.

- **Certificate of origin.** Certain nations require a signed statement as to the origin of the export item. This is usually obtained through a semi-official organization, such as a local chamber of commerce. This may be required even though the commercial invoice may contain this information.

- **Inspection certification.** Some purchasers and countries may require a certificate attesting to the specifications of the goods shipped, usually performed by a third party. This is often obtained from an independent testing organization.

- **Dock receipt, warehouse receipt.** These receipts are used to transfer accountability when the export item is moved by the domestic carrier to the port of embarkation and left with the international carrier for export.

- **Destination control statement.** This statement appears on the commercial invoice, bill of lading, or air waybill and shippers export declaration (SED), and serves to notify the carrier and all foreign parties that the item may only be exported to certain destinations.

- **Insurance certificate.** If the seller provides insurance, the insurance certificate states the type and amount of coverage. This is a negotiable instrument.

- **Shipper's export declaration (SED).** Used to control exports and compile trade statistics, this document is prepared for shipments valued in excess of $500 and is required by the U.S. Department of Commerce.

- **Export license.** U.S. export shipments are required by the U.S. Government to have an export license, either a General License or a Validated License. A complete discussion of licensing is found in Chapter 12.

- **Export packing list.** Considerably more detailed and informative than a standard domestic packing list, an export packing list itemizes the material in each individual package, and indicates the type of package—box, crate, drum, carton, etc. It shows the individual net, legal, tare and gross weights and measurements for each package (in both Imperial and metric systems). Package markings should be shown along with the shipper's

and buyer's references. The packing list should be either included in or attached to the outside of a package in a waterproof envelope marked "packing list enclosed." The list is used by the shipper or forwarding agent to ascertain the total shipment weight and volume, in addition to determining whether the correct cargo is being shipped. In addition, Customs officials (both U.S. and foreign) may use the list to check the cargo.

Documentation must be precise. Slight discrepancies or omissions may prevent U.S. merchandise from being exported, may result in U.S. firms not getting paid, or may even result in the seizure of the exporter's goods by U.S. or foreign government Customs. Collection documents are subject to precise time limits and may not be honored by a bank if out of date. Much of the documentation is routine for freight forwarders or customs brokers acting on the firm's behalf, but the exporter is ultimately responsible for accuracy of the documentation.

The amount of documents the exporter must deal with varies depending on the destination of the shipment. As each country has different import regulations, the exporter must be careful to provide proper documentation. If the exporter does not rely on the services of a freight forwarder, there are several methods of obtaining information on foreign import restrictions:

- Country Desk Officers in the Department of Commerce are specialists in individual country conditions. See Appendix IV for a list of the individual officers.

- Foreign government embassies and consulates in the United States can often provide information on import regulations.

- The Bureau of National Affairs *Export Shipping Manual* contains complete country-by-country shipping information, as well as tariff systems, import and exchange controls, mail regulations, and other special information. Contact the Bureau of National Affairs, 1231 25th Street, N.W., Washington, DC 20037. An annual subscription is $273.

- *The Air Cargo Tariff Guidebook* lists various regulations affecting air shipments on a country-by-country basis. Other information includes tariff rules and rates, transportation charges, air waybill information and special carrier regulations. Contact the Air Cargo Tariff, P.O. Box 7627, 1117 ZJ Schipol Airport, The Netherlands.

- The National Council On International Trade Documentation (NCITD) provides several low-cost publications that provide information on specific documentation commonly used in international trade. NCITD provides a free listing of their publications. Contact the National Council On International Trade Documentation, 350 Broadway, Suite 1200, New York, NY 10013. Telephone: (212) 925-1400.

Shipping

Inland transportation of an export order is handled in much the same way as that of a domestic one. The export marks should be added to the standard information shown on a domestic bill of lading and should show the name of the exporting carrier and the latest allowed arrival date at the port of export. The exporter should also include instructions for the inland carrier to notify the international freight forwarder by telephone on arrival.

When determining the method of international shipping, the exporter may find it useful to consult with a freight forwarder. Since carriers are often used for large and bulky shipments, the exporter should reserve space on the carrier well before actual shipment date (called the booking contract).

The exporter should consider the cost of shipment, delivery schedule, and accessibility to the shipped product of the foreign buyer when determining the method of international shipping. Although air carriers are more expensive, their cost may be offset by lower domestic shipping costs (by using a local airport rather than a coastal seaport) and quicker delivery times. This may give the U.S. exporter an edge over other competitors, whose service to their accounts may not be as timely.

Before shipping, the U.S. firm should be sure to check with the foreign buyer as to the destination of the goods. Often, the buyer may wish the goods to be shipped to a free trade zone or a free port, which allows exemption from import duties while goods are in the zone. A more complete description of these may be found in Chapter 12.

Insurance

Export shipments are usually insured against loss or damage in transit by cargo insurance. Though similar to domestic cargo insurance, this coverage is much broader and applies to shipments by U.S. mail and air freight, as well as sea cargo. Arrangements for cargo insurance may be made either by the buyer or seller, depending on the terms of sale. Exporters are advised to consult with international insurance carriers or freight forwarders for more information.

Damaging weather conditions, rough handling by carriers, and other common hazards to cargo make marine insurance important protection for U.S. exporters. If the terms of sale make the U.S. firm responsible for insurance, they should either obtain their own policy or insure cargo under a freight forwarder's policy for a fee. If the terms of sale make the foreign buyer responsible, the exporter should not assume (or even take the buyer's word) that adequate insurance has been obtained. If the buyer neglects to obtain coverage or obtains too little, damage to the cargo may cause a major financial loss to the exporter.

SHORT FORM BILL OF LADING
(Non-Negotiable Unless Consigned To Order)

NAME OF CARRIER

SHIPPER/EXPORTER (2) (COMPLETE NAME AND ADDRESS)	DOCUMENT NO. (5)
A B C COMPANY ANYTOWN USA	EXPORT REFERENCES (6)

CONSIGNEE (3) (COMPLETE NAME AND ADDRESS)	FORWARDING AGENT - REFERENCES (7) (COMPLETE NAME AND ADDRESS)
X Y Z COMPANY LONDON ENGLAND	POINT AND COUNTRY OF ORIGIN (8)

NOTIFY PARTY (4) (COMPLETE NAME AND ADDRESS)	DOMESTIC ROUTING/EXPORT INSTRUCTIONS (9)
SAME	

PIER/TERMINAL (10)
123 ELIZABETH P.A. N.J.

VESSEL (11) FLAG	PORT OF LOADING (12)	ONWARD INLAND ROUTING (15)
SS ATLANTIC	NEW YORK	

PORT OF DISCHARGE FROM VESSEL (13)	FOR TRANSSHIPMENT TO (14)	
LONDON	NONE	

PARTICULARS FURNISHED BY SHIPPER

MARKS AND NUMBERS (16)	NO. OF PKGS. (17)	DESCRIPTION OF PACKAGES AND GOODS (18)	GROSS WEIGHT (19)	MEASUREMENT (20)
X Y Z CO. LONDON ENGLAND MADE IN USA #1/5	5	BOXES: AUTO PARTS	___00#	45'

THESE COMMODITIES LIC___ ___ BY ___ ___INATION ENGLAND DIVERSION
CONTRARY TO U.S. ___

___IGHT - PREPAID

FREIGHT AND CHARGES PAYABLE AT

PREPAID ☐   **COLLECT** ☐

	PREPAID	COLLECT
TOTAL		

RECEIVED the goods or the containers, vans, trailers, pallet units or other packages said to contain goods herein mentioned, in apparent good order and condition, except as otherwise indicated, to be transported, delivered or transhipped as provided herein. All of the provisions written, printed or stamped on either side hereof are part of this bill of lading contract.

IN WITNESS WHEREOF, the Master or agent of said vessel has signed _____ bills of lading, all of the same tenor and date, one of which being accomplished, the others to stand void.

BY _R. Benson_
FOR THE MASTER

DATED _____   B/L NO. _____

Form 90-820 — Printed and Sold by Unz & Co., Division of Scott Printing Corp., 190 Baldwin Ave., Jersey City, N.J. 07306 — N.J. (201) 795-5400 ; N.Y (212) 344-2270 Toll Free (800) 631-3098

Form 33-555 — Rev. 1/66 — Printed and Sold by Unz & Co., Division of Scott Printing Corp., 190 Baldwin Ave., Jersey City, N.J. 07306 — N.J. (201) 795-5400 / N.Y. (212) 344-2270 Toll Free (800) 631-3098

(SPACES IMMEDIATELY BELOW ARE FOR SHIPPERS MEMORANDA—NOT PART OF DOCK RECEIPT)

DELIVERING CARRIER TO STEAMER:	CAR NUMBER—REFERENCE
FORWARDING AGENT—REFERENCES	EXPORT DEC. No.

DOCK RECEIPT
NON-NEGOTIABLE

SHIPPER: A B C COMPANY ANYTOWN USA

SHIP	VOYAGE NO.	FLAG	PIER	PORT OF LOADING
SS ATLANTIC			123 ELIZABETH PA NJ	NEW YORK

FOR. PORT OF DISCHARGE *(Where goods are to be delivered to consignee or on-carrier)* — LONDON | For TRANSSHIPMENT to *(If goods are to be transshipped or forwarded at port of discharge)*

PARTICULARS FURNISHED BY SHIPPER OF GOODS

MARKS AND NUMBERS	No. of PKGS.	DESCRIPTION OF PACKAGES AND GOODS	MEASURE-MENT	GROSS WEIGHT
X Y Z CO. LONDON ENGLAND MADE IN USA #1/5	5	BOXES: AUTO ~	45'	1500#
		~RECEIVING CLERK ~ CLEAN DOCK RECEIPT ACCEPTED		

Sample

DIMENSIONS AND WEIGHTS OF PACKAGES TO BE SHOWN ON REVERSE SIDE

DELIVERED BY:

RECEIVED THE ABOVE DESCRIBED MERCHANDISE FOR SHIPMENT AS INDICATED HEREON, SUBJECT TO ALL CONDITIONS OF THE UNDERSIGNED'S USUAL FORM OF DOCK RECEIPT AND BILL OF LADING. COPIES OF THE UNDERSIGNED'S USUAL FORM OF DOCK RECEIPT AND BILL OF LADING MAY BE OBTAINED FROM THE MASTER OF THE VESSEL OR THE VESSEL'S AGENT

LIGHTER TRUCK } ....

ARRIVED— DATE................TIME.........

UNLOADED— DATE................TIME.........

CHECKED BY ....

PLACED IN SHIP / ON DOCK LOCATION.............

AGENT FOR MASTER

BY *G. P. Lipetta* ....
RECEIVING CLERK

DATE.........................

SHIPPER'S EXPORT DECLARATION
OF SHIPMENTS FROM THE UNITED STATES
Export Shipments Are Subject To Inspection By U.S. Customs Service and/or The Office of Export Control
READ CAREFULLY THE INSTRUCTIONS ON BACK TO AVOID DELAY AT SHIPPING POINT

Declarations Should be Typewritten or Prepared in Ink

Form Approved: O.M.B. No. 41-R0397

CONFIDENTIAL — For use solely for official purposes authorized by the Secretary of Commerce. Use for unauthorized purposes is not permitted (Title 15, Sec. 10.91 (a) C.F.R.; Sec. 7(c) Export Administration Act of 1969, as amended, P.L. 91-184).

Authentication (When required)

DO NOT USE THIS AREA	DISTRICT	PORT	COUNTRY (For Customs use only)
	10	01	

File No. (For Customs use only)

1. FROM (U.S. port of export)
NEW YORK

2. METHOD OF TRANSPORTATION (Check one):
[X] VESSEL (Incl. ferry) [ ] AIR [ ] OTHER (Specify) _____

2a. EXPORTING CARRIER (If vessel, give name of ship, flag and pier number. If air, give name of airline.)
SS ATLANTIC

3. EXPORTER (Principal or seller — licensee)
A B C COMPANY
ADDRESS (Number, street, place, State)
ANYTOWN USA

4. AGENT OF EXPORTER (Forwarding agent)
A. FREIGHT FORWARDER, INC.
ADDRESS (Number, street, place, State)
ANYTOWN USA

5. ULTIMATE CONSIGNEE
X Y Z COMPANY
ADDRESS (Place, country)
LONDON ENGLAND

6. INTERMEDIATE CONSIGNEE
SAME
ADDRESS (Place, country)

7. FOREIGN PORT OF UNLOADING (For vessel and air shipments only)
LONDON

8. PLACE AND COUNTRY OF ULTIMATE DESTINATION (Not place of transshipment)
LONDON ENGLAND

MARKS AND NOS. (9)	NUMBERS AND KIND OF PACKAGES, DESCRIPTION OF COMMODITIES, EXPORT LICENSE NUMBER OR GENERAL LICENSE SYMBOL (Describe commodities in sufficient detail to permit verification of the Schedule B commodity numbers assigned. Do not use general terms.) (10)	SHIPPING (Gross) WEIGHT IN POUNDS (REQUIRED FOR VESSEL AND AIR SHIPMENTS ONLY) (11)	SPECIFY "F" OR "D" (12)	SCHEDULE B COMMODITY NO. (Include Commodity List item number) (13)	NET QUANTITY SCHEDULE B UNITS (State unit) (14)	VALUE AT U.S. PORT OF EXPORT (Selling price or cost if not sold, including inland freight, insurance and other charges to U.S. port of export) (Nearest whole dollar; omit cents figures) (15)
X Y Z CO. LONDON ENGLAND MADE IN USA #1/5	5 BOXES: AU1	1500#	D	123-1234	1400#	1000.00

These commodities licensed by U.S. for ultimate destination ......ENGLAND.......................... Diversion contrary to U.S. law prohibited.

VALIDATED LICENSE NO. _____   OR GENERAL LICENSE SYMBOL _____

16. BILL OF LADING OR AIR WAYBILL NUMBER

17. DATE OF EXPORTATION (Not required for shipments by vessel)

18. THE UNDERSIGNED HEREBY AUTHORIZES A. FREIGHT FORWARDER, INC.   ANYTOWN USA
(Name and address — Number, street, place, State)
TO ACT AS FORWARDING AGENT FOR EXPORT CONTROL AND CUSTOMS PURPOSES.

EXPORTER A B C CO.   BY (DULY AUTHORIZED OFFICER OR EMPLOYEE) *S. Alexander*

▶ **19. I CERTIFY THAT ALL STATEMENTS MADE AND ALL INFORMATION CONTAINED IN THIS EXPORT DECLARATION ARE TRUE AND CORRECT. I AM AWARE OF THE PENALTIES PROVIDED FOR FALSE REPRESENTATION.** (See paragraph I (s) and (o) on reverse side.)

SIGNATURE *C. N. Full*
(Duly authorized officer or employee of exporter or named forwarding agent)

FOR A B C CO.
(Name of corporation or firm, and capacity of signer; e.g., secretary, export manager, etc.)

ADDRESS ANYTOWN USA

▶ Declaration should be made by duly authorized officer or employee of exporter or of forwarding agent named by exporter.

ªIf shipping weight is not available for each Schedule B item listed in column (13) included in one or more packages, insert the approximate gross weight for each Schedule B item. The total of these estimated weights should equal the actual weight of the entire package or packages.

ᵇDesignate foreign merchandise (reexports) with an "F" and exports of domestic merchandise produced in the United States or changed in condition in the United States with a "D." (See instructions on reverse side.)

DO NOT USE THIS AREA

Form No. 38-825– Printed and Sold by Uns & Co., Division of Scott Printing Corp., 190 Baldwin Ave., Jersey City, N.J. 07306—N.J. (201) 795-5400 / N.Y. (212) 344-2270 Toll Free (800) 631-3098

PACKING LIST

............DEC. 15.....................**19.**80....
Place and Date of Shipment

To X Y Z COMPANY
LONDON ENGLAND

Gentlemen:

Under your Order No....123...the material listed below

was shipped 12/15/81 via TRUCK AND VESSEL
To LONDON

Shipment consists of:		Marks	
.....5.....Cases.............Packages		X Y Z CO.	
.........Crates.............Cartons		LONDON ENGLAND	
.........Bbls.............Drums		MADE IN USA	
.........Reels.....................		#1/5	

*LEGAL WEIGHT IS WEIGHT OF ARTICLE PLUS PAPER, BOX, BOTTLE, ETC., CONTAINING THE ARTICLE AS USUALLY CARRIED IN STOCK.

PACKAGE NUMBER	WEIGHTS IN LBS. or KILOS			DIMENSIONS			QUANTITY	ATE CONTENTS PACKAGE
	GROSS WEIGHT EACH	*LEGAL WEIGHT EACH	NET WEIGHT EACH	HEIGHT	WIDTH	LENGTH		
1/5	300		250	25	25	25		(J PARTS)

Sample

Getting paid

14

There are several basic methods of receiving payment for products sold abroad. As with domestic sales, a major factor that determines the method of payment is the amount of trust in the buyer's ability to pay. Within the United States, if the buyer has good credit, sales are usually made on open account; if not, cash in advance is required. For export sales, these same methods may be used; however, other methods are available that are often more advantageous to the exporter. Ranked in order from most secure for the exporter to least secure, the basic methods of payment are:

1. Cash in advance.
2. Letter of credit.
3. Documentary drafts for collection.
4. Open account.
5. Consignment sales.

Three of these methods—cash in advance, open account, and consignment sales—may appear to be more familiar since they are often used in domestic sales. These three are discussed first before describing the other two methods listed above.

Before continuing, a caution is needed. Since getting paid in full and on time is of utmost concern to exporters, risk is a major consideration. There are many factors that can give exporting a higher risk than domestic sales. However, there are also several methods of reducing risks. One of the most important factors for reducing risks is to know what risks exist. For that reason, before deciding among the various methods of payment described in this chapter, it is strongly advised that exporters discuss the potential transaction with an international banker.

Cash in advance

Cash in advance may seem to be the most desirable method of all since the shipper is relieved of collection problems and has immediate use of the money. On the other hand, advance payment creates cash flow problems and increases risks for the buyer, and thus the buyer may refuse to pay until the merchandise is received.

Open account

In a foreign transaction, an open account can be especially risky for the seller unless the buyer is a well known customer or has been thoroughly checked for credit worthiness. In addition, the exporter's capital is tied up until payment is made. This is especially important since, in many countries, payment is usually not sent until merchandise is received.

Consignment sales

In international consignment sales, the same basic procedure is followed as in the United States. The material is shipped to a foreign distributor to be sold on behalf of the exporter. The exporter retains title to the goods until they are sold by the distributor. Once sold, payment is sent to the exporter. With this method, the exporter has greatest risk and least control over the goods and may have to wait quite a while to get paid.

When this type of sale is contemplated, it may be wise to consider some form of political risk insurance. In addition, it may be necessary to conduct a credit check on the foreign distributor (see section on "Decreasing credit risks through credit checks" later in this chapter). Furthermore, the contract should establish who is responsible for property risk insurance covering merchandise until it is sold and payment received.

Drafts and letters of credit

For the new exporter and for exporters selling to new markets, the three methods just described are not customary in international trade. Instead, documentary drafts and letters of credit are preferred. These two methods, described below, have several common features and advantages.

Normally a third party, such as a bank, acts as an intermediary to satisfy both buyer and seller that each side is keeping its end of the bargain before goods or money are exchanged. Documents, such as shipping and insurance forms, must be presented to the bank to insure that conditions of the sale are met. This is true for both documentary drafts (also called "bills of exchange") and letters of credit. (See Chapter 13 for a description of documents used in export operations.) To speed communications, two banks are usually involved, one in the exporter's country and one in the buyer's country. These may be two branches of the same bank or different banks working together.

With letters of credit, the seller presents documents to a bank in the United States to prove that goods have been shipped according to conditions of the purchase order. This proof enables the bank to pay the seller on the spot or to guarantee payment according to terms stated (e.g., in 30, 60, 90 days or longer.) In the case of drafts, the buyer pays a bank in his or her country for the merchandise and then receives the documents necessary to obtain the goods that have been shipped. Drafts that require payment before goods are received are called "sight drafts." Drafts that obligate later payment, after goods are received, can be either "time drafts" or "date drafts."

Sight drafts

A sight draft is used when the seller wishes to retain title to a shipment until it reaches its destination and is paid for. Before the cargo can be released, the original order bill of lading or airway bill must be properly endorsed by the buyer and surrendered to the carrier.

In actual practice, the bill of lading or airway bill is endorsed by the shipper and sent to the buyer's bank or to another intermediary along with a sight draft, invoices, and other necessary supporting documents specified either by the buyer or the buyer's country (e.g., packing lists, consular invoices, insurance certificates). The bank notifies the buyer that they have received these documents and that, as soon as the amount of the draft is paid, it will turn over the bill of lading enabling the buyer to obtain the shipment.

When using a sight draft to control the transfer of title of a shipment, some risk remains because the buyer's ability or willingness to pay may change between the time the goods are shipped and the time the drafts are presented for payment. Also, the policies of the importing country may change. If the buyer cannot or will not pay for and claim the goods, then returning or disposing of them becomes the problem of the exporter.

Time drafts and date drafts

If the exporter wants to extend credit to the buyer, a time draft can be used to state that payment is due within a certain time after the buyer accepts the draft and receives the goods. By signing and writing "accepted" on the draft the buyer is formally obligated to pay in the stated time. When this is done the draft is called a "trade acceptance" and can either be kept by the exporter until maturity or sold to a bank at a discount for immediate payment (this is also discussed under financing in Chapter 11).

A date draft differs slightly from a time draft in that it specifies a date on which payment is due rather than a time period after the draft is accepted. When a sight draft or time draft is used, a buyer can delay payment by delaying acceptance of the draft. A date draft can prevent this.

Letters of credit

A letter of credit is a document issued by a bank at the buyer's request in favor of the seller. It provides the issuing bank's promise to pay a specified amount of money upon receipt by the bank of certain documents within a specified time. The documents ensure that conditions stated in the letter of credit, such as terms of sale, shipping date, insurance coverage, etc., have been met.

Letters of credit are similar to drafts but are more secure. If a buyer defaults on payment of a draft, then the exporter must spend money and effort attempting to collect. With a letter of credit, if it is specifically *irrevocable*, the bank must pay even if the buyer defaults. A revocable letter of credit is usually not advisable since it may be altered or revoked without the exporter's permission.

Further, if the letter of credit is *confirmed* by a U.S. bank, then the exporter still is paid by the U.S. bank, even if the buyer's foreign bank defaults. An unconfirmed letter of credit is not advisable if there is any reason to believe that the foreign bank will default—for example, if the bank does not have a good record or if the bank's government is politically or economically unstable.

If the letter of credit is unconfirmed, the U.S. bank may wait until it receives payment from the foreign bank before paying the exporter. Often, though, the U.S. bank pays the exporter as soon as the exporter presents the documents required. However, if the foreign bank defaults on payment, the U.S. bank has recourse to the exporter for the loss.

Costs of drafts and letters of credit

Banks may charge between .25 and 1 percent of the amount of payment for handling letters of credit and less for handling drafts. Normally, fees charged by both the foreign and U.S. banks for their collection services are charged to the account of the buyer. This should be explicitly stated in all quotations and on all drafts.

In most cases, the buyer is expected to pay the charges for the letter of credit but some buyers may not accept terms that require this added cost. In such cases, the exporter must either lose that potential sale or absorb the letter of credit costs. However, if an exporter knows little about the buyer or is unsure about the political or economic stability of the foreign country, then the security of a letter of credit justifies the added costs.

A typical letter of credit transaction

Here is what typically happens when payment is made by an irrevocable letter of credit confirmed by a U.S. bank:

1. After the exporter and customer agree on the terms of a sale, the customer arranges for his or her bank to open a letter of credit. (Delays may be encountered if, for example, the buyer has insufficient funds. In many developing countries foreign currencies, such as the U.S. dollar, may be scarce.)

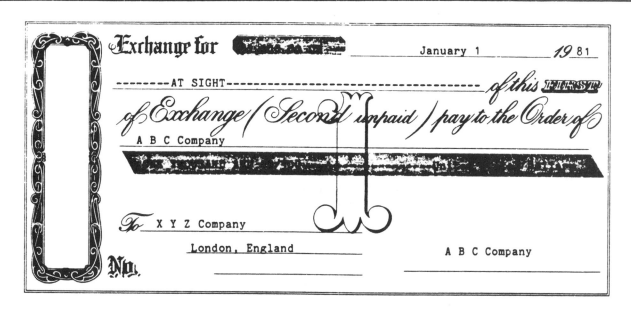

Exchange for ▓▓▓▓▓▓▓   January 1   19 81

--------AT SIGHT------------------------------------ *of this* **FIRST**

of Exchange (Second unpaid) pay to the Order of

A B C Company

To   X Y Z Company

London, England   A B C Company

No.

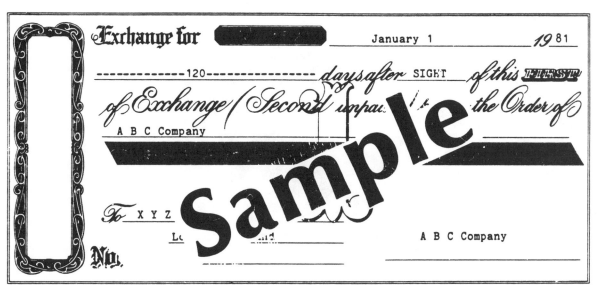

Exchange for ▓▓▓▓▓   January 1   19 81

------------120--------------- *days after* SIGHT *of this* **FIRST**

of Exchange (Second unpaid) the Order of

A B C Company

To   X Y Z

L   nd   A B C Company

No.

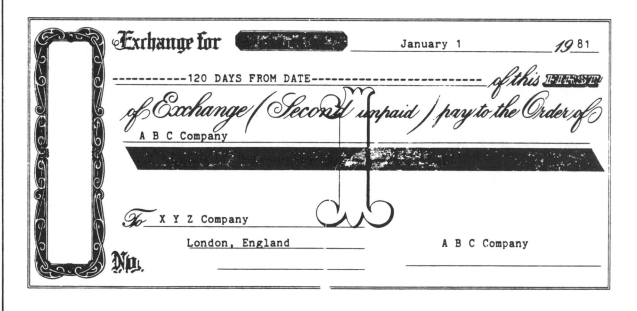

Exchange for ▓▓▓▓▓   January 1   19 81

-------120 DAYS FROM DATE----------------------- *of this* **FIRST**

of Exchange (Second unpaid) pay to the Order of

A B C Company

To   X Y Z Company

London, England   A B C Company

No.

CHEMICALBANK (B)

International Operations
P.O Box 44, Church Street Station
New York, N.Y. 10008

MARCH , 19XX (E)

Their Ref. No.   123456

Our Advice No. 000000
~~Received on all drafts and communications relative thereto~~

To

(A)   EXPORT CORPORATION OF AMERICA
123 FIRST STREET
NEW YORK, NEW YORK   1003_

~~Irrevocable~~
~~Confirmed~~
~~SPECIMEN~~

EXPORT CONFIRMED

Instructions
received from

BANCO DE BANCO   (C)
BOGOTA, COLOMBIA

For Account of (same if left blank)

GOMEZ Y FLORENCIO   (D)
BOGOTA, COLOMBIA

Gentlemen:

We are instructed by the above mentioned correspondent to advise you that they have or___ed in your favor their irrevocable credit, as indicated above, for a sum or sums not exceeding in all •
FIFTY THOUSAND DOLLARS UNITED STATES CURRENCY ($50,000___)

Available by
your draft(s)

At   SIGHT ON US   (H)

For FULL   Invoice value of merchandis___ ___n invoice as:

~~Sample~~

MACHINE SPARE PARTS. F.O.B. NEW Y___

YOUR DRAFT(S) MUST BE AC___
(F) 1.   YOUR COMMERCIAL INVOIC___ ___ AND 3 COPIES.
2.   FULL SET ON BOARD OCEAN ___ LADING ISSUED TO ORDER BLANK ENDORSED,
DATED LATEST APRIL 30, 19__ (G)

EVIDENCING SHIPMENT OF THE MERCHANDISE FROM NEW YORK TO BOGOTA.
PARTIAL SHIPMENTS NOT PERMITTED.
INSURANCE COVERED BY BUYERS IN COLOMBIA.

THE ABOVE MENTIONED CORRESPONDENT ENGAGES WITH YOU THAT ALL DRAFTS DRAWN UNDER AND
IN CONFORMITY WITH THE TERMS OF THIS ADVICE WILL BE DULY HONORED UPON DELIVERY OF
DOCUMENTS AS SPECIFIED IF PRESENTED AT THIS OFFICE (COMMERCIAL LETTER OF CREDIT
DEPARTMENT, 55 WATER STREET, SOUTH BUILDING, 17th FLOOR, NEW YORK CITY, NEW YORK
10041) ON OR BEFORE MAY 10, 19XX.

WE CONFIRM THE CREDIT AND HEREBY UNDERTAKE THAT ALL DRAFTS DRAWN AND PRESENTED AS
ABOVE SPECIFIED WILL BE DULY HONORED.

Very truly yours,

XXXXXXXXXXXXXXXXXXXXXXXXXXXXXXXXXXXXXXX
Authorized Signature

Provisions applicable to this credit
This credit is subject to the Uniform Customs and Practice for Documentary Credits (1983 Revision) International Chamber of Commerce Publication No. 4

2. The buyer's bank prepares an irrevocable letter of credit, including all instructions to the seller concerning the shipment.

3. The buyer's bank sends the irrevocable letter of credit to a U.S. bank requesting confirmation. The exporter may request that a particular U.S. bank be the confirming bank, but usually the foreign bank selects one of its U.S. correspondent banks.

4. The U.S. bank prepares a letter of confirmation to forward to the exporter, along with the irrevocable letter of credit.

5. The exporter reviews carefully all conditions in the letter of credit. The exporter's freight forwarder should be contacted to make sure that the shipping date can be met. If the exporter cannot comply with any of the conditions, the customer should be alerted at once.

6. The exporter arranges with the freight forwarder to deliver the goods to the appropriate port or airport.

7. When the goods are loaded, the forwarder completes the necessary documents.

8. The exporter (or the forwarder) presents documents indicating full compliance to the U.S. bank.

9. The bank reviews the documents. If they are in order, it issues the exporter a check. The documents are airmailed to the buyer's bank for review and transmitted to the buyer.

10. The buyer (or agent) gets the documents that may be needed to claim the goods.

An example of an irrevocable comfirmed letter of credit

The specimen of an irrevocable, confirmed letter of credit in figure 1 illustrates the various parts of a typical letter of credit. In this sample, the letter of credit was forwarded to the exporter, Export Corporation of America (A) by the drawee bank, Chemical Bank (B), as a result of the letter of credit being issued by the Banco de Banco, Bogota, Columbia (C), for the account of the importer, Gomez Y Florencia (D). The date of issue was March x, 19xx (E), and the beneficiary must submit proper documents (e.g., a commercial invoice in triplicate) (F) by March 31, 19xx (G) in order for a sight draft (H) to be honored.

Tips on using a letter of credit

When preparing quotations for prospective customers, exporters should keep in mind that banks do not pay amounts greater than specified in the letter of credit—even if higher charges for shipping, insurance or other factors are documented.

After receiving a letter of credit from a potential customer, the exporter should carefully compare its terms with the terms of its pro forma quotation. This is extremely important for if the terms are not precisely met the letter of credit may be invalid. If it is not possible to meet the terms or if any of the information is incorrect or even misspelled, the exporter should immediately get in touch with the customer and ask for an amendment to the letter of credit.

Late shipment and late presentation of documents are some of the most common errors to avoid when using letters of credits. Other common errors include presenting documents that are not properly signed or dated or that are not "clean" (a bill of lading is "clean" if no irregularities or damage is noted at the time goods are shipped).

Foreign exchange

For payments to be made in international transactions, foreign currencies must be exchanged, normally through commercial banks. One of the hazards of foreign trade is the uncertainty of the future exchange rates between currencies. It is possible that the relative value between the dollar and the buyer's currency will change between the time the deal is made and payment is received. If the exporter is not properly protected, a devaluation in the foreign currency could cause the exporter to lose dollars in the transaction. For example, if the buyer has agreed to pay 500,000 French francs for a shipment and the franc is valued at 20 cents, the seller would expect to receive $100,000. If the franc later decreased in value to be worth 19 cents, payment under the new rate would be only $95,000, a loss of $5,000 for the seller. Of course, it is also true that if the foreign currency increases in value that the exporter would get a windfall in extra profits. However, most exporters are not interested in speculating on foreign exchange fluctuations and prefer to avoid risks.

One of the simplest ways for a U.S. exporter to avoid this type of risk is to quote prices and demand payment in U.S. dollars. This places the burden and risk on the buyer to make the currency exchange. Exporters should also be aware of problems of currency convertibility; not all currencies are freely or quickly convertible into U.S. dollars.

If the buyer requests to make payment in a foreign currency, the exporter should consult an international banker before negotiating the sales contract. Banks can offer advice on the foreign exchange risks that exist; further, most international banks can help one hedge against such a risk, if needed, by agreeing to purchase the foreign currency at a fixed price in dollars regardless of the value of the currency when the customer pays. When this is done the bank assumes foreign exchange risks in return for a fee or discount on the transaction. If this mechanism is used, the fee should be included in the price quotation.

Countertrade and barter

Many developing countries with high foreign trade deficits, large international debt, and small holdings of foreign currencies restrict the amount of foreign exchange that can be purchased by importers to pay for goods. This is also true for many of the State controlled economies in Eastern Europe. In order to make sales to these countries, some form of countertrade may be required.

Simple barter is the direct exchange of goods or services between two parties; no currency is involved. Countertrade is a more complex transaction that includes the exchange of some currency as well as goods. For example, a countertrade contract may specify that the seller be paid in currency on the condition, stipulated by separate agreement, that the seller agrees to find markets for specified products from the buyer's country.

Countertrade transactions are quite complex and difficult to arrange. Usually only very large multinational corporations, international banks, or trading companies have enough expertise and resources to put together countertrade deals. However, small or medium-sized U.S. exporters can take advantage of countertrade opportunities by trading through one of these larger intermediaries. In addition, some trading houses offer services in the field of countertrade. Keep in mind, however, that the fees charged for countertrade transactions are quite steep (often the obtained products have to be discounted by 20 percent or more). Carrying out such a transaction alone exposes the exporter to the trouble of having to sell its products and the goods obtained.

The U.S. Department of Commerce can advise and assist U.S. exporters faced with countertrade requirements. The Department's services are intended to be applied early in an export transaction to help collect needed information, identify options, avoid risks and problems, and locate private sector sources of assistance. For information, contact the Office of Trade Finance, International Trade Administration, U.S. Department of Commerce, Washington, DC. Telephone: (202) 377-3277.

Deceasing credit risks through credit checks

This chapter has referred to three methods of reducing credit risks:

1. Selecting a safe method of payment—the safest being a confirmed, irrevocable letter of credit.

2. Obtaining credit risk insurance (see Chapter 11 for more information on this method).

3. Obtaining credit information on potential foreign buyers and distributors.

Generally, it is a good idea to check a buyer's credit even if credit risk insurance or relatively safe payment methods are employed. Banks are often able to provide credit reports on foreign companies, either through their own foreign branches or through a correspondent bank. In addition to banks, private credit institutions also offer international credit checking services.

The Department of Commerce's World Trader's Data Reports (WTDRs) also provide useful information for credit checks. A WTDR may be requested, for a fee, for any foreign company. Although the WTDR is itself not a credit report, it does contain some financial information and also identifies other U.S. companies that do business with the reported firm. These companies may then be contacted directly by the exporter to find out about their payment experience with the firm. (See Chapter 4 for more information on WTDRs.)

Collection problems: What to do when something goes wrong

In international trade, problems involving bad debts are more easily avoided than rectified when they occur. Credit checks and the other methods just discussed can limit risks involved. Nonetheless, just as in a company's domestic business, exporters occasionally encounter problems with buyers who default on payments. When this occurs in international trade, it can be both difficult and expensive to obtain payment. Even when the exporter has insurance to cover commercial credit risks, a default by a buyer is still costly. The exporter must exhaust all reasonable means of obtaining payment before an insurance claim will be honored, and often there is a significant delay until the insurance payment is made.

The simplest (and least costly) solution to a payment problem is to contact and negotiate with the customer. With patience, understanding, and flexibility, an exporter can often resolve conflicts to the satisfaction of both sides. This is especially the case when a simple misunderstanding or technical problem is to blame and there is no question of bad faith. Even though the exporter may be required to compromise on points—perhaps even on the price of the committed goods—the company may save a valuable customer and profit in the long run.

If, however, negotiations fail and the sum involved is large enough to warrant the effort, a company should obtain the assistance and advice of its bank, legal counsel, and other qualified experts. If both parties can agree to take their dispute to an arbitration agency, this is preferable to legal action, since arbitration is often faster and less costly. The International Chamber of Commerce handles the majority of international arbitrations, and is usually acceptable to foreign companies since it is not affiliated with any single country. For information, contact the Vice President for Arbitration, U.S. Council of the International Chamber of Commerce. Telephone: (212) 354-4480. The American Arbitration Association also handles international disputes; for information telephone: (212) 484-4000.

U.S. Government trade complaint service

Trade complaint service is available to aid U.S. exporters who find themselves in a trade dispute as a result of a specific overseas commercial transaction. These disputes, which are processed through the Commerce Department's District Offices, must meet certain criteria. After a firm has made every effort to settle the complaint without U.S. Government assistance, cases are accepted when it can be clearly shown that communications have broken down and the value of the claim is more than $1,000. Simple collection claims are not accepted.

The Department makes every effort to restore communications between the parties of the dispute in order to arrive at an amicable settlement. When legal proceedings are initiated, U.S. Government assistance is normally withdrawn.

After-sales service

15

The success of many export transactions depends on factors other than the quality and price of the product or service. These factors must be considered if the exporter is looking for repeat export business. One of the most important considerations for the U.S. firm is how to service products shipped overseas, followed by the need to maintain long-distance customer relations. In pursuing these objectives, what kind of support can be expected from local dealers? These issues, and others, may very well determine the long-term success rate of a company's exporting activities.

Maintenance, repair, and training

When exporting a product that requires after-sales service, several options are available:

- Disregard service issues altogether.

- Locate a local (i.e. to service the products.

- Train the distributor (if utilized) to provide repair and maintenance.

- Establish service personnel in the country or be prepared to provide these services long-distance.

Each option has advantages and disadvantages that must be evaluated in light of the level of service needed by the product, as well as the exporter's long-term plans. Generally, it is difficult to be price competitive when contracting with an overseas service organization for post-sales service. One viable alternative to the U.S. firm is to establish such service on a short-term basis until the distributors can be trained to provide this service directly. This option, of course, is an expensive approach for the long-term.

To maintain a long-term relationship with representatives, the exporter must take into account the provision of service to overseas customers. Exporting ventures that overlook this issue are inadvisable, since such action may permanently damage the foreign reputation of a U.S. firm and its product, creating a prohibitive barrier to international expansion at a later time.

One option is to engage a local organization to service the exported products. While this alternative may require little or no commitment of new personnel by the U.S. firm, it suffers from several disadvantages. First of all, considerable sums may be needed to prepare the local organization for servicing activities through training and indoctri-

nation. Second, the organization can be difficult to control, possibly charging a premium for its service activities or being unpredictable in cases of warranty service. Third, the exporting company may not know what priority the local service organization attaches to the servicing of the exported products. Fourth, the responsibility for service may still rest with the exporter in the mind of foreign customers. They may interpret unwillingness to send service personnel as a lack of commitment to the sale and quality of this product in their market. As a result, sales may not reflect demand, and competition (be it local or foreign) may be able to gain a larger share of the market.

Training a distributor to deliver service suffers from similar disadvantages of cost. However, if a close and long lasting business relationship with a particular firm can be established, then this option may be a viable one. It requires not only a one-time training expenditure, but an ongoing training relationship, since foreign distributors may have personnel turnover and the product may be put to new uses or be further developed.

For these reasons, it is important for the U.S. firm to continue to oversee servicing of its products if it intends to develop the market. The exporter may find that, apart from the expenses associated with maintaining an ongoing business relationship with an overseas distributor, the distributor must be compensated for providing the service—a fact that may show up in the price the distributor is willing to pay for the product. Finally, failure to deliver service on a product eliminates the opportunity to learn more about the foreign customers that are being served, their product applications, and their current and future product needs.

Two options are available for providing service directly. First, service can be provided long-distance by dispatching service personnel in response to product breakdowns. While such an option is possible, it is very costly and may not satisfy customers due to the time lapse before service personnel arrive. Even if the product is not prone to breakdowns, foreign customers generally feel happier and more secure if they can see a local presence and if they know that a service person can be reached easily.

Stationing service personnel permanently in the country is another alternative, one that is definitely appreciated by foreign customers. The expense of such an activity may be prohibitive in the early stages of market entry, but when making long-term plans for significant market penetration, this may be the best alternative. In such an instance, service expenses should be considered as part of the investment for market development.

Another option involves cooperation with other firms that have similar servicing needs. Through the mechanism of the export trading company, which is discussed in Chapter 4, U.S. firms can now cooperate in their international marketing efforts without a violation of antitrust statutes. By sending a service technician abroad to work for two or three different manufacturers with similar products or servicing needs, firms can drastically reduce expenditures while delivering a local presence and excellent after-sales follow-up.

Overall, the delivery of service can make or break a sale. In order to remain internationally competitive, an exporter must provide the best service possible. The support delivered for a product determines how enthusiastic customers are about placing another order. In addition, a premium price can be commanded for a product based on servicing capabilities. Indeed, service can be made a primary sales tool.

Feedback and customer relations

Rarely should an exporter rely entirely on secondary sources for information critical to business.

While sales figures may accurately reflect how well the firm is doing today, they are not always good indicators of future sales, changing market conditions, customer needs, or untapped market opportunities. There are several different sources for this kind of information: In-country agents or distributors; a firm's sales staff who may periodically visit distributors; an export management or trading company; and a first hand view of market conditions by the exporter.

There are several advantages to visiting the country involved in exporting. It is important to get the flavor of an export market: Look, smell, touch, discuss. How are the products being received? What is the competition doing? What do their products look like? Are the distributors and customers really happy? Complaints or problems that might be too trivial to show up in a report or a telex may come out over a cup of coffee. And, in many instances, a telex or occasional visit by a lower level employee may not convince foreign contacts of the seriousness of a company's intentions.

Flexibility and cultural adaptation should be guiding principles when traveling abroad on business. The exporter should acquire through reading or training a basic knowledge of the business culture, management attitudes, business methods, and consumer habits of the country in which he or she is doing business. For a more complete discussion of cultural practices, refer to Chapter 8.

Beyond exporting

16

Exporting goods manufactured in the U.S. is but one option open to American businesses interested in reaching an international market. Another important opportunity lies in manufacturing abroad, which should be considered as well.

Case studies show that firms usually export before they establish foreign operations. Exporting firms and those firms setting up foreign manufacturing may wish to be closer to their established customers to minimize transportation costs, to improve product adaptation or servicing capability, or to take advantage of a local identity in marketing. But this is not always the case. Certain products, such as inexpensive consumer items, may be priced out of foreign markets by the time freight and handling costs, import duties and taxes, agents' commissions, and other costs are added to the export price. Also, some countries prohibit the importation of certain items, but allow manufacture. To overcome these barriers, or to maintain or enlarge market share, exporters may wish to consider manufacturing their product abroad.

There are three basic ways that foreign manufacturing can be accomplished:

- Technology licensing;

- Wholly owned branch and subsidiary operations; and

- Joint ventures.

In choosing the course of action, the firm needs to consider the risk associated with each route, the costs, the firm's abilities and experience, the actions of competitors, the nature of the business, and U.S. and foreign government regulations and practices. Regardless of the method used to manufacture overseas, two overriding keys to success are mutual trust and written (legal) agreements.

Technology licensing

Technology licensing is a contractual arrangement in which the licensor's patents, trademarks, service marks, copyrights, or know-how may be sold or otherwise made available to a licensee for compensation negotiated in advance between the parties. Such compensation, known as **royalties,** may consist of a lump sum royalty, a "running" royalty (royalty based on volume of production), or a combination of both. U.S. companies frequently license their patents, trademarks, copyrights, and know-how to a foreign company that then manufactures and sells products based on the technology in a country or group of countries authorized by the licensing agreement.

A technology licensing agreement usually enables a U.S. firm to enter a foreign market quickly, yet poses fewer financial and legal risks than owning and operating a foreign manufacturing facility or participating in an overseas joint venture. Licensing also permits U.S. firms to overcome many of the **tariff and non-tariff barriers** that frequently hamper export of U.S. manufactured products. For these reasons, licensing can be a particularly attractive method of exporting for small companies or companies with little international trade experience, although licensing is profitably employed by large and small firms alike.

Technology licensing is not limited to the manufacturing sector. **Franchising** is also an important form of technology licensing used by many service industries. In franchising, the franchisor (licensor) permits the franchisee (licensee) to employ its trademark or service mark in a contractually specified manner for the marketing of goods or services. The franchisor usually continues to support the operation of the franchisee's business through the provision of advertising, accounting, training, and related services and in many instances also supplies products needed by the franchisee as well.

Like all forms of exporting, technology licensing has certain potential drawbacks. The negative aspects of licensing are weakened control over the transferred technology because of its transfer to an unaffiliated firm and the fact that licensing usually produces fewer profits than exporting U.S. manufactured goods or successfully operating an overseas manufacturing facility or joint venture. In certain third world countries, there also may be problems in adequately protecting the licensed technology from unauthorized use by third parties.

When considering the licensing of technology, it is important to remember that a foreign licensee often may attempt to use the licensed technology to manufacture products that are marketed in the U.S. or third countries in direct competition with the licensor or its other licensees. In many instances, U.S. licensors may wish to impose territorial restrictions on their foreign licensees, depending upon U.S. or foreign antitrust laws and the licensing laws of the host country. U.S. and foreign patent, trademark, and copyright laws also can often be used to bar unauthorized sales by foreign licensees, provided that the United States licensor has valid patent, trademark, or copyright protection in the United States or the third countries involved. In addition, unauthorized exports to the U.S. by foreign licensees can often be prevented by filing unfair import practices complaints with the U.S. International Trade Commission and by registering U.S. trademarks and copyrights with the U.S. Customs Service.

As in all overseas transactions, it is very important to investigate not only the prospective license, but the licensee's country as well. The government of the host country very often must approve the licensing agreement before it goes into effect. Such governments, for example, may prohibit royalty payments that exceed a certain rate or contractual provisions barring the licensee from exporting products manufactured with or embodying the licensed technology to third countries.

The prospective licensor always must take into account the host country's foreign patent, trademark and copyright laws, exchange controls, product liability laws, possible countertrading or barter requirements, antitrust and tax laws, and attitudes toward repatriation of royalties and dividends. The existence of a tax treaty or bilateral investment treaty between the United States and the prospective host country is an important indicator of the overall commercial relationship. Prospective U.S. licensors, especially of advanced technology, also should determine whether they need to obtain an export license from the U.S. Department of Commerce.

International technology licensing agreements, in a few instances, can unlawfully restrain trade in violation of U.S. or foreign antitrust laws. U.S. antitrust law, as a general rule, prohibits international technology licensing agreements that unreasonably restrict imports of competing goods or technology into the United States or unreasonably restrain U.S. domestic competition or exports.

Whether or not a restraint is reasonable is a fact-specific determination that considers the availability of competing goods or technology, market shares, barriers to entry, the business justifications for and the duration of contractual restraints, valid patents, trademarks, and copyrights, as well as certain other factors. The U.S. Department of Justice's *Antitrust Guide for International Operations* (1977) contains useful advice regarding the legality of various types of international transactions, including technology licensing. In those instances in which significant Federal antitrust issues are presented, U.S. licensors may wish to consider applying for an export trade certificate of review from the U.S. Department of Commerce (discussed in Chapter 4) or requesting a U.S. Department of Justice Business Review letter.

The United States is not the only country with antitrust laws that affect technology licensing. Foreign countries, particularly the European Economic Community (Common Market), also have strict antitrust laws on this subject. The European Economic Community recently issued detailed regulations governing patent licensing and ancillary licensing of trademarks and know-how. These regulations entitled "Commission Regulation (EEC) No. 2349/84 on the Application of Article 85(3) of the Treaty [of Rome] to Certain Categories of Patent Licensing Agreements," became effective on January 1, 1985, and should be carefully considered by anyone currently licensing or contemplating the licensing of technology to the Common Market.

Because of the potential complexity of international technology licensing agreements, firms should seek qualified legal advice in the United States before entering into such an agreement. In many instances, U.S. licensors should also retain qualified legal counsel in the host country in order to obtain advice on applicable local laws and to receive assistance in securing the foreign government's approval of the agreement. Sound legal advice and thorough investigation of the prospective licensee and the host country increases the likelihood that the licensing agreement will be a profitable transaction and help decrease or avoid potential problems.

Wholly owned branch and subsidiary operations

Unlike a technology licensing agreement, a wholly owned branch or subsidiary operation abroad requires a substantial investment and the ability to operate successfully in a foreign country. However, with 100 percent ownership, the U.S. firm is assured that it can operate in the manner most advantageous to its corporate goals, within the limits set by the host country's laws.

In a wholly owned branch or subsidiary, unlike a joint venture, the U.S. firm exercises sole control over sales policy and production and can unilaterally initiate more efficient production and management methods, subject to local laws and labor contract restrictions. Transferring technology to a wholly owned branch or subsidiary operation also offers more complete patent, trademark, and know-how protection than licensing technology to an unaffiliated firm.

Moreover, the use of a wholly owned branch or subsidiary operation allows the U.S. firm to take full advantage of any investment or tax incentives that may be offered by the host country to firms establishing new manufacturing facilities. This is especially true in some countries that grant additional relief if the product is manufactured for export, thus improving the host country's balance-of-payments position. Finally, problems with minority shareholders will be avoided.

A wholly owned branch or subsidiary operation can be established by the acquisition of an existing facility or construction of a new one. Acquisition is usually the quicker and more economical method. The acquisition method usually enables a U.S. firm to benefit from the reputation and good will of the acquired firm. However, certain acquisitions, particularly those involving major existing or potential competitors in U.S. or foreign markets, may be subject to challenge under U.S. or foreign (e.g., Federal Republic of Germany) antitrust laws. Qualified antitrust counsel can frequently avoid, or at least reduce, such difficulties by restructuring the acquisition or negotiating with government antitrust officials.

Joint ventures

There are a number of business and legal reasons why a wholly owned foreign branch or subsidiary may not be the best export strategy for a U.S. company. In such cases, the firm may wish to consider a joint venture with a firm in the host country. International joint ventures are used in a wide variety of manufacturing, mining, and service industries and are frequently undertaken in conjunction with technology licensing by the U.S. firm to the joint venture.

The host country may require that a certain percentage (often 51 percent) of manufacturing or mining operations be owned by nationals of that country, thereby requiring U.S. firms to operate through joint ventures. in addition to such legal requirements, U.S. firms may find it desirable to enter into a joint venture with a foreign firm to help spread the high costs and risks frequently associated with foreign operations.

Moreover, the local partner may bring to the joint venture knowledge of the customs and tastes of the people, an established distribution network, and valuable business and political contacts. Having local partners also decreases the foreign status of the firm and may provide some protection against discrimination or expropriation, should conditions change.

There are, of course, possible disadvantages to international joint ventures. A major potential drawback to joint ventures, especially in countries that limit foreign companies to 49 percent or less participation, is the loss of effective managerial control. A loss of effective managerial control can result in reduced profits, increased operating costs, inferior product quality and exposure to product liability and environmental litigation and fines. U.S. firms that wish to retain effective managerial control will find this issue an important topic in negotiations with the prospective joint venture partner and frequently the host government as well.

As in the case of technology licensing agreements, joint ventures can raise U.S. or foreign antitrust issues in certain circumstances, particularly when the prospective joint venture partners are major existing or potential competitors in the affected national markets. Firms may wish to consider applying for an **export trade certificate of review** from the U.S. Department of Commerce (discussed in Chapter 4) or a **Business Review Letter** from the U.S. Department of Justice when there are significant Federal antitrust issues raised by the proposed international joint venture.

Because of the complex legal issues frequently raised by international joint venture agreements, it is very important, before entering into any such agreement, to seek legal advice from qualified U.S. counsel experienced in this aspect of international trade. Many of the export counseling sources in Chapter 2 can help direct a U.S. company to local counsel suitable for its needs.

U.S. firms contemplating international joint ventures also should consider retaining experienced counsel in the host country. U.S. firms can find it very disadvantageous to rely upon their potential joint venture partners to negotiate host government approvals and advise them on legal issues, since their prospective partners' interests may not always coincide with their own. Qualified foreign counsel can be very helpful in obtaining government approvals and providing on-going advice regarding the host country's patent, trademark, copyright, tax, labor, corporate, commercial, antitrust and exchange control laws.

Appendices

The twelve most common mistakes of potential exporters

The following may be considered the 12 most common mistakes and pitfalls made by new exporters.

1. **Failure to obtain qualified export counseling and to develop a master international marketing plan before starting an export business.** —To be successful, a firm must first clearly define goals, objectives, and the problems encountered. Secondly, it must develop a definitive plan to accomplish an objective despite the problems involved. Unless the firm is fortunate enough to possess a staff with considerable export expertise, it may not be able to take this crucial first step without qualified outside guidance.

2. **Insufficient commitment by top management to overcome the initial difficulties and financial requirements of exporting.** —It may take more time and effort to establish a firm in a foreign market than in domestic ones. Although the early delays and costs involved in exporting may seem difficult to justify when compared to established domestic trade, the exporter should take a long-range view of this process and carefully monitor international marketing efforts through these early difficulties. If a good foundation is laid for export business, the benefits derived should eventually outweigh the investment.

3. **Insufficient care in selecting overseas distributors.** —The selection of each foreign distributor is crucial. The complications involved in overseas communications and transportation require international distributors to act with greater independence than their domestic counterparts. Also, since a new exporter's history, trademarks, and reputation are usually unknown in the foreign market, foreign customers may buy on the strength of a distributor's reputation. A firm should therefore conduct a personal evaluation of the personnel handling its account, the distributor's facilities, and the management methods employed.

4. **Chasing orders from around the world instead of establishing a basis for profitable operations and orderly growth.** —If exporters expect distributors to actively promote their accounts, the distributors must be trained, assisted, and their performance must be continually monitored. This requires a company marketing executive permanently located in the distributor's geographical region. New exporters should concentrate their efforts in one or two geographical areas until there is sufficient business to support a company representative. Then, while this initial core area is expanded, the exporter can move into the next selected geographical area.

5. **Neglecting export business when the U.S. market booms.** —Too many companies turn to exporting when business falls off in the United States. When domestic business starts to boom again, they neglect their export trade or relegate it to a secondary place. Such neglect can seriously harm the business and motivation of their overseas representatives, strangle the U.S. company' own export trade and leave the firm without recourse when domestic business falls off once more. Even if domestic business remains strong, the company may eventually realize that they have only succeeded in shutting off a valuable source of additional profits.

6. **Failure to treat international distributors on an equal basis with domestic counterparts.** —Often, companies carry out institutional advertising campaigns, special discount offers, sales incentive programs, special credit term programs, warranty offers, etc., in the U.S. market but fail to make similar assistance available to their international distributors. This is a mistake that can destroy the vitality of overseas marketing efforts.

7. **Assuming that a given market technique and product will automatically be successful in all countries.** —What works in one market may not work in others. Each market has to be treated separately to insure maximum success.

8. **Unwillingness to modify products to meet regulations or cultural preferences of other countries.** —Local safety and security codes, as well as import restrictions, cannot be ignored by foreign distributors. If necessary modifications are not made at the factory, the distributor must do them—usually at greater cost and, perhaps, not as well. It should also be noted that the resulting smaller profit margin makes the account less attractive.

9. **Failure to print service, sale, and warranty messages in locally understood languages.** —Although a distributor's top management may speak English, it is unlikely that all sales

personnel (let alone service personnel) have this capability. Without a clear understanding of sales messages or service instructions, these persons may be less effective in performing their functions.

10. **Failure to consider use of an export management company.**—If a firm decides it cannot afford its own export department (or has tried one unsuccessfully), it should consider the possibility of appointing an appropriate export management company (EMC).

11. **Failure to consider licensing or joint-venture agreements.**—Import restrictions in some countries, insufficient personnel/financial resources, or a too limited product line cause many companies to dismiss international marketing as unfeasible. Yet, many products that can compete on a national basis in the United States can be successfully marketed in most markets of the world. A licensing or joint venture arrangement may be the simple, profitable answer to any reservations. In general, all that is needed for success is flexibility in using the proper combination of marketing techniques.

12. **Failure to provide readily available servicing for the product.**—A product without the necessary service support can acquire a bad reputation in a short period, potentially preventing further sales.

Fast match

A quick, easy to way to match your international business requirements to the programs, services, and publications described in this Guide.

IF YOU ARE SEEKING INFORMATION OR ASSISTANCE REGARDING → USE ↓

	Potential Markets	Market Research	Direct Sales Leads	Agents/Distributors	Licenses	Credit Analysis	Financial Assistance	Risk Insurance	Tax Incentives	Export Counseling	Export Regulations	Overseas Contracts	Marketing Strategies	Trade Complaints	Customs Advantages	Carnet	See Page(s)
U.S. & Foreign Commercial Service	●	●	●		●					●	●		●	●			5, 15, 27
District Export Councils		●								●							6
Trade Opportunities Program	●	●	●	●	●							●					6, 27, 57
Agent/Distributor Service		●		●													6, 27
Overseas Business Reports	●	●															7, 14
Foreign Economic Trends	●	●															14
Small Business Administration	●	●					●			●							7, 12, 16, 48
International Chambers of Commerce											●					●	76
Export Statistics Profiles	●	●															12, 13
Export Information System Data Reports	●	●															12, 14
Annual Worldwide Industry Reviews	●	●															12, 13
International Market Research	●	●															12, 13, 14
Country Market Surveys	●	●															12, 13
Custom Statistical Service	●	●															12, 13
Product Market Profile	●	●															14
Market Share Reports	●	●															14
Country Market Profiles	●	●															14
Country Trade Statistics	●	●															12, 14
Background Notes	●	●													●		14
International Economic Indicators	●	●															15
World Traders Data Reports	●					●											20, 40, 76
Commercial News USA	●		●	●													26, 28
Export-Import Bank							●										26, 46
Export Mailing List Service	●	●	●	●													27
Commerce Trade Shows	●	●	●	●	●	●							●				28
Commerce Trade Missions	●	●	●	●	●	●							●				29
Export Development Offices		●	●														30, 35
Catalog Exhibitions			●														30
Major Projects Program						●						●					30
Overseas Private Investment Corporation							●	●									48
Private Export Funding Corporation							●										49
Foreign Sales Corporation							●		●								56
Commerce Business Daily	●		●														32, 57
Free Ports & Free Trade Zones															●		56, 66

87

Export glossary

Acceptance—This term has several related meanings:

1. A time draft (or bill of exchange) which the drawee has accepted and is unconditionally obligated to pay at maturity. The draft must be presented first for acceptance—the drawee becomes the "acceptor"—then for payment. The word "accepted" and the date and place of payment must be written on the face of the draft.

2. The drawee's act in receiving a draft and thus entering into the obligation to pay its value at maturity.

3. (Broadly speaking) Any agreement to purchase goods under specified terms. An agreement to purchase goods at a stated price and under stated terms.

Ad valorem—According to value. See **Duty.**

Advance against documents—A loan made on the security of the documents covering the shipment.

Advising bank—A bank, operating in the exporter's country, that handles letters of credit for a foreign bank by notifying the exporter that the credit has been opened in his or her favor. The advising bank fully informs the exporter of the conditions of the letter of credit without necessarily bearing responsibility for payment.

Advisory capacity—A term indicating that a shipper's agent or representative is not empowered to make definitive decisions or adjustments without approval of the group or individual represented. Compare **Without reserve**.

Agent—See **Foreign sales agent.**

Air waybill—A bill of lading that covers both domestic and international flights transporting goods to a specified destination. This is a non-negotiable instrument of air transport that serves as a receipt for the shipper, indicating that the carrier has accepted the goods listed and obligates itself to carry the consignment to the airport of destination according to specified conditions. Compare **Inland bill of lading, Ocean bill of lading,** and **Through bill of lading.**

Alongside—A phrase referring to the side of a ship. Goods to be delivered "alongside" are to be placed on the dock or barge within reach of the transport ship's tackle so that they can be loaded aboard the ship.

Antidiversion clause—See **Destination control statement.**

Arbitrage—The process of buying **Foreign exchange**, stocks, bonds, and other commodities in one market and immediately selling them in another market at higher prices.

Asian dollars—U.S. dollars deposited in Asia and the Pacific Basin. Compare **Eurodollars.**

ATA Carnet—See **Carnet.**

Balance of trade—The difference between a country's total imports and exports; if exports exceed imports, a favorable balance of trade exists; if not, a trade deficit is said to exist.

Barter—Trade in which merchandise is exchanged directly for other merchandise without use of money. Barter is an important means of trade with countries using currency that is not readily convertible.

Beneficiary—The person in whose favor a **Letter of credit** is issued or a **Draft** is drawn.

Bill of exchange—See **Draft.**

Bill of lading—A document that establishes the terms of a contract between a shipper and a transportation company under which freight is to be moved between specified points for a specified charge. Usually prepared by the shipper on forms issued by the carrier, it serves as a document of title, a contract of carriage, and a receipt for goods. Also see **Air waybill, Inland bill of lading, Ocean bill of lading,** and **Through bill of lading.**

Bonded warehouse—A warehouse authorized by **Customs** authorities for storage of goods on which payment of **Duties** is deferred until the goods are removed.

Booking—An arrangement with a steamship company for the acceptance and carriage of freight.

Buying agent—See **Purchasing agent.**

Carnet—A customs document permitting the holder to carry or send merchandise temporarily into certain foreign countries (for display, demonstration, or similar purposes) without paying duties or posting bonds. (*See Chapter 15*).

Cash against documents (C.A.D.)—Payment for goods in which a commission house or other intermediary transfers title documents to the buyer upon payment in cash.

Cash in advance (C.I.A.)—Payment for goods in which the price is paid in full before shipment is made. This method is usually used only for small purchases or when the goods are built to order.

Cash with order (C.W.O.)—Payment for goods in which the buyer pays when ordering and in which the transaction is binding on both parties.

Certificate of inspection—A document certifying that merchandise (such as perishable goods) was in good condition immediately prior to its shipment. (See Chapter 13.)

Certificate of manufacture—A statement (often notarized) in which a producer of goods certifies that manufacture has been completed and that the goods are now at the disposal of the buyer.

Certificate of origin—A document, required by certain foreign countries for tariff purposes, certifying the country of origin of specified goods (See Chapter 10.)

C & F—"Cost and freight." A pricing term indicating that the cost of the goods and freight charges are included in the quoted price; the buyer arranges for and pays insurance. (See Chapter 10.)

Charter party—A written contract, usually on a special form, between the owner of a vessel and a "charterer" who rents use of the vessel or a part of its freight space. The contract generally includes the freight rates and the ports involved in the transportation.

C & I—"Cost and insurance." A pricing term indicating that the cost of the product and insurance are included in the quoted price. The buyer is responsible for freight to the named port of destination.

C.I.F.—"Cost, insurance, freight." A pricing term indicating that the cost of the goods, insurance, and freight are included in the quoted price. (See Chapter 10.)

Clean bill of lading—A receipt for goods issued by a carrier that indicates that the goods were received in "apparent good order and condition," without damages or other irregularities. Compare **Foul bill of lading.**

Clean draft—A **Draft** to which no documents have been attached.

Collection papers—All documents (**Commercial invoices, Bills of lading**, etc.) submitted to a buyer for the purpose of receiving payment for a shipment.

Commercial attache—The commerce expert on the diplomatic staff of his or her country's embassy or large consulate.

Commercial invoice—An itemized list of goods shipped, usually included among a exporter's **Collection papers**. (See Chapter 13.)

Commission agent—See **Purchasing agent.**

Common carrier—An individual, partnership, or corporation that transports persons or goods for compensation.

Confirmed letter of credit—A letter of credit, issued by a foreign bank, with validity confirmed by a U.S. bank. An exporter who requires a confirmed letter of credit from the buyer is assured of payment by the U.S. bank even if the foreign buyer or the foreign bank defaults. See **Letter of credit.** (Also see Chapter 14.)

Consignment—Delivery of merchandise from an exporter (the consignor) to an agent (the consignee) under agreement that the agent sell the merchandise for the account of the exporter. The consignor retains title to the goods until the consignee has sold them. The consignee sells the goods for commission and remits the net proceeds to the consignor.

Consular declaration—A formal statement, made to the consul of a foreign country, describing goods to be shipped.

Consular invoice—A document, required by some foreign countries, describing a shipment of goods and showing information such as the consignor, consignee, and value of the shipment. Certified by a consular official of the foreign country, it is used by the country's customs officials to verify the value, quantity, and nature of the shipment. (See Chapter 13.)

Convertible currency—A currency that can be bought and sold for other currencies at will.

Correspondent bank—A bank that, in its own country, handles the business of a foreign bank.

Countertrade—The sale of goods or services that are paid for in whole or in part by the transfer of goods or services from a foreign country. (See **Barter.**)

Credit risk insurance—Insurance designed to cover risks of nonpayment for delivered goods. Compare **Marine insurance.**

Customs—The authorities designated to collect duties levied by a country on imports and exports. The term also applies to the procedures involved in such collection.

Customhouse broker—An individual or firm licensed to enter and clear goods through Customs.

Date draft—A draft that matures in a specified number of days after the date it is issued, without regard to the date of **Acceptance** (Definition 2). See **Draft, Sight draft** and **Time draft**. (Also see Chapter 14.)

Deferred payment credit—Type of **Letter of credit** providing for payment some time after presentation of shipping documents by exporter.

Demand draft—See **Sight draft.**

Destination control statement—Any of various statements that the U.S. Government requires to be displayed on export shipments and that specify the destinations for which export of the shipment has been authorized. (See Chapter 13.)

Devaluation—The official lowering of the value of one country's currency in terms of one or more foreign currencies. (E.g., if the U.S. dollar is devalued in relation to the French franc, one dollar will "buy" fewer francs than before.)

DISC—Domestic international sales corporation. (See Chapter 12.)

Discrepancy—Letter of credit—When documents presented do not conform to the letter of credit, it is referred to as a "discrepancy."

Dispatch—An amount paid by a vessel's operator to a charterer if loading or unloading is completed in less time than stipulated in the charter party.

Distributor—A foreign agent who sells for a supplier directly and maintains an inventory of the supplier's products.

Dock receipt—A receipt issued by an ocean carrier to acknowledge receipt of a shipment at the carrier's dock or warehouse facilities. Also see **Warehouse receipt.**

Documentary draft—A **Draft** to which documents are attached.

Documents against acceptance (D/A)—Instructions given by a shipper to a bank indicating that documents transferring title to goods should be delivered to the buyer (or drawee) only upon the buyer's acceptance of the attached draft.

Draft (or Bill of exchange)—An unconditional order in writing from one person (the drawer) to another (the drawee), directing the **Drawee** to pay a specified amount to a named **Drawer** at a fixed or determinable future date. (See Chapter 14.) See **Date draft, Sight draft, Time draft.**

Drawback—Articles manufactured or produced in the United State with the use of imported components or raw materials and later exported are entitled to a refund of up to ninety-nine percent of the duty charged on the imported components. The refund of duty is known as a "drawback."

Drawee—The individual or firm on whom a draft is drawn and who owes the stated amount. Compare **Drawer.** Also see **Draft.**

Drawer—The individual or firm that issues or signs a draft and thus stands to receive payment of the stated amount from the drawee. Compare **Drawee.** Also see **Draft.**

Dumping—Exporting/importing merchandise into a country below the costs incurred in production and shipment.

Duty—A tax imposed on imports by the customs authority of a country. Duties are generally based on the value of the goods (ad valorem duties), some other factor such as weight or quantity (specific duties), or a combination of value and other factors (compound duties).

EMC—See **Export management company.**

ETC—See **Export trading company.**

Eurodollars—U.S. dollars placed on deposit in banks outside the United States; usually refers to deposits in Europe.

Ex—"From." When used in pricing terms such as "Ex Factory" or "Ex Dock," it signifies that the price quoted applies only at the point of origin (in the two examples, at the seller's factory or a dock at the import point). In practice, this kind of quotation indicates that the seller agrees to place the goods at the disposal of the buyer at the specified place within a fixed period of time.

Exchange permit—A government permit sometimes required by the importer's government to enable the importer to convert his or her own country's currency into foreign currency with which to pay a seller in another country.

Exchange rate—The price of one currency in terms of another, i.e., the number of units of one currency that may be exchanged for one unit of another currency.

Eximbank—The Export-Import Bank of the United States (See Chapter 11.)

Export broker—An individual or firm that brings together buyers and sellers for a fee but does not take part in actual sales transactions.

Export commission house—An organization which, for a commission, acts as a purchasing agent for a foreign buyer.

Export declaration—See **Shipper's export declaration.**

Export license—A government document that permits the "Licensee" to engage in the export of designated goods to certain destinations. (See **General and Validated licenses** and Chapter 12.)

Export management company—A private firm that serves as the export department for several manufacturers, soliciting and transacting export business on behalf of its clients in return for a commission, salary, or retainer plus commission. (See Chapter 2.)

Export trading company—A firm similar or identical to an export management company. (See Chapter 2.)

Factoring houses—See Chapter 11.

F.A.S.—"Free alongside." A pricing term indicating that the quoted price includes the cost of delivering the goods alongside a designated vessel. (See Chapter 10.)

FCIA—Foreign credit insurance association. (See Chapter 11.)

F.I.—"Free in." A pricing term indicating that the charterer of a vessel is responsible for the cost of loading and unloading goods from the vessel.

Floating policy—See **Open policy.**

F.O.—"Free out." A pricing term indicating that the charterer of a vessel is responsible for the cost of loading goods from the vessel.

F.O.B.—"Free on board." A pricing term indicating that the quoted price includes the cost of loading the goods into transport vessels at the specified place. (*See Chapter 10.*)

Force majeure—The title of a standard clause in marine contracts exempting the parties for non-fulfillment of their obligations as a result of conditions beyond their control, such as earthquakes, floods, or war.

Foreign exchange—The currency or credit instruments of a foreign country. Also, transactions involving purchase and/or sale of currencies.

Foreign freight forwarder—See **Freight forwarder.**

Foreign sales agent—An individual or firm that serves as the foreign representative of a domestic supplier and seeks sales abroad for the supplier.

Foreign trade zone—See **Free trade zone.**

Foul bill of lading—A receipt for goods issued by a carrier with an indication that the goods were damaged when received. Compare **Clean bill of lading.**

Free port—An area such as a port city into which merchandise may legally be moved without payment of duties.

Free trade zone—A port designated by the government of a country for duty-free entry of any non-prohibited goods. Merchandise may be stored, displayed, used for manufacturing, etc., within the zone and reexported without duties being paid. Duties are imposed on the merchandise (or items manufactured from the merchandise) only when the goods pass from the zone into an area of the country subject to the Customs Authority.

Freight forwarder—An independent business which handles export shipments for compensation. (A freight forwarder is among the best sources of information and assistance on U.S. export regulations and documentation, shipping methods, and foreign import regulations.)

GATT—"General Agreement on Tariffs and Trade." A multilateral treaty intended to help reduce trade barriers between the signatory countries and to promote trade through tariff concessions.

General export license—Any of various export licenses covering export commodities for which **Validated export licenses** are not required. No formal application or written authorization is needed to ship exports under a General export license. (*See Chapter 12.*)

Gross weight—The full weight of a shipment, including goods and packaging. Compare **Tare weight.**

Import license—A document required and issued by some national governments authorizing the importation of goods into their individual countries.

Inland bill of lading—A bill of lading used in transporting goods overland to the exporter's international carrier. Although a **Through bill of lading** can sometimes be used, it is usually necessary to prepare both an inland bill of lading and an **Ocean bill of lading** for export shipments. Compare **Air waybill, Ocean bill of lading,** and **Through bill of lading.**

International freight forwarder—See **Freight forwarder.**

IOGA (Industry-Organized, Government-Sponsored) Trade Mission—See *Chapter 7.*

Irrevocable letter of credit—A letter of credit in which the specified payment is guaranteed by the bank if all terms and conditions are met by the drawee. Compare **Revocable letter of credit.** (*Also see Chapter 14.*)

Letter of credit (L/C)—A document, issued by a bank per instructions by a buyer of goods, authorizing the seller to draw a specified sum of money under specified terms, usually the receipt by the bank of certain documents within a given time. (*See Chapter 14.*)

Licensing—A business arrangement in which the manufacturer of a product (or a firm with proprietary rights over certain technology, trademarks, etc.) grants permission to some other group or individual to manufacture that product (or make use of that proprietary material) in return for specified royalties or other payment.

Manifest—See **Ship's manifest.**

Marine insurance—Insurance that compensates the owners of goods transported overseas in the event of loss that cannot be legally recovered from the carrier. Also covers air shipments. Compare **Credit risk insurance.**

Marking (or marks)—Letters, numbers, and other symbols placed on cargo packages to facilitate identification. (*See Chapter 13.*)

Ocean bill of lading—A **Bill of lading (B/L)** indicating that the exporter consigns a shipment to an international carrier for transportation to a specified foreign market. Unlike an **Inland B/L,** the **Ocean B/L** also serves as a collection document. If it is a "straight" **B/L,** the foreign buyer can obtain the shipment from the carrier by simply showing proof of identity. If a "negotiable" **B/L** is used, the buyer must first pay for the goods, post a bond, or meet other conditions agreeable to the seller. Compare **Air waybill, Inland bill of lading,** and **Through bill of lading.**

On board bill of lading (B/L)—A **Bill of lading** in which a carrier certifies that goods have been placed on board a certain vessel.

Open account—A trade arrangement in which goods are shipped to a foreign buyer without guarantee of payment. The obvious risk this method poses to the supplier makes it essential that the buyer's integrity be unquestionable.

Open insurance policy—A marine insurance policy that applies to all shipments made by an exporter over a period of time rather than to one shipment only.

"Order" bill of lading (B/L)—A negotiable **Bill of lading** made out to the order of the shipper.

Packing list—A list showing the number and kinds of items being shipped, as well as other information needed for transportation purposes. (*See Chapter 13.*)

Parcel post receipt—The postal authorities' signed acknowledgment of delivery to receiver of a shipment made by parcel post.

PEFCO (Private Export Funding Corporation)—lends to foreign buyers to finance exports from U.S. (*See Chapter 11.*)

Perils of the sea—A marine insurance term used to designate heavy weather, stranding, lightning, collision, and sea water damage.

Phytosanitary Inspection Certificate—A certificate, issued by the U.S. Department of Agriculture to satisfy import regulations for foreign countries, indicating that a U.S. shipment has been inspected and is free from harmful pests and plant diseases.

Political risk—In export financing the risk of loss due to such causes as currency inconvertibility, government action preventing entry of goods, expropriation or confiscation, war, etc.

Pro forma invoice—An invoice provided by a supplier prior to the shipment of merchandise, informing the buyer of the kinds and quantities of goods to be sent, their value, and important specifications (weight, size, etc.).

Purchasing agent—An agent who purchases goods in his or her own country on behalf of foreign importers such as government agencies and large private concerns.

Quota—The quantity of goods of a specific kind that a country permit to be imported without restriction or imposition of additional **Duties.**

Quotation—An offer to sell goods at a stated price and under specified conditions.

Remitting bank—Bank that sends the **Draft** to overseas bank for collection.

Representative—See **Foreign sales agent.**

Revocable letter of credit—A **Letter of credit** that can be cancelled or altered by the **Drawee** (buyer) after it has been issued by the drawee's bank. Compare **Irrevocable letter of credit.** (*Also see Chapter 14.*)

Schedule B—Refers to "Schedule B, Statistical Classification of Domestic and Foreign Commodities Exported from the United States." All commodities exported from the United States must be assigned a seven-digit Schedule B number.

Shipper's export declaration—A form required by the U.S. Treasury Department for all shipments and prepared by a shipper, indicating the value, weight, destination, and other basic information about an export shipment. (*See Chapter 13.*)

Ship's manifest—An instrument in writing, signed by the captain of a ship, that lists the individual shipments constituting the ship's cargo.

Sight draft (S/D)—A draft that is payable upon presentation to the drawee. Compare **Date draft, Time draft.** (*See Chapter 14.*)

Spot exchange—The purchase or sale of foreign exchange for immediate delivery.

Standard Industrial Classification (SIC)—A standard numerical code system used by the U.S. Government to classify products and services.

Standard International Trade Classification (SITC)—A standard numerical code system developed by the United Nations to classify commodities used in international trade.

Steamship conference—A group of steamship operators that operate under mutually agreed upon freight rates.

Straight bill of lading—A non-negotiable **Bill of lading** in which the goods are consigned directly to a named consignee.

Tare weight—The weight of a container and packing materials without the weight of the goods it contains. Compare **Gross weight.**

Tenor (or a Draft)—Designation of a payment as being due at sight, a given number of days after sight, or a given number of days after date.

Through bill of lading—A single **Bill of lading** converting both the domestic and international carriage of an export shipment. An **Air waybill,** for instance, is essentially a through bill of lading used for air shipments. Ocean shipments, on the other hand, usually require two separate documents—an **Inland bill of lading** for domestic carriage and an **Ocean bill of lading** for international carriage. **Through bills of lading** are insufficient for ocean shipments. Compare **Air waybill, Inland bill of lading, Ocean bill of lading.**

Time draft—A draft that matures either a certain number of days after acceptance or a certain number of days after the date of the draft. Compare **Date draft, Sight draft.** (*See Chapter 14.*)

Tramp steamer—A ship not operating on regular routes or schedules.

Transaction statement—A document that delineates the terms and conditions agreed upon between the importer and exporter.

Trust receipt—Release of merchandise by a bank to a buyer in which the bank retains title to the merchandise. The buyer, who obtains the goods for manufacturing or sales purposes, is obligated to maintain the goods (or the proceeds from their sale) distinct from the remainder of his or her assets and to hold them ready for repossession by the bank.

Validated export license—A required document issued by the U.S. Government authorizing the export of specific commodities. This license is for a specific transaction or time period in which the exporting is to take place. Compare **General export license**. (*Also see Chapter 12.*)

Warehouse receipt—A receipt issued by a warehouse listing goods received for storage.

Wharfage—A charge assessed by a pier or dock owner for handling incoming or outgoing cargo.

Without reserve—A term indicating that a shipper's agent or representative is empowered to make definitive decisions and adjustments abroad without approval of the group or individual represented. Compare **Advisory capacity**.

Directory of Federal export assistance

A. U.S. Department of Commerce
B. Small Business Administration
C. Export-Import Bank
D. U.S. Department of Agriculture
E. Overseas Private Investment Corporation (OPIC)
F. Department of the Treasury/ U.S. Customs Service
G. Agency for International Development
H. U.S. Trade Representative

A. U.S. Department of Commerce

The U.S. Department of Commerce can provide a wealth of information to exporters. The first step an exporter should take is to contact the nearest US&FCS District Office (listed by State in Appendix X). For more specific information on who to contact in Washington, DC, the Export Counseling Center (below) can help guide the exporter to the right person or office.

To send inquiries to or to communicate with the following offices, the address should include the office name, the office room number, followed by: U.S. Department of Commerce, Washington, DC 20230 (exceptions noted).

Area Code: 202

U.S. and Foreign Commercial Service

Office of Domestic Operations

* Export Counseling Center: Room 1066 (Export counseling and marketing assistance).............................. 377-3181

Export Promotion Services

* Office of Information Product Development and Distribution: P.O. Box 14207, Washington, DC 20044 (Information on foreign markets, customers, and trade leads)............... 377-2432

* Office of Marketing Programs: (Trade show and trade mission information) Room 2116 377-4231

* Information on *Commercial News USA* and other Commerce export-related publications)... 377-5367

Office of Foreign Operations

Regional Coordinators for:

* Africa, Near East and South Asia: Room 3104 377-2736
* East Asia and Pacific: Room 3104 377-2736
* Europe: Room 3122 377-1599
* Western Hemisphere: Room 3122 377-1599

Trade Development

Product/Service Specialists:
* Aerospace: Room 6877 377-8228
* Automotive Affairs and Consumer Goods: Room 4324 377-0823
* Basic Industries: Room 4045 377-0614
* Capital Goods & International Construction: Rm 2001B 377-5023
* Export Trading Company Affairs: Room 5618 377-5131
* International Major Projects: Room 2007 377-5225
* Science and Electronics: Room 1001A 377-4466
* Services: Room 1128 377-5261
* Textiles and Apparel: Room 3100 377-3737
* Trade Information and Analysis: Room 3814B 377-1316

Trade Administration

Office of Export Administration
* Exporter's Service Staff: (Export licensing, controls, etc.) Room 1099 377-4811

Office of Antiboycott Compliance: Room 3886 377-2381

Minority Business Development Agency

Minority Export Development Consulting Program Office: Room 5093 377-2881

International Economic Policy

Country Desk Officers can provide specific country information relating to international trade. The following is a list of country desk officers.

Listing of ITA desk officers

Country	Desk officer	Phone	Room
Afghanistan	Stan Bilinski	377-2954	2029-B
Albania	James Ellis	377-2645	3419
Algeria	Jeffrey Johnson	377-4652	2033
Angola	Simon Bensimon	377-0357	3317
Argentina	Mark Siegelman	377-5427	3021
ASEAN	George Paine	377-3875	2032
Australia	Tony Costanza	377-3646	2310
Austria	Philip Combs	377-2434	3411
Bahamas	Libby Roper	377-2527	3029-A
Bahrain	Claude Clement	377-5545	2039
Bangladesh	Christine Coady	377-2954	2029-B
Barbados	Vacant	377-2527	3029-A
Belgium	Boyce Fitzpatrick	377-2920	3415
Belize	Robert Dormitzer	377-3527	3029-A
Benin	James Robb	377-4564	3317
Bermuda	Libby Roper	377-2527	3029-A
Bhutan	Richard Harding	377-2954	2029-B
Bolivia	Roger Turner	377-4302	3314
Botswana	Reginald Biddle	377-5148	3317
Brazil	Robert Bateman	377-3871	3017
Brunei	Gary Bouck	377-3875	2310
Bulgaria	James Ellis	377-2645	3419
Burkina Faso	John Crown	377-4564	3317
Burma	Kyaw Win	377-5334	3820
Burundi	Simon Bensimon	377-0357	3318
Cambodia	JeNelle Matheson	377-4681	2323
Cameroon	Philip Michelini	377-0357	3317
Canada	Thomas Brewer	377-3101	3314
Cape Verde	Renee Hancher	377-4564	3317
Caymans	Libby Roper	377-2527	3029-A
Central African Rep.	Philip Michelini	377-0357	3317
Chad	Fred Stokelin	377-4564	3317
Chile	Herbert Lindow	377-4302	3027
Columbia	Richard Muenzer	377-4302	3027
Comoros	Fred Stokelin	377-4564	3317
Congo	Philip Michelini	377-0357	3317
Costa Rica	Fred Tower	377-2527	3029-A
Cuba	Ted Johnson	377-2527	3029-A
Cyprus	Ann Corro	377-3945	3044
Czechoslovakia	James Ellis	377-2645	3419
Denmark	Maryanne Lyons	377-3254	3413
D'Jibouti	Fred Stokelin	377-4564	3320
Dominican Rep.	Bill DesRochers	377-2527	3016
East Caribbean	Desmond Foynes	377-2527	3022
Ecuador	Herbert Lindow	377-4302	3027
Egypt	Cynthia Anthony	377-4652	2033
El Salvador	Robert Dormitzer	377-5563	3029-A
Equatorial Guinea	Simon Bensimon	377-0357	3318
Ethiopia	Fred Stokelin	377-4564	3320
European Community	Charles Ludolph	377-5276	3034
Finland	Maryanne Lyons	377-3254	3413
France	Ken Nichols	377-8008	3042
French Guyana	Libby Roper	377-2523	3029-A
Gabon	Philip Michelini	377-0357	3317
Gambia	Jim Robb	377-4564	3317
German Democratic Rep.	James Ellis	377-2645	3419
Germany (West)	Velizar Stanoyevitch	377-2434	3411
Ghana	John Crown	377-4564	3317
Greece	Ann Corro	377-3945	3044
Grenada	Vacant	377-2527	3029-A

Listing of ITA desk officers—Continued

Country	Desk officer	Phone	Room
Guatemala	Ted Johnson	377-5563	3022
Guadeloupe	Libby Roper	377-2527	3029-A
Guinea	Jim Robb	377-4564	3317
Guidea-Bissau	Jim Robb	377-4564	3317
Guyana	Robert Dormitzer	377-2527	3029-A
Haita	Libby Roper	377-2521	3029-A
Honduras	Robert Dormitzer	377-2527	3029-A
Hong Kong	Janelle Matheson	377-2462	2323
Hungary	Karen Ware	377-2645	3421
Iceland	Maryanne Lyons	377-3254	3413
India	Richard Harding/ Christine Coady/ Renee Hancher	377-2954	2029-B
Indonesia	Don Ryan/ Linda Droker	377-3875	2032
Iran	Thomas Sams	377-5767	2039
Iraq	Thomas Sams	377-5767	2039
Ireland	Boyce Fitzpatrick	377-2920	3415
Israel	Kathleen Keim	377-4652	2039
Italy	Noel Negretti	377-2177	3045
Ivory Coast	Jim Robb	377-4388	3317
Jamaica	Lavern Kelly	377-2527	3029-A
Japan	Maureen Smith	377-4527	2318
Jordan	Thomas Sams	377-5767	2038
Kampuchea	JeNelle Matheson	377-4681	2323
Kenya	Fred Stokelin	377-4564	3317
Korea	Scott Goddin	377-4399	2034
Kuwait	Elise Kleinwaks	377-5767	2039
Laos	Jeff Lee	377-3583	2325
Lebanon	Thomas Sams	377-5767	2039
Lesotho	Reginald Biddle	377-5148	3317
Liberia	Jim Robb	377-4564	3317
Libya	Jeffrey Johnson	377-5737	2039
Luxembourg	Boyce Fitzpatrick	377-2920	3415
Macao	Jeff Lee	377-3853	2325
Madagascar	Simon Bensimon	377-0357	3317
Malaysia	Jeff Hardee	377-3875	2310
Malawi	Jeff Hardee	377-3875	2310
Maldives	Renee Hancher	377-2954	2029-B
Mali	John Crown	377-4564	3320
Malta	Robert McLaughlin	377-5401	3415
Martinique	Libby Roper	377-2527	3029-A
Mauritania	John Crown	377-4564	3317
Martitius	Simon Bensimon	377-0357	3317
Mexico	Sandra O'Leary	377-2332	3028
Mongolia	Lillian Monk	377-3932	3217
Morocco	Cheryl McQueen	377-5737	2039
Mozambique	Reginald Biddle	377-5148	3317
Namibia	Davis Coale	377-5148	3319
Nepal	Renee Hancher	377-2954	2029-B
Netherlands	Robert McLaughlin	377-5401	3415
Netherlands Antilles	Vacant	377-2527	3029-A
New Zealand	Gary Bouck	377-3647	2310
Nicaragua	Ted Johnson	377-2527	3029-A
Niger	John Crown	377-4564	3317
Nigeria	James Robb	377-4388	3321
Norway	James Devlin	377-4414	3413
Oman	Claude Clement	377-5545	2039
Pacific Islands	Tony Costanza	377-3647	2310
Pakistan	Stan Bilinski	377-2954	1029-B

Listing of ITA desk officers—Continued

Country	Desk officer	Phone	Room
Panama	Fred Tower	377-2527	3029-A
Paraguay	Brian Hannon	377-5427	3021
Peoples Republic of China	Jeff Lee	377-3583	2317
Peru	Richard Muenzer	377-4302	3027
Philippines	George Paine	377-3875	2310
Poland	Edgar Fulton	377-2645	3419
Portugal	Jeremy Keller	377-8010	3042
Puerto Rico	Fred Tower	377-2527	3029-A
Qatar	Claude Clement	377-5545	2039
Romania	Edgar Fulton	377-2645	3419
Rwanda	Simon Bensimon	377-0357	3317
Sao Tome & Principe	Simon Bensimon	377-0357	3317
Saudi Arabia	Elise Kleinwaks	377-5767	2039
Senegal	Jim Robb	377-4564	3317
Seychelles	Fred Stokelin	377-4564	3320
Sierra Leone	Jim Robb	377-4564	3317
Singapore	Jeff Hardee	377-3875	2310
Somalia	Fred Stokelin	377-4564	3317
South Africa	Davis Coale	377-5148	3317
Spain	Randy Miller	377-4509	3042
Sri Lanka	Renee Hancher	377-2954	2029-B
St. Bartholomey	Libby Roper	377-2527	3029-A
St. Martin	Libby Roper	377-2527	3029-A
Sudan	Fred Stokelin	377-4564	3317
Suriname	Robert Dormitzer	377-2527	3029-A
Swaziland	Reginald Biddle	377-5148	3317
Sweden	James Devlin	377-4414	3413
Switzerland	Lavondus Thomas	377-2897	3044
Syria	Tom Sanis	377-5767	2039
Taiwan	Christine Carter	377-4957	2034
Tanzania	Fred Stokelin	377-4564	3317
Thailand	Donald Ryan/ Linda Droker	377-3875	2032
Togo	John Crown	377-4564	3317
Trinidad & Tobago	Vacant	377-2527	3029-A
Tunisia	Cheryl McQueen	377-5737	2039
Turks & Caicos Islands	Libby Roper	377-2527	3029-A
Turkey	Goeffrey Jackson	377-2434	3042
Uganda	Fred Stokelin	377-4564	3317
U.S.S.R.	Jack Brougher	377-4655	3414
United Arab Emirates	Claude Clement	377-5545	2039
United Kingdom	Paul Norloff/ Brenda Hogan	377-4104	4212
Uruguay	Brian Hannon	377-5427	3021
Venezuela	Kevin Miles	377-4302	3027
Vietnam	JeNelle Matheson	377-4681	2323
Virgin Islands (U.K.)	Vacant	377-2527	3029-A
Virgin Islands (U.S.)	Fred Tower	377-2912	3016
Yemen	Thomas Sams	377-5767	2039
Yugoslavia	John Priamou	377-5373	3046
Zaire	Simon Bensimon	377-0357	3317
Zambia	Reginald Biddle	377-5148	3317
Zimbabwe	Davis Coale	377-5148	3317

B. Small Business Administration (SBA)

All export programs administered through SBA are available through SBA Field Offices (see Appendix V). More information about the programs can be obtained through:

Small Business Administration
(SBA)... (202) 653-7794
Office of International Trade
1441 L Street, NW.
Washington, DC 20416

C. Export Import Bank

Export Import Bank
811 Vermont Ave., NW.
Washington, DC 20571   Area Code: 202

Export Trading Company
  Assistance 566-8944

Engineering Division 566-8802

Small Business Assistance
  Hotline 800-424-5201

D. U.S. Department of Agriculture

U.S. Department of Agriculture
14th Street and Independence Avenue, SW.
Washington, DC 20250   Area Code: 202

Foreign Agricultural Service

Commodity and Marketing Programs:

  Dairy, Livestock and Poultry................. 447-8031
  Grain and Feed Division........................ 447-6219
  Horticulture and Tropical Plants 447-6590
  Oilseed and Oilseed Products............. 447-7037
  Tobacco, Cotton and Seed................... 382-9516
  Forest Products 382-8138

Export Programs Division........................ 447-3031

Minority and Small Business Coordinator 447-3833

Agricultural Information & Marketing
  Service (AIMS) 447-7103

E. Overseas Private Investment Corporation (OPIC)

Overseas Private Investment Corporation
(OPIC)....................................... (202) 457-7200
1615 M St., NW., Suite 400
Washington, DC 20527

F. U.S. Department of Treasury

U.S. Department of Treasury
15th Street and Pennsylvania Ave., NW.
Washington, DC 20220

U.S. Customs Strategic Investigation Division
(Exodus Command Center)............ (202) 566-9464

G. Agency for International Development (AID)

Agency for International Development (AID)
Department of State Building
320 21st Street, NW.
Washington, DC 20523

Office of Business Relations .... (202) 235-1840

H. Office of the United States Trade Representative

Winder Building
600 17th Street, NW.
Washington, DC 20506   Area Code: 202

General Counsel 395-3150
Private Sector Laison 395-6120
Agricultural Affairs & Commodity
  Policy 395-6127
The Americas Trade Policy 395-6135
East-West & Non-Market
  Economies 395-4543
Europe & Japan...................................... 395-4620
General Agreement on Tariff &
  Trade (GATT).. 395-6843
Industrial & Energy Trade Policy 395-7320
Investment Policy................................... 395-3510
Pacific, Asia, Africa & North-South
  Trade Policy 395-3430

Sources of assistance by State

State Trade Development Services

State	Seminars/ conferences	One-on-one counseling	Market studies prepared	Language bank	Referrals to local export services	Newsletter	How-to handbook	Sales leads disseminated	Trade shows	Trade missions	Foreign offices reps.	Operational financing program
WYOMING										•		
WISCONSIN	•	•			•	•	•	•	•	•	•	
WEST VIRGINIA	•									•		
WASHINGTON	•	•	•	•		•	•	•	•	•	•	
VIRGINIA	•	•	•				•		•		•	
VERMONT	•										•	
UTAH	•	•					•	•	•	•	•	
TEXAS	•	•					•	•	•		•	
TENNESSEE	•	•	•		•		•	•	•	•		
SOUTH DAKOTA	•	•	•	•				•				
SOUTH CAROLINA	•	•	•		•			•	•	•	•	
RHODE ISLAND	•	•	•		•	•		•	•	•	•	
PENNSYLVANIA	•	•	•		•	•		•	•		•	
OREGON	•	•				•	•	•	•			
OKLAHOMA	•	•	•	•	•	•	•	•	•	•		
OHIO	•	•	•	•	•	•		•	•	•	•	•
NORTH DAKOTA	•	•						•	•			
NORTH CAROLINA	•	•	•	•	•	•		•	•	•	•	
NEW YORK	•	•			•	•		•	•	•	•	
NEW MEXICO	•	•			•		•	•			•	
NEW JERSEY	•	•			•	•		•	•	•		
NEW HAMPSHIRE	•	•			•		•	•	•			
NEVADA	•			•		•				•		
NEBRASKA	•	•		•	•		•	•	•			
MONTANA	•	•	•					•	•			
MISSOURI	•	•	•		•	•	•	•	•	•	•	
MISSISSIPPI	•	•	•			•	•	•	•	•		•
MINNESOTA	•	•			•	•		•	•	•	•	•
MICHIGAN	•	•	•			•	•	•	•	•	•	
MASSACHUSETTS	•	•	•		•				•			
MARYLAND	•	•				•		•		•	•	
MAINE	•							•		•		
LOUISIANA (d)												
KENTUCKY	•	•			•		•	•	•	•	•	
KANSAS	•	•			•	•	•	•	•	•		
IOWA	•	•	•	•			•	•	•	•	•	
INDIANA	•	•		•				•	•	•	•	•
ILLINOIS	•	•	•		•			•	•	•	•	•
IDAHO	•							•	•	•		
HAWAII	•	•			•			•	•	•		
GEORGIA	•	•	•		•			•	•	•	• (c)	
FLORIDA	•	•	•					•	•	•	•	
DELAWARE	•				•			•	•			
CONNECTICUT	•	•	•		•	•		•	•		•	
COLORADO	•	•	•		•			•	•	•		
CALIFORNIA	•	•		•		• (a)	• (b)	•	•	•		•
ARKANSAS	•	•	•		•	•		•	•	•		
ARIZONA	•	•	•			•		•	•	•		
ALASKA									•	•	•	
ALABAMA	•	•			•		•	•	•	•	•	

Notes: See next page for notes and explanation of programs.

State trade development services explanation and footnotes

* **Seminars/conferences**— State sponsors seminars for exporters, either basic, specific function, or specific market.

* **One-on-one counseling**—State staff provides actual export counseling to individual businesses in addition to making appropriate referrals.

* **Market studies prepared**—State staff prepares specific market studies for individual companies.

* **Language bank**—State program to match foreign-speaking visitors with bilingual local residents who provide volunteer translation services.

* **Referrals to local export services**—Matching exporters with exporter services, e.g. matchmaker fair, export service directory, individual referrals, etc.

* **Newsletter**—State publishes an international trade newsletter.

* **How-to handbook**—State publishes a basic how-to-export handbook.

* **Sales leads disseminated**—State collects and distributes sales leads to in-State businesses.

* **Trade shows**—State assists with and accompanies or represents businesses on trade shows.

* **Trade missions**—State assists with and accompanies business on trade missions.

* **Foreign offices/reps**—State office or contractual representative located abroad.

* **Operational financing program**—State export financing assistance program that is currently operational.

Footnotes:

(a) California issues a bimonthly column to local chambers and trade groups for publication in their newsletters.

(b) California produces a "road map" to low cost and free trade services.

(c) Georgia's foreign offices are only active in attracting reverse investment.

(d) Louisiana has recently established a new Office of International Trade, Finance and Development within the Department of Commerce and Industry. The Office is expected to offer a full range of trade promotion services.

Source: National Association of State Development Agencies, State Export Program Database, January, 1985.

State & local sources of assistance

Alabama

U.S. Department of Commerce
US&FCS District Office
3rd Floor, Berry Building
2015 2nd Avenue North
Birmingham, Alabama 35203
(205) 254-1331

U.S. Small Business Administration
908 South 20th Street, Suite 202
Birmingham, Alabama 35205
(205) 254-1344

Alabama World Trade Association
777 Central Bank Building
Huntsville, Alabama 35801
(205) 539-8121

Office of International Trade
Department of Economic and
    Community Affairs
P.O. Box 2939
Montgomery, Alabama 36105-0939
(205) 284-8721

Alaska

U.S. Department of Commerce
US&FCS District Office
701 C Street
P.O. Box 32
Anchorage, Alaska 99513
(907) 271-5041

U.S. Small Business Administration
701 C Street, Room 1068
Anchorage, Alaska 99501
(907) 271-4022

U.S. Small Business Administration
101 12th Avenue, Box 14
Fairbanks, Alaska 99701
(907) 452-0211

Alaska State Chamber of Commerce
310 Second Street
Juneau, Alaska 99801
(907) 586-2323

Anchorage Chamber of Commerce
415 F Street
Anchorage, Alaska 99501
(907) 272-2401

Department of Commerce
and Economic Development
Pouch D
Juneau, Alaska 99811
(907) 465-3580

Fairbanks Chamber of Commerce
First National Center
100 Cushman Street
Fairbanks, Alaska 99707
(907) 452-1105

Arizona

U.S. Department of Commerce
US&FCS District Office
Fed. Bldg. & U.S. Courthouse
230 N. 1st Ave., Rm. 3412
Phoenix, Arizona 85025
(602) 254-3285

U.S. Small Business Administration
3030 N. Central Avenue, Suite 1201
Phoenix, Arizona 85012
(602) 241-2200

U.S. Small Business Administration
301 W. Congress Street, Room 3V
Tucson, Arizona 85701
(602) 762-6715

Arizona World Trade Association
34 West Monroe, Suite 900
Phoenix, Arizona 85003
(602) 254-5521

Director of International Trade
Office of Economic Planning and Development
1700 W. Washington Street, Room 505
Phoenix, Arizona 85007
(602) 255-3737

Foreign Trade Zone No. 48
Papago Agency
P.O. Box 578
Sells, Arizona 85634
(602) 383-2611

Foreign Trade Zone No. 60
Border Industrial Development, Inc.
P.O. Box 578
Nogales, Arizona 85621
(602) 281-0600

Arkansas

U.S. Department of Commerce
US&FCS District Office
320 West Capitol Avenue, Room 635
Little Rock, Arkansas 72201
(501) 378-5794

U.S. Small Business Administration
320 W. Capitol Avenue, Room 601
Little Rock, Arkansas 72201
(501) 378-5871

Arkansas Exporters Round Trade
1660 Union National Plaza
Little Rock, Arkansas 72201
(501) 375-5377

International Marketing
Department of Economic Development
1 Capitol Mall
Little Rock, Arkansas 72201
(501) 371-7678

World Trade Club of Northeast Arkansas
P. O. Box 2566
Jonesboro, Arkansas 72401
(501) 932-7550

California

U.S. Department of Commerce
US&FCS District Office
11777 San Vicente Boulevard, Room 800
Los Angeles, California 90049
(213) 209-6707

U.S. Department of Commerce
US&FCS District Office
Federal Building, Room 15205
450 Golden Gate Avenue
Box 36013
San Francisco, California 94102
(415) 556-5860

U.S. Small Business Administration
2202 Monterey Street, Room 108
Fresno, California 93721
(209) 487-5189

U.S. Small Business Administration
350 South Figueroa Street, 6th Floor
Los Angeles, California 90071
(213) 688-2956

U.S. Small Business Administration
660 J Street, Room 215
Sacramento, California 95814
(916) 440-4461

U.S. Small Business Administration
880 Front Street, Room 4-S-29
San Diego, California 85701
(619) 293-5540

U.S. Small Business Administration
450 Golden Gate Avenue, Room 15307
San Francisco, California 94102

U.S. Small Business Administration
211 Main Street, 4th Floor
San Francisco, California 94105
(415) 556-0642

U.S. Small Business Administration
111 W. St. John Street, Room 424
San Jose, California 95113
(408) 275-7584

U.S. Small Business Administration
2700 N. Main Street, Room 400
Santa Ana, California 92701
(714) 836-2494

California State World Trade Commission
1121 L Street, Suite 310
Sacramento, California 95814
(916) 324-5511

Department of Economic
  and Business Development
1030 13th Street, Room 200
Sacramento, California 95814
(916) 322-1394

California Chamber of Commerce
International Trade Department
1027 10th Street
P.O. Box 1736
Sacramento, California 95808
(916) 444-6670

Century City Chamber of Commerce
International Business Council
2020 Avenue of the Stars, Plaza Level
Century City, California 90067
(213) 553-4062

Custom Brokers & Freight Forwarders
  Association
303 World Trade Center
San Francisco, California 94111
(415) 982-7788

Economic Development Corporation
  of Los Angeles County
1052 W. 6th Street, Suite 510
Los Angeles, California 90017
(213) 482-5222

Export Managers Association of California
10919 Vanowen Street
North Hollywood, California 91605
(213) 985-1158

Foreign Trade Association of
  Southern California
350 S. Figueroa Street, #226
Los Angeles, California 90071
(213) 627-0634

Inland International Trade
  Association, Inc.
Bob Watson
World Trade Center
W. Sacramento, California 95691
(916) 371-8000

International Marketing Association
  of Orange County
Cal State Fullerton
Marketing Department
Fullerton, California 92634
(714) 773-2223

Long Beach Area Chamber of Commerce
International Business Association
50 Oceangate Plaza
Long Beach, California 90802
(213) 436-1251

Los Angeles Area Chamber of Commerce
International Commerce Division
404 S. Bixel Street
Los Angeles, California 90017
(213) 629-0722

Los Angeles International Trade
  Development Corporation
555 S. Flower Street, #2014
Los Angeles, California 90071
(213) 622-4832

Oakland World Trade Association
1939 Harrison Street
Oakland, California 94612
(415) 388-8829

San Diego Chamber of Commerce
101 West "C" Street
San Diego, California 92101
(619) 232-0124

San Francisco Chamber of Commerce
San Francisco World Trade Association
465 California Street, 9th Floor
San Francisco, California 94104
(415) 392-4511

Santa Clara Valley World Trade Association
P.O. Box 6178
San Jose, California 95150
(408) 998-7000

Valley International Trade Association
  (San Fernando Valley)
1323 Carmelina Avenue, Suite 214
Los Angeles, California 90025
(213) 207-1802

World Trade Association of Orange County
Hutton, 200 E. Sandpointe #480
Santa Ana, California 92707
(714) 549-8151

World Trade Association of San Diego
P.O. Box 81404
San Diego, California 92138
(619) 298-6581

World Trade Council of San Mateo Co.
4 West Fourth Avenue, Suite 501
San Mateo, California 94402
(415) 342-7278

Colorado

U.S. Department of Commerce
US&FCS District Office
U.S. Customhouse, Room 119
721 19th Street
Denver, Colorado 80202
(303) 837-3246

U.S. Small Business Administration
U.S. Customhouse, Room 407
721 19th Street
Denver, Colorado 80202
(303) 844-2607

Colorado Association of Commerce
  and Industry
1390 Logan Street
Denver, Colorado 80202
(303) 831-7411

Denver Chamber of Commerce
1301 Welton Street
Denver, Colorado 80204
(303) 534-3211

Foreign Trade Office
Department of Commerce & Development
1313 Sherman Street, Room 523
Denver, Colorado 80203
(303) 866-2205

Connecticut

U.S. Department of Commerce
US&FCS District Office
Federal Building, Room 610-B
450 Main Street
Hartford, Connecticut 06103
(203) 722-3530

U.S. Small Business Administration
One Hartford Square West
Hartford, Connecticut 06106
(203) 722-3600

International Division
Department of Economic Development
210 Washington Street
Hartford, Connecticut 06106
(203) 566-3842

Delaware

U.S. Department of Commerce
US&FCS District Office
—See listing for Philadelphia, Pennsylvania

U.S. Small Business Administration
844 King Street, Room 5207
Wilmington, Delaware 19801
(302) 573-6294

Delaware State Chamber of Commerce
One Commerce Center, Suite 200
Wilmington, Delaware 19801
(302) 655-7221

Delaware-Eastern Pennsylvania Export Council
9448 Federal Building
600 Arch Street
Philadelphia, Pennslyvania 19106
(215) 597-2850

Division of Economic Development
Box 1401
630 State College Road
Dover, Delaware 19901
(302) 736-4271

Florida

U.S. Department of Commerce
US&FCS District Office
Federal Building, Suite 224
51 SW. First Avenue
Miami, Florida 33130
(305) 350-5267

U.S. Small Business Administration
400 W. Bay Street, Room 261
Jacksonville, Florida 32202
(904) 791-3782

U.S. Small Business Administration
2222 Ponce de Leon Boulevard, 5th Floor
Miami, Florida 33134
(305) 350-5521

U.S. Small Business Administration
700 Twigs Street, Room 607
Tampa, Florida 33602
(813) 228-2594

U.S. Small Business Administration
3550 45th Street, Suite 6
West Palm Beach, Florida 33407
(305) 689-2223

Bureau of International
  Trade and Development
Department of Commerce
Collins Building
Tallahassee, Florida 32301
(904) 488-6124

Georgia

U.S. Department of Commerce
US&FCS District Office
1365 Peachtree Street, NE, Suite 504
Atlanta, Georgia 30309
(404) 881-7000

U.S. Department of Commerce
US&FCS District Office
Federal Building, Room A-107
120 Barnard Street
Savannah, Georgia 31401
(912) 944-4204

U.S. Small Business Administration
1720 Peachtree Road, NW., 6th Floor
Atlanta, Georgia 30309
(404) 881-4749

U.S. Small Business Administration
52 North Main Street, Room 225
Statesboro, Georgia 30458
(912) 489-8719

Department of Industry and Trade
1400 N. OMNI International
Atlanta, Georgia 30303
(404) 656-3746

International Trade Division
Division of Marketing
Department of Agriculture
19 Martin Luther King, Jr., Drive
Atlanta, Georgia 30334
(404) 656-3600

Hawaii

U.S. Department of Commerce
US&FCS District Office
4106 Federal Building

300 Ala Moana Boulevard
P.O. Box 50026
Honolulu, Hawaii 96850
(808) 546-8694

U.S. Small Business Administration
2213 Federal Building
300 Ala Moana Boulevard
Honolulu, Hawaii 96850
(808) 546-8950

Chamber of Commerce of Hawaii
World Trade Association
735 Bishop Street
Honolulu, Hawaii 96813
(808) 531-4111

Economic Development Corporation of Honolulu
1001 Bishop Street
Suite 855, Pacific Tower
Honolulu, Hawaii 96813
(808) 545-4533

International Services Agency
Department of Planning &
  Economic Development
P.O. Box 2359
Honolulu, Hawaii 96804
(808) 548-3048

Idaho

U.S. Department of Commerce
US&FCS District Office
 —See listing for Salt Lake City, Utah

U.S. Small Business Administration
1005 Main Street, 2nd Floor
Boise, Idaho 83701
(208) 334-1696

Division of Economic & Community Affairs
Office of the Governor
State Capitol, Room 108
Boise, Idaho 83720
(208) 334-2470

Department of Agriculture
International Trade Division
120 Klotz Lane
P.O. Box 790
Boise, Idaho 83701

District Export Council
Statehouse, Room 225
Boise, Idaho 83720
(208) 334-2200

Idaho International Institute
1112 South Owyhee
Boise, Idaho 83705
(208) 342-4723

Idaho World Trade Association
Box 660
Twin Falls, Idaho 83301
(208) 326-5116

World Trade Committee
Greater Boise Chamber of Commerce
P.O. Box 2368
Boise, Idaho 83701
(208) 344-5515

Illinois

U.S. Department of Commerce
US&FCS District Office
Mid-Continental Plaza Building, Room 1406
55 East Monroe Street
Chicago, Illinois 60603
(312) 353-4450

U.S. Small Business Administration
219 South Dearborn Street
Room 838
Chicago, Illinois 60604
(312) 886-0848

U.S. Small Business Administration
Four North, Old State Capitol Plaza
Springfield, Illinois 62701
(217) 492-4416

American Association of Exporters
 and Importers
7763 S. Kedzie Avenue
Chicago, Illinois 60652
(312) 471-1958

Chamber of Commerce of
 Upper Rock Island County
622 19th Street
Moline, Illinois 61265
(309) 762-3661

Chicago Association of Commerce
 and Industry
World Trade Division
130 S. Michigan Avenue
Chicago, Illinois 60603
(312) 786-0111

Chicago Economic Development Commission
International Business Division
20 N. Clark Street, 28th Floor
Chicago, Illinois 60602
(312) 744-8666

Customs Brokers and Foreign Freight
Forwarders Association of Chicago, Inc.
P.O. Box 66365
Chicago, Illinois 60666
(312) 992-4100

Department of Commerce
 & Community Affairs,
International Business Division
310 South Michigan Avenue, Suite 1000
Chicago, Illinois 60604
(312) 793-7164

Foreign Credit Insurance Association
20 North Clark Street, Suite 910
Chicago, Illinois 60602
(312) 641-1915

Illinois Department of Agriculture
1010 Jorie Boulevard
Oak Brook, Illinois 60521
(312) 920-9256

Illinois Manufacturers' Association
175 West Jackson Blvd., Suite 1321
Chicago, Illinois 60604
(312) 922-6575

Illinois State Chamber of Commerce
International Trade Division
20 N. Wacker Drive, Suite 1960
Chicago, Illinois 60606
(312) 372-7373

International Business Council
 MidAmerica (IBCM)
401 North Wabash Avenue, Suite 538
Chicago, Illinois 60611
(312) 222-1424

Mid-America International
 Agri-Trade Council (MIATCO)
300 West Washington Boulevard Suite 1001
Chicago, Illinois 60606
(312) 368-4448

Northwest International Trade Club
P.O. Box 454
Elk Grove Village, Illinois 60007
(312) 793-2086

Overseas Sales & Marketing
  Association of America, Inc.
3500 Devon Avenue
Lake Bluff, Illinois 60044
(312) 679-6070

Peoria Area Chamber of Commerce
230 SW. Adams Street
Peoria, Illinois 61602
(309) 676-0755

World Trade Club of
  Northern Illinois
515 N. Court
Rockford, Illinois 61101
(815) 987-8100

Indiana

U.S. Department of Commerce
US&FCS District Office
One North Capitol
Indianapolis, Indiana 46204-2248
(317) 232-8846

U.S. Department of Commerce
US&FCS District Office
357 U.S. Courthouse & Federal Office Building
46 East Ohio Street
Indianapolis, Indiana 46204
(317) 269-6214

U.S. Small Business Administration
575 N. Pennsylvania Street, Room 578
Indianapolis, Indiana 46204
(317) 269-7272

U.S. Small Business Administration
501 East Monroe Street, Room 160
South Bend, Indiana 46601
(219) 232-8361

Fort Wayne Chamber of Commerce
International Development Group
826 Ewing Street
Fort Wayne, Indiana 46802
(219) 434-1435

Greater Lafayette
Tippecanoe World Trade Council
Chamber of Commerce
P.O. Box 348
Lafayette, Indiana 47902
(317) 742-4041

Indiana Manufacturers Association
115 N. Pennsylvania Street, No. 950
Indianapolis, Indiana 46204
(317) 632-2474

Indiana State Chamber of Commerce
1 North Capitol, No. 200
Indianapolis, Indiana 46204
(317) 634-6407

Indianapolis Chamber of Commerce
Development and World Trade
320 N. Meridan
Indianapolis, Indiana 46204
(317) 267-2900

Indianapolis Economic Development Corporation
48 Monument Circle
Indianapolis, Indiana 46204
(317) 236-6363

Michiana World Trade Club
230 W. Jefferson Blvd.
P.O. Box 1677
South Bend, Indiana 46634
(219) 234-0051

TransNational Business Club
College of Business
Ball State University
Muncie, Indiana 47306
(317) 285-5207

Tri State World Trade Council
329 Main Street
Evansville, Indiana 47708
(812) 425-8147

World Trade Club of Indiana, Inc.
P.O. Box 986
Indianapolis, Indiana 46206
(317) 261-1169

Iowa

U.S. Department of Commerce
US&FCS District Office
817 Federal Building
210 Walnut Street
Des Moines, Iowa 50309
(515) 284-4222

U.S. Small Business Administration
373 Collins Road, N.E.
Cedar Rapids, Iowa 52402
(319) 399-2571

U.S. Small Business Administration
749 Federal Building
210 Walnut Street
Des Moines, Iowa 50309
(515) 284-4222

International Trade
Iowa Development Commission
600 East Court Avenue, Suite A
Des Moines, Iowa 50309
(515) 281-3581

Iowa Association of Business
  & Industry
706 Employers Mutual Building
Des Moines, Iowa 50309
(515) 281-3138

Iowa-Illinois International
  Trade Association
112 East Third Street
Davenport, Iowa 52801
(319) 322-1706

Siouxland Int. Trade Association
Legislative & Agriculture Affairs
101 Pierce Street
Sioux City, Iowa 51101
(712) 255-7903

Kansas

U.S. Department of Commerce
US&FCS District Office
—See listing for Kansas City, Missouri

U.S. Small Business Administration
110 East Waterman Street
Wichita, Kansas 67202
(316) 269-6571

Department of Economic Development
International Trade Development
  Division
503 Kansas Avenue, 6th Floor
Topeka, Kansas 66603
(913) 296-3483

International Trade Institute
1627 Anderson
Manhattan, Kansas 66502
(913) 532-6799

Kansas District Export Council
c/o Sunflower Manufacturing Company
Box 628
Beloit, Kansas 67420
(913) 738-2261

Kentucky

U.S. Department of Commerce
US&FCS District Office
U.S. Post Office & Courthouse Building,
  Room 636-B
Louisville, Kentucky 40202
(502) 582-5066

U.S. Small Business Administration
600 Federal Place, Room 188
Louisville, Kentucky 40201
(502) 582-5971

Kentuckiana World Commerce Council
P.O. Box 58456
Louisville, Kentucky 40258
(502) 583-5551

Kentucky District Export Council
601 West Broadway, Room 636-B
Louisville, Kentucky 40202
(502) 582-5066

Louisville Economic Development Cabinet
609 West Jefferson Street
Louisville, Kentucky 40201
(502) 586-3051

Office of International Marketing
Kentucky Commerce Cabinet
Capitol Plaza Tower, 24th Floor
Frankfort, Kentucky 40601
(502) 564-2170

TASKIT (Technical Assistance to Stimulating
  Kentucky International Trade)
College of Business and Economic
University of Kentucky
Lexington, Kentucky 40506-0205
(606) 257-7663

Louisiana

U.S. Department of Commerce
US&FCS District Office
432 International Trade Mart
2 Canal Street
New Orleans, Louisiana 70130
(504) 589-6546

U.S. Small Business Administration
1661 Canal Street, Suite 2000
New Orleans, Louisiana 70112
(504) 589-6685

U.S. Small Business Administration
500 Fannin Street
Room 6B14
Shreveport, Louisiana 71101
(318) 226-5196

Chamber of Commerce/New Orleans
  and the River Region
301 Camp Street
New Orleans, Louisiana 70130
(504) 527-6900

Office of International Trade
  Finance and Development
Louisiana Department of Commerce
P.O. Box 44185
Baton Rouge, Louisiana 70804
(504) 342-5361

World Trade Club of
  Greater New Orleans
1132 International Trade Mart
2 Canal Street
New Orleans, Louisiana 70130
(504) 525-7201

Maine

U.S. Department of Commerce
US&FCS District Office
—See listing for Boston, Massachusetts

U.S. Small Business Administration
40 Western Avenue, Room 512
Augusta, Maine 04333
(207) 622-8378

State Development Office
State House, Station 59
Augusta, Maine 04333
(207) 289-2656

Maryland

U.S. Department of Commerce
US&FCS District Office
415 U.S. Customhouse
Gay and Lombard Streets
Baltimore, Maryland 21202
(301) 962-3560

U.S. Small Business Administration
8600 La Salle Road, Room 630
Towson, Maryland 21204
(301) 962-4392

Baltimore Economic Development Corp.
36 S. Charles Street, Suite 2400
Baltimore, Maryland 21201
(301) 837-9305

Division of Economic Development
45 Calvert Street
Annapolis, Maryland 21401
(301) 269-3944

The Export Club
326 N. Charles Street
Baltimore, Maryland 21201
(301) 727-8831

Massachusetts

U.S. Department of Commerce
US&FCS District Office
441 Stuart Street, 10th Floor
Boston, Massachusetts 02116
(617) 223-2312

U.S. Small Business Administration
150 Causeway Street, 10th Floor
Boston, Massachusetts 02114
(617) 223-3224

U.S. Small Business Administration
1550 Main Street
Springfield, Massachusetts 01103
(413) 785-0268

Associated Industries of Massachusetts
462 Boylston Street
Boston, Massachusetts 02116
(617) 262-1180

Brockton Regional Chamber of Commerce
One Centre Street
Brockton, Massachusetts 02401
(617) 586-0500

Central Berkshire Chamber of Commerce
Berkshire Common
Pittsfield, Massachusetts 01201
(413) 499-4000

Chamber of Commerce of the Attleboro Area
42 Union Street
Attleboro, Massachusetts 02703
(617) 222-0801

Fall River Area Chamber of Commerce
P.O. Box 1871
200 Pocasset Street
Fall River, Massachusetts 02722
(617) 676-8226

Greater Boston Chamber of Commerce
125 High Street
Boston, Massachusetts 02110
(617) 426-1250

Greater Fitchburg Chamber of Commerce
344 Main Street
Fitchburg, Massachusetts 01420
(617) 343-6487

Greater Gardner Chamber of Commerce
301 Central Street
Gardner, Massachusetts 01440

Greater Lawrence Chamber of Commerce
300 Essex Street
Lawrence, Massachusetts 01840
(617) 687-9404

Greater Springfield Chamber of Commerce
600 Bay State West Plaza, Suite 600
1500 Main Street
Springfield, Massachusetts 01115
(413) 734-5671

Massachusetts Department of Commerce
  & Development
100 Cambridge Street
Boston, Massachusetts 02202
(617) 727-3218

Massachusetts Department of Food & Agriculture
100 Cambridge Street
Boston, Massachusetts 02202
(617) 727-3108

New Bedford Area Chamber of Commerce
Room 407, First National Bank Building
New Bedford, Massachusetts 02742
(617) 999-5231

North Suburban Chamber of Commerce
25-B Montvale Avenue
Woburn, Massachusetts 01801
(617) 933-3499

Office of Economic Affairs
One Ashburton Place
Boston, Massachusetts 02108
(617) 367-1830

South Middlesex Area Chamber of Commerce
615 Concord Street
Framingham, Massachusetts 01701
(617) 879-5600

South Shore Chamber of Commerce
36 Miller Stile Road
Quincy, Massachusetts 02169
(617) 479-1111

Waltham/West Suburban Chamber of Commerce
663 Main Street
Waltham, Massachusetts 02154
(617) 894-4700

Watertown Chamber of Commerce
75 Main Street
Watertown, Massachusetts 02172
(617) 926-1017

Worcester Chamber of Commerce
Suite 350—Mechanics Tower
100 Front Street
Worcester, Massachusetts 01608
(617) 753-2924

Michigan

U.S. Department of Commerce
US&FCS District Office
445 Federal Building
231 West Lafayette
Detroit, Michigan 48226
(313) 226-3650

U.S. Small Business Administration
515 Patrick V. McNamara Building
477 Michigan Avenue, Room 515
Detroit, Michigan 48226
(313) 226-6075

U.S. Small Business Administration
220 W. Washington Street, Room 310
Marquette, Michigan 49885
(906) 225-1108

Ann Arbor Chamber of Commerce
207 East Washington
Ann Arbor, Michigan 48104
(313) 665-4433

City of Detroit
Community & Economic Development
    Department
150 Michigan Avenue, 7th Floor
Detroit, Michigan 48226
(313) 224-6533

Detroit Customhouse Brokers &
    Foreign Freight Forwarders
    Association
1237-45 First National Building
Detroit, Michigan 48226
(313) 961-4130

Downriver Community Conference
15100 Northline
Southgate, Michigan 48195
(313) 283-8933

Flint Area Chamber of Commerce
708 Root
Flint, Michigan 49503
(313) 232-7101

(Greater) Detroit Chamber of Commerce
150 Michigan Avenue
Detroit, Michigan 48226
(313) 964-4000

(Greater) Grand Rapids Chamber of Commerce
17 Fountain Street, NW.
Grand Rapids, Michigan 49502
(616) 459-7221

(Greater) Port Huron-Marysville
    Chamber of Commerce
920 Pine Grove Avenue
Port Huron, Michigan 48060
(313) 985-7101

(Greater) Saginaw Chamber of Commerce
901 S. Washington
Saginaw, Michigan 48606
(517) 752-7161

Kalamazoo Chamber of Commerce
500 W. Crosstown Parkway
Kalamazoo, Michigan 49008
(616) 381-4000

Macomb County Chamber of Commerce
10 North Avenue
P.O. Box 855
Mt. Clemens, Michigan 48043
(313) 463-1528

Michigan Department of Agriculture
Office of International Trade
P.O. Box 30017
Lansing, Michigan 48909
(517) 373-1054

Michigan Manufacturers Association
124 East Kalamazoo
Lansing, Michigan 48933
(517) 372-5900

Michigan State Chamber of Commerce
Small Business Programs
200 N. Washington Square, Suite 400
Lansing, Michigan 48933
(517) 371-2100

Muskegon Area Chamber of Commerce
1065 Fourth Street
Muskegon, Michigan 49441
(616) 722-3751

Office of International Development
Michigan Department of Commerce
Law Building, 5th Floor
Lansing, Michigan 48909
(517) 373-6390

Twin Cities Area Chamber of Commerce
777 Riverview Drive, Building V
Benton Harbor, Michigan 49022
(616) 925-0044

West Michigan World Trade Club
445 Sixth Street, NW.
Grand Rapids, Michigan 49504
(616) 451-7651

    World Trade Club of Detroit
150 Michigan Avenue
Detroit, Michigan 48226
(313) 964-4000

Minnesota

U.S. Department of Commerce
US&FCS District Office
108 Federal Building
110 S. 4th Street
Minneapolis, Minnesota 55401
(612) 349-3338

U.S. Small Business Administration
100 North 6th Street, Suite 610
Minneapolis, Minnesota 55403
(612) 349-3550

Minnesota Export Finance Authority
90 W. Plato Boulevard
St. Paul, Minnesota 55107
(612) 297-4659

Minnesota World Trade Association
33 E. Wentworth Avenue, 101
West St. Paul, Minnesota 55118
(612) 457-1038

Minnesota Trade Office
90 W. Plato Boulevard
St. Paul, Minnesota 55107
(612) 297-4222

Mississippi

U.S. Department of Commerce
US&FCS District Office
300 Woodrow Wilson Boulevard, Suite 328
Jackson, Mississippi 39213
(601) 960-4388

U.S. Small Business Administration
100 West Capitol Street, Suite 322
Jackson, Mississippi 39269
(601) 960-4378

U.S. Small Business Administration
111 Fred Haise Boulevard, 2nd Floor
Biloxi, Mississippi 39530
(601) 435-3676

International Trade Club of
   Mississippi, Inc.
P.O. Box 16673
Jackson, Mississippi 39236
(601) 981-7906

Marketing Division
Mississippi Department of
   Economic Development
P.O. Box 849
Jackson, Mississippi 39205
(601) 359-3444

Missouri

U.S. Department of Commerce
US&FCS District Office
120 South Central, Suite 400
St. Louis, Missouri 53105
(314) 425-3301

U.S. Department of Commerce
US&FCS District Office
601 E. 12th Street, Room 635
Kansas City, Missouri 64106
(816) 374-3142

U.S. Small Business Administration
818 Grande Avenue
Kansas City, Missouri 64106
(816) 374-3419

U.S. Small Business Administration
309 North Jefferson, Room 150
Springfield, Missouri 65803
(417) 864-7670

International Business Development
Department of Commerce &
Economic Development
P.O. Box 118
Jefferson City, Missouri 65102
(314) 751-4855

International Trade Club
   of Greater Kansas City
920 Main Street, Suite 600
Kansas City, Missouri 64105
(816) 221-1460

Missouri Department of Agriculture
International Marketing Division
P.O. Box 630
Jefferson City, Missouri 65102
(314) 751-5611

Missouri District Export Council
120 S. Central, Suite 400
St. Louis, Missouri 63105
(314) 425-3302

World Trade Club of St. Louis, Inc.
111 North Taylor Avenue
Kirkwood, Missouri 63122
(314) 965-9940

Montana

U.S. Department of Commerce
US&FCS District Office
—See listing for Denver, Colorado

U.S. Small Business Administration
301 South Park, Room 528
Helena, Montana 59626
(406) 449-5381

U.S. Small Business Administration Post-of-Duty
2601 First Avenue North, Room 216
Billings, Montana 59101
(406) 657-6047

Governor's Office of Commerce &
   Small Business Development
State Capitol
Helena, Montana 59620
(406) 444-3923

Nebraska

U.S. Department of Commerce
US&FCS District Office
Empire State Building, 1st Floor
300 South 19th Street
Omaha, Nebraska 68102
(402) 221-3664

U.S. Small Business Administration
Empire State Building
300 South 19th Street
Omaha, Nebraska 68102
(402) 221-4691

International Division
Nebraska Department of Economic Development
P.O. Box 94666
301 Centennial Mall South
Lincoln, Nebraska 68509
(402) 471-3111

Midwest International Trade Association
c/o NBC, 13th & 0 Streets
Lincoln, Nebraska 68108
(402) 472-4321

Omaha Chamber of Commerce
International Affairs
1301 Harney Street
Omaha, Nebraska 68102
(402) 346-5000

Nevada

U.S. Department of Commerce
US&FCS District Office
1755 East Plumb Lane, Room 152
Reno, Nevada 89502
(702) 784-5203

U.S. Small Business Administration
301 East Steward Street
Las Vegas, Nevada 89125
(702) 385-6611

U.S. Small Business Administration
50 South Virginia Street, Room 238
Reno, Nevada 89505
(702) 784-5268

Commission on Economic Development
600 East Williams, Suite 203
Carson City, Nevada 89710
(702) 885-4325

Department of Economic Development
Capitol Complex
Carson City, Nevada 89701
(701) 885-4325

Economic Development Authority of
  Western Nevada
P.O. Box 11710
Reno, Nevada 89510
(702) 322-4004

Latin Chamber of Commerce
P.O. Box 7534
Las Vegas, Nevada 89125-2534
(702) 835-7367

Nevada Development Authority
P.O. Box 11128
Las Vegas, Nevada 89111

Nevada District Export Council
P.O. Box 11007
Reno, Nevada 89520
(702) 784-3401

New Hampshire

U.S. Department of Commerce
US&FCS District Office
—See listing for Boston, Massachusetts

U.S. Small Business Administration
55 Pleasant Street, Room 211
Concord, New Hampshire 03301
(603) 244-4041

Foreign Trade & Commercial Development
Department of Resources &
  Economic Development
105 Loudon Road, Building 2
Concord, New Hampshire 03301
(603) 271-2591

New Jersey

U.S. Department of Commerce
US&FCS District Office
3131 Princeton Pike, 4-D, Ste. 211
Trenton, New Jersey 08648
(609) 989-2100

U.S. Small Business Administration
60 Park Place, 4th Floor
Newark, New Jersey 07102
(201) 645-2434

U.S. Small Business Administration
1800 East Davis Street, Room 110
Camden, New Jersey 08104
(609) 757-5183

Department of Commerce &
  Economic Development
Division of International Trade
744 Broad Street, Room 1709
Newark, New Jersey 07102
(201) 648-3518

World Trade Association of New Jersey
5 Commerce Street
Newark, New Jersey 07102
(201) 623-7070

New Mexico

U.S. Department of Commerce
US&FCS District Office
517 Gold, SW., Ste 4303
Albuquerque, New Mexico 87102
(505) 766-2386

Department of Development
International Trade Division
Bataan Memorial Building
Santa Fe, New Mexico 87503
(505) 827-6208

New Mexico Department of Agriculture
P.O. Box 5600
Las Cruces, New Mexico 88003
(505) 646-4929

New Mexico Foreign Trade and
  Investment Council
Mail Stop 150, Alvarado Square
Albuquerque, New Mexico 87158
(505) 848-4632

New Mexico Industry Development Corporation
5301 Central Avenue, NE., Suite 705
Albuquerque, New Mexico 87110
(505) 262-2247

New York

U.S. Department of Commerce
US&FCS District Office
1312 Federal Building
111 West Huron Street
Buffalo, New York 14202
(716) 846-4191

U.S. Department of Commerce
US&FCS District Office
Federal Office Building, Room 3718
26 Federal Plaza, Foley Square
New York, New York 10278
(212) 264-0634

U.S. Small Business Administration
26 Federal Plaza, Room 3100
New York, New York 10278
(212) 264-4355

U.S. Small Business Administration
35 Pinelawn Road, Room 102E
Melville, New York 11747
(516) 454-0750

U.S. Small Business Administration
100 S. Clinton Street, Room 1071
Syracuse, New York 13260
(315) 423-5383

U.S. Small Business Administration
111 West Huron Street, Room 1311
Buffalo, New York 14202
(716) 846-4301

U.S. Small Business Administration
333 East Water Street
Elimira, New York 14901
(607) 733-4686

U.S. Small Business Administration
445 Broadway, Room 2368
Albany, New York 12207
(518) 472-6300

U.S. Small Business Administration
100 State Street, Room 601
Rochester, New York 14614
(716) 263-6700

Albany-Colonie Regional
    Chamber of Commerce
14 Corporate Woods Boulevard
Albany, New York 12211
(518) 434-1214

American Association of
    Exporters and Importers
11 West 42nd Street
New York, New York 10036
(212) 944-2230

Buffalo Area Chamber of Commerce
Economic Development
107 Delaware Avenue
Buffalo, New York 14202
(716) 849-6677

Buffalo World Trade Association
146 Canterbury Square
Williamsville, New York 14221
(716) 634-8439

Foreign Credit Insurance
    Association
One World Trade Center, 9th Floor
New York, New York 10048
(212) 432-6300

International Business Council of the
    Rochester Area Chamber of Commerce
International Trade & Transportation
55 St. Paul Street
Rochester, New York 14604
(716) 451-2220

Long Island Association, Inc.
80 Hauppage Road
Commack, New York 11725
(516) 499-4400

Long Island Association, Inc.
World Trade Club
Legislative & Economic Affairs
80 Hauppage Road
Commack, New York 11725
(516) 499-4400

Mohawk Valley World Trade Council
P.O. Box 4126
Utica, New York 13540
(315) 797-9530 ext. 319

National Association of Export Companies
200 Madison Avenue
New York, New York 10016
(212) 561-2025

New York Chamber of Commerce & Industry
200 Madison Avenue
New York, New York 10016
(212) 561-2028

New York State Department of Commerce
International Division
230 Park Avenue
New York, New York 10169
(212) 309-0502

Rochester Area Chamber of Commerce
World Trade Department
International Trade & Transportation
55 St. Paul Street
Rochester, New York 14604
(716) 454-2220

Tappan Zee International Trade Association
1 Blue Hill Plaza
Pearl River, New York 10965
(914) 735-7040

U.S. Council of the International
    Chamber of Commerce
1212 Avenue of the Americas
New York, New York 10036
(212) 354-4480

Westchester County Association, Inc.
World Trade Club of Westchester
235 Mamaroneck Avenue
White Plains, New York 10605
(914) 948-6444

World Commerce Association of
    Central New York
1 MONY Plaza
Syracuse, New York 13202
(315) 470-1343

World Trade Club of New York, Inc.
200 Madison Avenue
New York, New York 10016
(212) 561-2028

World Trade Institute
1 World Trade Center
New York, New York 10048
(212) 466-4044

North Carolina

U.S. Department of Commerce
US&FCS District Office
203 Federal Building
324 West Market Street
P.O. Box 1950
Greensboro, North Carolina 27402
(919) 378-5345

U.S. Small Business Administration
230 South Tryon Street, Room 700
Charlotte, North Carolina 28202
(704) 371-6563

U.S. Small Business Administration
215 South Evans Street, Room 102E
Greenville, North Carolina 27834
(919) 752-3798

Department of Commerce
International Division
430 North Salisburg Street
Raleigh, North Carolina 27611
(919) 733-7193

North Carolina Department of Agriculture
P.O. Box 27647
Raleigh, North Carolina 27611
(919) 733-7912

North Carolina World Trade Association
AMF Marine International
P.O. Box 2690
High Point, North Carolina 27261
(919) 899-6621

North Dakota

U.S. Department of Commerce
US&FCS District Office
—See listing for Omaha, Nebraska

U.S. Small Business Administration
657 2nd Avenue, North, Room 218
Fargo, North Dakota 58108
(701) 237-5771

North Dakota Economic
    Development Commission
International Trade Division
1050 E. Interstate Avenue
Bismarck, North Dakota 58505
(701) 224-2810

Fargo Chamber of Commerce
321 N. 4th Street
Fargo, North Dakota 58108
(701) 237-5678

Ohio

U.S. Department of Commerce
US&FCS District Office
9504 Federal Building
550 Main Street
Cincinnati, Ohio 45202
(513) 684-2944

U.S. Department of Commerce
US&FCS District Office
666 Enclid Avenue, Room 600
Cleveland, Ohio 44114
(216) 522-4750

U.S. Small Business Administration
1240 East 9th Street, Room 317
Cleveland, Ohio 44199
(216) 552-4180

U.S. Small Business Administration
85 Marconi Boulevard
Columbus, Ohio 43215
(614) 469-6860

U.S. Small Business Administration
550 Main Street, Room 5028
Cincinnati, Ohio 45202
(513) 684-2814

Cleveland World Trade Association
690 Huntington Building
Cleveland, Ohio 44115
(216) 621-3300

Columbus Area Chamber of Commerce
Economic Development
37 N. High Street
Columbus, Ohio 43216
(614) 221-1321

Columbus Council on World Affairs
57 Jefferson Street
Columbus, Ohio 43215
(614) 461-0632

Commerce & Industry Association
    of Greater Elyria
Elyria, Ohio 44036
(216) 322-5438

Dayton Council on World Affairs
300 College Park
Dayton, Ohio 45469
(513) 229-2319

Dayton Development Council
1880 Kettering Tower
Dayton, Ohio 45423
(513) 226-8222

Department of Development
International Trade Division
30 East Broad Street
P.O. Box 1001
Columbus, Ohio 43216
(614) 466-5017

(Greater) Cincinnati Chamber of Commerce
Export Development
120 West 5th Street
Cincinnati, Ohio 45202
(513) 579-3122

(Greater) Cincinnati World Trade Club
120 W. 5th Street
Cincinnati, Ohio 45202
(513) 579-3122

International Business & Trade Association
    of Akron Regional Development Board
Akron, Ohio 44308
(216) 376-5550

North Central Ohio Trade Club
Chamber of Commerce
Mansfield, Ohio 44902
(419) 522-3211

Ohio Department of Agriculture
Ohio Department Building, Room 607
65 South Front Street
Columbus, Ohio 43215
(614) 466-8789

Ohio Foreign Commerce Association, Inc.
26250 Euclid Avenue, Suite 333
Cleveland, Ohio 44132
(216) 696-7000

Toledo Area International Trade Association
Toledo, Ohio 43604
(419) 243-8191

Oklahoma

U.S. Department of Commerce
US&FCS District Office
4024 Lincoln Boulevard
Oklahoma City, Oklahoma 73105
(405) 231-5302

U.S. Small Business Administration
200 NW. 5th Street, Suite 670
Oklahoma City, Oklahoma 73102
(405) 231-4301

Department of Economic Development
International Trade Division
4024 N. Lincoln Boulevard
P.O. Box 53424
Oklahoma City, Oklahoma 73152
(405) 521-3501

(Metropolitan) Tulsa Chamber of Commerce
Economic Development Division
616 South Boston Avenue
Tulsa, Oklahoma 74119
(918) 585-1201

Oklahoma City Chamber of Commerce
Economic and Community Development
One Santa Fe Plaza
Oklahoma City, Oklahoma 73102
(405) 278-8900

Oklahoma City International Trade Association
c/o Ditch Witch International
P.O. Box 66
Perry, Oklahoma 73077
(405) 336-4402

Oklahoma District Export Council
4024 Lincoln Boulevard
Oklahoma City, Oklahoma 73105
(405) 231-5302

Oklahoma State Chamber of Commerce
4020 Lincoln Boulevard
Oklahoma City, Oklahoma 73105
(405) 424-4003

Tulsa World Trade Association
1821 N. 106th East Avenue
Tulsa, Oklahoma 74116
(918) 836-0338

Oregon

U.S. Department of Commerce
US&FCS District Office
1220 SW. 3rd Avenue, Room 618
Portland, Oregon 97204
(503) 221-3001

U.S. Small Business Administration
1220 SW. 3rd Avenue, Room 676
Portland, Oregon 97204
(503) 221-5221

Department of Economic Development
International Trade Division
921 SW. Washington, Suite 425
Portland, Oregon 97205
(503) 229-5625 or (800) 452-7813

Eugene Area Chamber of Commerce
1401 Willamette
P.O. Box 1107
Eugene, Oregon 97440
(503) 484-1314

Institute for International Trade
  and Commerce
Portland State University
1912 SW. 6th Avenue, Room 260
Portland, Oregon 97207
(503) 229-3246

Oregon District Export Council
1220 SW. 3rd Avenue, Room 618
Portland, Oregon 97209
(503) 292-9219

Western Wood Products Association
Yem Building
Portland, Oregon 97204
(503) 224-3930

Pennsylvania

U.S. Department of Commerce
US&FCS District Office
9448 Federal Building
600 Arch Street
Philadelphia, Pennsylvania 19106
(215) 597-2866

U.S. Department of Commerce
US&FCS District Office
2002 Federal Building
1000 Liberty Avenue
Pittsburgh, Pennsylvania 15222
(412) 644-2850

U.S. Small Business Administration
231 St. Asaphs Road, Suite 400
Philadelphia, Pennsylvania 19004
(215) 596-5889

U.S. Small Business Administration Branch Office
100 Chestnut Street, Suite 309
Harrisburg, Pennsylvania 17101
(717) 782-3840

U.S. Small Business Administration Branch Office
20 North Pennsylvania Avenue
Wilkes-Barre, Pennsylvania 18701
(717) 826-6497

U.S. Small Business Administration District Office
960 Pennsylvania Avenue, 5th Floor
Pittsburgh, Pennsylvania 15222
(412) 644-2780

American Society of International
    Executives, Inc.
Dublin Hall, Suite 419
Blue Bell, Pennsylvania 19422
(215) 643-3040

(City of) Philadelphia
Municipal Services Bldg., Room 1660
Philadelphia, Pennsylvania 19102
(215) 686-3647

Economic Development Council
    of Northwestern Pennsylvania
1151 Oak Street
Pittston, Pennsylvania 18640
(717) 655-5581

Erie Manufacturers Association
P.O. Box 1779
Erie, Pennsylvania 16507
(814) 453-4454

(Greater) Pittsburgh
    Chamber of Commerce
411 Seventh Avenue
Pittsburgh, Pennsylvania 15219
(412) 392-4500

International Trade Development Association
Box 113
Furlong, Pennsylvania 18925
(215) 822-6993

Pennsylvania Department of Agriculture
    Bureau of Agricultural Development
2301 North Cameron Street
Harrisburg, Pennsylvania 17110
(717) 783-8460

Pennsylvania Department of Commerce
Bureau of Domestic & International Commerce
408 South Office Building
Harrisburg, Pennsylvania 17120
(717) 787-6500

Philadelphia Export Network
3508 Market Street, Suite 100
Philadelphia, Pennsylvania 19104
(215) 898-4189

Reading Foreign Trade Association
35 N. 6th Street
Reading, Pennsylvania 19603
(215) 320-2976

Smaller Manufacturers Council
339 Boulevard of the Allies
Pittsburgh, Pennsylvania 15222
(412) 391-1622

Southwestern Pennsylvania
    Economic Development District
355 Fifth Avenue, Room 1411
Pittsburgh, Pennsylvania 15222
(412) 391-1240

Western Pennsylvania District
    Export Council
1000 Liberty Avenue, Room 2002
Pittsburgh, Pennsylvania 15222
(412) 644-2850

Women's International Trade
    Association
P.O. Box 40004
Continental Station
Philadelphia, Pennsylvania 19106
(215) 923-6900

World Trade Association of
    Philadelphia, Inc.
820 Land Title Building
Philadelphia, Pennsylvania 19110
(215) 563-8887

World Trade Club of Northwest Pennsylvania
P.O. Box 1232
Kingston, Pennsylvania 18704
(717) 287-9624

Rhode Island

U.S. Department of Commerce
US&FCS District Office
—See listing for Boston, Massachusetts

U.S. Small Business Administration
380 Westminster Mall
Providence, Rhode Island 02903
(401) 351-7500

Department of Economic Development
7 Jackson Walkway
Providence, Rhode Island 02903
(401) 277-2601

South Carolina

U.S. Department of Commerce
US&FCS District Office
Strom Thurmond Federal Building, Suite 172
1835 Assembly Street
Columbia, South Carolina 29201
(803) 765-5345

U.S. Small Business Administration
Strom Thurmond Federal Building, Suite 172
1825 Assembly, 3rd Floor
Columbia, South Carolina 29202
(803) 765-5376

South Carolina District Export Council
Strom Thurmond Federal Building, Suite 172
1835 Assembly Street
Columbia, South Carolina 29201
(803) 765-5345

South Carolina International Trade Club
Strom Thurmond Federal Building
Suite 172, 1835 Assembly Street
Columbia, South Carolina 29201
(803) 765-5345

South Carolina State Development Board
International Division
P.O. Box 927
Columbia, South Carolina 29202
(803) 758-2235

South Dakota

U.S. Department of Commerce
US&FCS District Office
—See listing for Omaha, Nebraska

U.S. Small Business Administration
101 South Main Avenue, Suite 101
Sioux Falls, South Dakota 57102
(605) 336-2980

Rapid City Area Chamber of Commerce
P.O. Box 747
Rapid City, South Dakota 57709
(605) 343-1774

Sioux Falls Chamber of Commerce
127 E. 10th Street
Sioux Falls, South Dakota 57101
(605) 336-1620

South Dakota Bureau of Industrial
   and Agricultural Development
221 S. Central
Pierre, South Dakota 57501
(605) 773-5032

Tennessee

U.S. Department of Commerce
US&FCS District Office
Suite 1114, Parkway Towers
404 James Robertson Parkway
Nashville, Tennessee 37219-1505
(615) 736-5161

U.S. Small Business Administration
404 James Robertson Parkway, Suite 1012
Nashville, Tennessee 37219
(615) 251-5881

Chattanooga World Trade Council
1001 Market Street
Chattanooga, Tennessee 37402
(615) 765-2121

Department of Economic &
   Community Development
Export Promotion Office
Andrew Jackson State Building, Room 10
Nashville, Tennessee 37219
(615) 741-5870

East Tennessee International Trade Club
c/o United American Bank
P.O. Box 280
Knoxville, Tennessee 37901
(615) 971-2027

Memphis World Trade Club
P.O. Box 3577
Memphis, Tennessee 38103
(901) 346-1001

Mid-South Exporters' Roundtable
P.O. Box 3521
Memphis, Tennessee 38103
(901) 761-3490

Middle Tennessee World Trade Council
P.O. Box 17367
Nashville, Tennessee 37202
(615) 329-4931

Tennessee Department of Agriculture
Ellington Agricultural Center
P.O. Box 40627, Melrose Station
Nashville, Tennessee 37204
(615) 360-0103

Tennessee District Export Council
c/o Aladdin Industries
P.O. Box 100255
Nashville, Tennessee 37210
(615) 748-3575

Texas

U.S. Department of Commerce
US&FCS District Office
1100 Commerce Street, Room 7A5
Dallas, Texas 75242
(214) 767-0542

U.S. Department of Commerce
US&FCS District Office
2625 Federal Building
515 Rusk Street
Houston, Texas 77002
(713) 229-2578

U.S. Small Business Administration
300 East 8th Street, Room 780
Austin, Texas 78701
(512) 482-5288

U.S. Small Business Administration
400 Mann Street, Suite 403
Corpus Christi, Texas 78408
(512) 888-3331

U.S. Small Business Administration
1100 Commerce Street, Room 3C36
Dallas, Texas 75242
(214) 767-0605

U.S. Small Business Administration
4100 Rio Bravo, Suite 300
El Paso, Texas 79902
(915) 543-7586

U.S. Small Business Administration
221 West Lancaster Avenue, Room 1007
Ft. Worth, Texas 76102
(817) 334-5463

U.S. Small Business Administration
222 East Van Buren Street, Room 500
Harlingen, Texas 78550
(512) 423-8934

U.S. Small Business Administration
2525 Murworth, Room 112
Houston, Texas 77054
(713) 660-4401

U.S. Small Business Administration
1611 Tenth Street, Suite 200
Lubbock, Texas 79401
(806) 762-7466

U.S. Small Business Administration
100 South Washington Street, Room 3C36
Marshall, Texas 75670
(214) 935-5257

U.S. Small Business Administration
727 East Duranyo Street, Room A-513
San Antonio, Texas 78206
(512) 229-6250

Amarillo Chamber of Commerce
Amarillo Building
1301 S. Polk
Amarillo, Texas 79101
(806) 374-5238

Dallas Chamber of Commerce
1507 Pacific
Dallas, Texas 75201
(214) 954-1111

Dallas Council on World Affairs
The Fred Lange Center
1310 Annex, Suite 101
Dallas, Texas 75204
(214) 827-7960

El Paso Chamber of Commerce
10 Civic Center Plaza
El Paso, Texas 79944
(915) 544-7880

Foreign Credit Insurance Association
600 Travis
Suite 2860
Houston, Texas 77002
(713) 227-0987

Fort Worth Chamber of Commerce
700 Throckmorton
Fort Worth, Texas 76102
(817) 336-2491

Greater San Antonio Chamber of Commerce
P.O. Box 1628
San Antonio, Texas 78296
(512) 227-8181

Houston Chamber of Commerce
1100 Milam Building, 25th Floor
Houston, Texas 77002
(713) 651-1313

Houston World Trade Association
1520 Texas Avenue, Suite 239
Houston, Texas 77002
(713) 225-0967

Lubbock Chamber of Commerce
14th Street & Avenue K
P.O. Box 561
Lubbock, Texas 79408
(806) 763-4666

North Texas Customs Brokers
& Foreign Freight Forwarders Association
P.O. Box 225464
DFW Airport, Texas 75261
(214) 456-0730

Odessa Chamber of Commerce
P.O. Box 3626
Odessa, Texas 79760
(915) 322-9111

Texas Department of Agriculture
Export Services Division
P.O. Box 12847, Capitol Station
Austin, Texas 78711
(512) 475-2760

Texas Economic Development Commission
International Trade Department
P.O. Box 13561
Austin, Texas 78711
(512) 475-6156

Texas Industrial Development Council, Inc.
P.O. Box 1002
College Station, Texas 77841
(409) 845-2911

U.S. Chamber of Commerce
4835 LBJ Freeway, Suite 750
Dallas, Texas 75324
(214) 387-0404

World Trade Association of
Dallas/Fort Worth
P.O. Box 29334
Dallas, Texas 75229
(214) 760-9105

Utah

U.S. Department of Commerce
US&FCS District Office
U.S. Post Office Building, Room 340
350 South Main Street
Salt Lake City, Utah 84101
(801) 524-5116

U.S. Small Business Administration
125 South State Street, Room 2237
Salt Lake City, Utah 84138
(314) 524-5800

Salt Lake Area Chamber of Commerce
Export Development Committee
19 E. 2nd Street
Salt Lake City, Utah 84111

Utah Economic & Industrial
Development Division
6150 State Office Building
Salt Lake City, Utah 84114
(801) 533-5325

World Trade Association of Utah
10 Exchange Place
Suite 301-302
Salt Lake City, Utah 84111
(801) 531-1515

Vermont

U.S. Department of Commerce
US&FCS District Office
—See listing for Boston, Massachusetts

U.S. Small Business Administration
87 State Street, Room 204
Montpelier, Vermont 05602
(802) 229-0538

Department of Economic Development
Pavilion Office Building
Montpelier, Vermont 05602
(802) 828-3221

Virginia

U.S. Department of Commerce
US&FCS District Office
8010 Federal Building
400 North 8th Street
Richmond, Virginia 23240
(804) 771-2246

U.S. Small Business Administration
3015 Federal Building
400 North 8th Street
Richmond, Virginia 23240
(804) 771-2617

International Trade Association
   of Northern Virginia
P.O. Box 2982
Reston, Virginia 22090

International Trade Development
Division of Industrial Development
1010 Washington Building
Richmond, Virginia 23219
(804) 786-3791

Newport News Export Trading System
Department of Development
Peninsula Export Program
2400 Washington Avenue
Newport News, Virginia 32607
(804) 247-8751

Piedmont Foreign Trade Council
P.O. Box 1374
Lyhnchburg, Virginia 24505
(804) 782-4231

Vextrac/Export Trading Company
   of the Virginia Port Authority
600 World Trade Center
Norfolk, Virginia 23510
(804) 623-8000

(Virginia) Chamber of Commerce
611 E. Franklin Street
Richmond, Virginia 23219
(804) 644-1607

Virginia Department of Agriculture &
   Consumer Services
1100 Bank Street, Room 710
Richmond, Virginia 23219
(804) 786-3501

Virginia District Export Council
P.O. Box 10190
Richmond, Virginia 23240
(804) 771-2246

Washington

U.S. Department of Commerce
706 Lake Union Building
1700 Westlake Avenue North
Seattle, Washington 98109
(206) 442-5616

U.S. Small Business Administration
915 Second Avenue, Room 1792
Seattle, Washington 98174
(206) 442-5534

U.S. Small Business Administration
W920 Riverside Avenue, Room 651
Spokane, Washington 99210
(509) 456-5310

Department of Commerce &
   Economic Development
International Trade & Investment Division
312 1st Avenue North
Seattle, Washington 89109
(206) 348-7149

Economic Development Council of Puget Sound
1218 Third Avenue, Suite 1900
Seattle, Washington 98101
(206) 622-2868

Inland Empire World Trade Club
P.O. Box 3727
Spokane, Washington 99220
(509) 489-0500

Seattle Chamber of Commerce
   Trade & Transportation Division
One Union Square, 12th Floor
Seattle, Washington 98101
(206) 447-7263

Washington Council on International
   Trade
Suite 420
Fourth and Vine Building
Seattle, Washington 98121
(206) 621-8485

Washington State Department of Agriculture
406 General Administration Building
Olympia, Washington 98504
(206) 753-5046

Washington State International Trade Fair
312 First Avenue North
Seattle, Washington 98109
(206) 682-6911

World Affairs Council
Mayflower Park Hotel
405 Olive Way
Seattle, Washington 98101
(206) 682-6986

World Trade Club of Bellevue
100 116th Avenue S.E.
Bellevue, Washington 98005
(206) 454-2464

World Trade Club of Seattle
1402 Third Avenue, Suite 414
Seattle, Washington 98101
(206) 621-0344

West Virginia

U.S. Department of Commerce
US&FCS District Office
3000 New Federal Office Building
500 Quarrier Street
Charleston, West Virginia 25301
(304) 347-5123

U.S. Small Business Administration
168 West Main Street
Clarksburg, West Virginia 26301
(304) 923-3706

U.S. Small Business Administration
628 Charleston National Plaza
Charleston, West Virginia 25301
(304) 347-5220

Governor's Office of Economic &
    Community Development
State Capitol, Room B-517
Charleston, West Virginia 25305
(304) 348-2234

West Virginia Chamber of Commerce
P.O. Box 2789
Charleston, West Virginia 25330
(304) 342-1115

West Virginia District Export Council
P.O. Box 26
Charleston, West Virginia 25321
(304) 343-8874

West Virginia Manufacturers Association
1313 Charleston National Plaza
Charleston, West Virginia 25301
(304) 342-2123

Wisconsin

U.S. Department of Commerce
US&FCS District Office
605 Federal Building
517 East Wisconsin Avenue
Milwaukee, Wisconsin 53202
(414) 291-3473

U.S. Small Business Administration
212 East Washington Avenue, Room 213
Madison, Wisconsin 53703
(608) 264-5261

U.S. Small Business Administration
500 South Barstow Street, Room 17
Eau Claire, Wisconsin 54701
(715) 834-9012

U.S. Small Business Administration
310 West Wisconsin Avenue, Room 400
Milwaukee, Wisconsin 53203
(414) 291-3941

Milwaukwee Association of Commerce
756 N. Milwaukee Street
Milwaukee, Wisconsin 53202
(414) 273-3000

Small Business Development Center
602 State Street
Madison, Wisconsin 53703
(608) 263-7766

Wisconsin Department of Development
123 West Washington Avenue
Madison, Wisconsin 53702
(608) 266-1767

Wyoming

U.S. Department of Commerce
US&FCS District Office
—See listing for Denver, Colorado

U.S. Small Business Administration
100 East "B" Street, Room 4001
Casper, Wyoming 82602
(307) 261-5761

Department of Economic Planning
Industrial Development Division
Barrett Building, 3rd Floor
Cheyenne, Wyoming 82002
(307) 777-7285

Contacts for top overseas markets

Argentina

American Embassy Commercial Section
4300 Columbia, 1425
Buenos Aires, Argentina
APO Miami 34034
Tel: 744-7611/8811/9911
Telex: 18156 USICA AR

American Chamber of Commerce in Argentina
Virrey Loreto 2477/81
1426 Buenos Aires, Argentina
Tel: 782-6016
Telex: 21517 CIARG AR

Embassy of Argentina Commercial Section
1667 K St., NW., Suite 610
Washington, DC 20006
Tel: (202) 939-6400
Telex: 89-2537 EMBARG WSH

Australia

American Embassy Commercial Section
Moonah Pl.
Canberra, A.C.T. 2600, Australia
APO San Francisco 96404
Tel: (062) 705000
Telex: 62104 USAEMB

American Consulate General—Melbourne
 Commercial Section
24 Albert Rd.
South Melbourne, Victoria 3205
Australia
APO San Francisco 96405
Tel: (03)699-2244
Telex: 30982 AMERCON

American Consulate General—Sydney
 Commercial Section
36th Fl., T&G Tower, Hyde Park Square
Park and Elizabeth Sts.
Sydney 2000, N.S.W., Australia
APO San Francisco 96209
Tel: 264-7044
Telex: 74223 FCSSYD

American Consulate General—Perth
Commercial Section
246 St. George's Ter.,
Perth, WA 6000, Australia

American Chamber of Commerce in Australia
60 Margaret Street
Sydney, N.S.W., 2000 Australia
Tel: 221-3055
Telex: 72729

Embassy of Australia Commercial Section
1601 Massachusetts Ave., NW.
Washington, DC 20036
Tel: (202) 797-3201

Bahamas

American Embassy Commercial Section
Mosmar Building
Queen Street
P.O. Box N-8197
Nassau, Bahamas
Tel: (809) 322-1181/1700
Telex: 20-138 AMEMB NS 138

Embassy of the Bahamas Commercial Section
600 New Hampshire Avenue, NW., Suite 865
Washington, DC 20037
Tel: (202) 338-3940
Telex: 440 244 BHMS

Belgium

American Embassy Commercial Section
27 Boulevard du Regent
B-1000 Brussels, Belgium
APO New York 09667-1000
Tel: (02) 513-3830
Telex: 846-21336

American Chamber of Commerce in Belgium
c/o Essochem, Europe, Inc.
B-1040 Brussels, Belgium
Tel: (02) 720-9130
Telex: 62788

Embassy of Belgium Commercial Section
3330 Garfield Street, NW.
Washington, DC 20008
Tel: (202) 333-6900
Telex: 89 566 AMBEL WSH

Brazil

American Embassy Commercial Section
Avenida das Nocoes, Lote 3
Brasilia, Brazil
APO Miami 34030
Tel: (061) 223-0120
Telex: 061-1091

American Consulate General—Rio de Janeiro
 Commerical Section
Avenida Presidente Wilson, 147
Rio de Janeiro, Brazil
APO Miami 34030
Tel: (021) 292-7117
Telex: AMCONSUL 021-21466

American Consulate General—Sao Paulo
   Commercial Section
Rua Padre Joao Manoel, 933
Caixa Postal 8063
Sao Paulo, Brazil
APO Miami 34030
Tel: (011) 881-6511
Telex: 011-22183

American Chamber of Commerce in Brazil—
   Sao Paulo
Caixa Postal 1980
01051, Sao Paulo, SP—Brazil
Tel: (011) 212-3132
Telex: 1132311 CASE BR

American Chamber of Commerce in Brazil—
   Rio de Janeiro
20.040 Rio de Janiero, RJ—Brazil
Tel: 203-2477
Telex: 2123539 RJRT BR
Cable: REYNOTABA

American Chamber of Commerce in Brazil—
   Salvador
c/o TABARAMA—Tabacos do Brazil Ltda.
Caixa Postal 508
40.000 Salvador, Bahia—Brazil
Tel: 241-1844

Embassy of Brazil Commercial Section
3006 Massachusetts Avenue, NW.
Washington, DC 20008
Tel: (202) 745-2700
Telex: 440371 BRASMB 89430 BRASMB

Canada

American Embassy Commercial Section
100 Wellington Street
Ottawa, Canada, K1P5T1
Tel: (613) 238-5335
Telex: 0533582

American Consulate General—Calgary
   Commercial Section
615 Macleod Trail S.E., Rm. 1050
Calgary, Alberta, Canada T2G 4T8
Tel: (403) 266-8962
Telex: 038-21332

American Consulate General—
   Montreal Commercial Section
Suite 1122
South Tower
Place Desjardins
Montreal, Quebec
Canada, H5B1G1
Tel: (514) 281-1886
Telex: 05-268751

American Consulate General—
   Toronto Commercial Section
360 University Avenue
Toronto, Ontario
Canada, M5G1S4
Tel: (416) 595-1700
Telex: 065-24132

American Consulate General—
   Vancouver Commercial Section
1075 West Georgia Street, 21st Floor
Vancouver, British Columbia
Canada, V6E4E9
Tel: (604) 685-4311
Telex: 04-55673

Embassy of Canada Commercial Section
1746 Massachusetts Avenue, NW.
Washington, DC 20036
Tel: 785-1400
Telex: 8 9664 DOMCAN A WSH

Chile

American Embassy Commercial Section
Edificio Codina
Agustinas 1343
Santiago, Chile
APO Miami 34033
Tel: 710133/90 or 710326/75
Telex: 240062-ICA-CL

American Chamber of Commerce in Chile
Pedro de Valdivia 291
Santiago, Chile
Tel: 223-3037
Telex: 645129 CMDLC CZ

Embassy of Chile Commercial Section
1732 Massachusetts Avenue, NW.
Washington, DC 20036
Tel: (202) 785-1746
Telex: 89-2663 EMBACHILE WSH

China, People's Republic of

American Embassy Commercial Section
Guang Hua Lu 17
Beijing, China
FPO San Francisco 96655
Tel: 52-2033
Telex: AMEMB CN 22701

American Consulate General—
   Guangzou Commercial Section
Dong Fang Hotel
Box 100
FPO San Francisco 96659
Tel: 69900 x 1000

American Consulate General—
   Shanghai Commercial Section
1469 Huai Hai Middle Rd.
Box 200
FPO San Francisco 96659
Tel: 379-880

American Consulate General—
   Shenyang Commercial Section
40 Lane 4, Section 5
Sanjing St., Heping District
Box 45
FPO San Francisco 96659-0002
Tel: 2 90038/34/54/68
Telex: 80011 AMCS CN

American Chamber of Commerce in China
Jian Guo Hotel
Jian Guo Men Wai
Beijing, People's Republic of China
Tel: 59-5261
Telex: 210179 GJPEK CN

Embassy of the People's Republic of China
    Commercial Section
2300 Connecticut Avenue, NW.
Washington, DC 20008
Tel: (202) 328-2520

Columbia

American Embassy Commercial Section
Calla 38, No. 8-61
Bogota, Colombia
APO Miami 34038
Tel: 285-1300/1688
Telex: 44843

American Chamber of Commerce in
    Colombia Bogota
Trv. 18, No. 78-80
Apartado Aereo 75240
Bogota, Colombia
Tel: 256-8800
Telex: 44635

American Chamber of Commerce in
    Colombia—Cali
Apartado Aereo 101
Cali, Valle, Colombia
Tel: 689-506, 689-409
Telex: 55442

Embassy of Colombia Commercial Section
2118 Leroy Place, NW.
Washington, DC 20008
Tel: (202) 387-8338
Telex: 197 624 COLE UT

Denmark

American Embassy Commercial Section
Dag Hammarskjolds Alie 24
2100 Copenhagen, Denmark
APO New York 09170
Tel: (01) 423144
Telex: 22216

Embassy of Denmark Commercial Section
3200 Whitehaven Street, NW.
Washington, DC 20008
Tel: (202) 234-4300
Telex: 089525 DEN EMB WSH
64444 DEN EMB WSH

Dominican Republic

American Embassy Commercial Section
Calle Cesar Nicolas Penson con Calle
    Leopoldo Navarro
Santo Domingo, Dominican Republic
APO Miami 34041-0008
Tel: 682-2171
Telex: 3460013

American Chamber of Commerce
    in the Dominican Republic
P.O. Box 1221
Santo Domingo, Dominican Republic
Tel: 565-1661
Telex: 0034 TATEM DR

Embassy of the Dominican Republic
    Commercial Section
1715 22nd Street, NW.
Washington, DC 20007
Tel: (202) 332-6280
Telex: 44-0031 DOR EMB

Ecuador

American Embassy Ecuador
120 Avenida Patria
Quito, Ecuador
APO Miami 34039
Tel: 548-000
Telex: 02-2329 USICAQ ED

American Consulate General-Guayaquil
    Commercial Section
9 de Octubre y Garcia Moreno
Guayaquil, Ecuador
APO Miami 34039
Tel: 511-570
Telex: 04-3452 USICAG ED

American Chamber of Commerce in Ecuador
P.O. Box 9103 Suc. Almagro
Quito, Ecuador
Tel: 523-152, 523-693

American Chamber of Commerce in Ecuador
Escobedo 1402 y Chile
P.O. Box 4767
Guayaquil, Ecuador
Tel: 529-855, 516-707

Embassy of Ecuador Commercial Section
2535 15th Street, NW.
Washington, DC 20009
Tel: (202) 234-7200
Telex: 440129 ECUAI

Egypt

American Embassy Commercial Section
5 Sharia Latin America
Cairo, Arab Republic of Egypt
FPO New York 09527
Tel: 28219/774666
Telex: 93773 AMEMB

American Consulate General-Alexandria
    Commercial Section
110 Avenue Horreya
Alexandria, Republic of Egypt
FPO New York 09527
Tel: 801911/25607/22861/28458

American Chamber of Commerce in Egypt
Cairo Marriott Hotel, Suite 1537
P.O. Box 33 Zamalek
Cairo, Egypt
Tel: 340-8888
Telex: 20870

Embassy of Egypt Commercial Section
2715 Connecticut Avenue, NW.
Washington, DC 20008
Tel: (202) 265-9111
Telex: 89-2481 COMRAU WSH
64-251 COMRAU WSH

France

American Embassy Commercial Section
2 Avenue Gabriel
75382 Paris Cedex 08
Paris, France
APO New York 09777
Tel: 296-1202/261-8075
Telex: 650-221

American Consulate General-Marseille
Commercial Section
No. 9 Rue Armeny 13006
13006 Marseille, France
Tel: 54-92-00
Telex: 430597

American Consulate General-Strasbourg
Commercial Section
15 Avenue D'Alsace
67082 Strasbourg, Cedex
Strasbourg, France
APO New York 09777
Tel: (88) 35-31-04/05/06
Telex: 870907

American Chamber of Commerce in France
53, Avenue Montaigne
75008 Paris, France
Tel: (1) 359-2349

Embassy of France Commercial Section
4101 Reservoir Road, NW.
Washington, DC 20007
Tel: (202) 944-6000
Telex: 248320 FRCC UR

Germany (West)

American Embassy Commercial Section
Deichmanns Ave.
5300 Bonn 2, Federal Republic of Germany
APO New York 09080
Tel: (0228) 339-3390
Telex: 885-452

American Mission—Berlin Commercial Section
Clayallee 170
D-1000 Berlin 33 (Dahlem),
Federal Republic of Germany
APO New York 09742
Tel: (030) 819-7561
Telex: 183-701 USBER-D

American Consulate General—
Dusseldorf Commercial Section
Cecilienalle 5
4000 Dusseldorf 30,
Federal Republic of Germany
APO New York 09711

American Consulate General—
Frankfurt am Main Commercial Section
Siesmayerstrasse 21
6000 Frankfurt,
Federal Republic of Germany
APO New York 09213
Tel: (0611) 740071
Telex: 412589 USCON-D

American Consulate General—
Hamburg Commercial Section
Alsterufer 27/28
2000 Hamburg 36,
Federal Republic of Germany
APO New York 09215-0002
Tel: (040) 44-1061
Telex: 213777

American Consulate General—
Munich Commercial Section
Koeniginstrasse 5
8000 Muenchen 22
APO New York 09108,
Federal Republic of Germany
Tel: (089) 23011
Telex: 5-22697 ACGM D

American Consulate General—
Stuttgart Commercial Section
Urbanstrasse 7
7000 Stuttgart, Federal Republic of Germany
APO New York 09154
Tel: (0711) 210221
Telex: 07-22945

American Chamber of Commerce in Germany
Flying Tigers
Flughafen, Luftfrachtzentrum
6000 Frankfurt 75, Federal Republic of Germany

Embassy of the Federal Republic of Germany
4645 Reservoir Road
Washington, DC 20007
Tel: (202) 298-4000
Telex: 8 9481 DIPLOGERMA WSH

Hong Kong

American Consulate General—
Hong Kong Commercial Section
26 Garden Road
Hong Kong
FPO San Francisco 96659-0002
Tel: 239011
Telex: 63141 USDOC HX

American Chamber of Commerce in Hong Kong
Lark International, Ltd.
15/F World Commerce Center
Harbour City, 11 Canton Road
TST Kowloon, Hong Kong
Tel: 5-26595

Hong Kong Office/British Embassy
3100 Massachusetts Avenue, NW.
Washington, DC 20008
Tel: (202) 898-4591
Telex: 440484 HK WSH UY

India

American Embassy Commercial Section
Shanti Path, Chanakyapuri
110021 New Delhi, India
Tel: 600651
Telex: USCS IN 031-4589

American Consulate General—
  Bombay Commercial Section
Lincoln House
78 Bhulabhai Desai Road
Bombay 400026, India
Tel: 822611/8
Telex: 011-6525 ACON IN

American Consulate General—
  Calcutta Commercial Section
5/1 Ho Chi Minh Sarani
Calcutta 700071, India
Tel: 44-3611/6
Telex: 021-2483

American Consulate General—
  Madras Commercial Section
Mount Road
Madras 600006, India
Tel: 8304116

Embassy of India Commercial Section
2536 Massachusetts Avenue, NW.
Washington, DC 20008
Tel: (202) 939-7000

Indonesia

American Embassy Commercial Section
Medan Merdeka Selatan 5
Jakarta, Indonesia
APO San Francisco 96356
Tel: 340001-9
Telex: 44218 AMEMB JKT

American Consulate—
  Medan Commercial Section
Jalan Imam Bonjol 13
Medan, Indonesia
APO San Francisco 96356
Tel: 322200
Telex: 51764

American Consulate—
  Surabaya Commercial Section
Jalan Raya Dr. Sutomo 33
Surabaya, Indonesia
APO San Francisco 96356
Tel: 69287/8
Telex: 031-334

American Chamber of Commerce in Indonesia
Citibank Building, 8th Pl.
Jalan M. H. Thamrin 55
Jakarta, Indonesia
Telex: 48116 CIBSEM IA

Embassy of Indonesia Commercial Section
2020 Massachusetts Avenue, NW.
Washington, DC 20036
Tel: (202) 293-1745

Iraq

American Interests Commercial Section
Belgian Embassy
Opp. For. Ministry Club
Masbah Quarter
P.O. Box 2447 Alwiyah
Baghdad, Iraq
Tel: 719-6138/9
Telex: 212287 USINT IK

Embassy of Iraq Commercial Section
1801 P Street, NW.
Washington, DC 20036
Tel: (202) 483-7500
Telex: 64437 IRAQI YA
64464 IRAQI YA

Ireland

American Embassy Commercial Section
42 Elgin Road
Ballsbridge
Dublin, Ireland
Tel: 688777
Telex: 25240

American Chamber of Commerce in Ireland
20 College Green
Dublin 2, Ireland
Tel: 712733
Telex: 31187 UCIL/EI

Embassy of Ireland Commercial Section
2234 Massachusetts Avenue, NW.
Washington, DC 20008
Tel: (202) 462-3939
Telex: 64160 HIBERNIA 64160
440419 HIBERNIA 440419

Israel

American Embassy Commercial Section
71 Hayarkon Street
Tel Aviv, Israel
APO New York 09672
Tel: 03-654338
Telex: 33376

American Chamber of Commerce in Israel
35 Shaul Hamelech Blvd.
P.O. Box 33174
Tel Aviv, Israel
Tel: (03) 252341/2
Telex: 32139 BETAM IL

Embassy of Israel Commercial Section
1621 22nd Street, NW.
Washington, DC 20008
Tel: (202) 364-5400

Italy

American Embassy Commercial Section
Via Veneto 119/A
00187 Rome, Italy
APO New York 09794
Tel: (6) 46742
Telex: 610450 AMBRMA

American Consulate General—
  Milan Commercial Section
Plazza Repubblica 32
20124 Milano
c/o U.S. Embassy
Box M
APO New York 09794
Tel: 498-2241/2/3

American Chamber of Commerce in Italy
c/o Peat, Marwick, Mitchell & Co.
Via San Paolo 15
20121 Milano, Italy

Embassy of Italy Commercial Section
1601 Fuller Street, NW.
Washington, DC 20009
Tel: (202) 328-5500
Telex: 90-4076 ITALY EMB WSH

Japan

American Embassy Commercial Section
10-1 Akasaka, 1-chome
Minato-ku (107)
Tokyo, Japan
APO San Francisco 96503
Tel: 583-7141
Telex: 2422118

American Consulate General—
  Osaka Commercial Section *
Sankei Building, 9th Floor
4-9, Umeda 2-chome
Kita-ku
Osaka (530), Japan
APO San Francisco 96503
Tel: (06) 341-2754/7

* Includes American merchandise display.

American Consulate—
  Fukuoka Commercial Section
5-26 Ohori 2-chome
Chuo-ku
Fukuoka (810), Japan
Box 10
FPO Seattle 98766
Tel: (092) 751-9331/4
Telex: 725679

American Chamber of Commerce in
  Japan-Tokyo
c/o Burroughs Company Ltd.
13-1, Shimomiyabicho
Shinjuku-ku
Tokyo (162), Japan
Tel: 03-235-3327
Telex: 2322378 Burtok J

American Chamber of Commerce in Japan-
  Okinawa
P.O. Box 235, Koza
Okinawa City (904), Japan
Tel: 098935-2684
Telex: J79873 NANSEI OK
Cable: AMCHAM OKINAWA

Embassy of Japan Commercial Section
2520 Massachusetts Avenue, NW.
Washington, DC 20008
Tel: (202) 234-2266
Telex: 89 540

Kuwait

American Embassy Commercial Section
P.O. Box 77 SAFAT
Kuwait
Tel: 424-151 through 9

American Chamber of Commerce in Kuwait
P.O. Box 77 Safat
Kuwait City, Kuwait
Tel: 2555597
Telex: 46902 SGT CNT KT

Embassy of Kuwait Commercial Section
2940 Tilden Street, NW.
Washington, DC 20008
Tel: (202) 966-0702
Telex: 64142 KUWAIT WSH

Malaysia

American Embassy Commercial Section
AIA Building 376 Jalan Tun Razak
P.O. Box 10035
Kuala Lumpur, 01-02, Malaysia
Tel: 489011
Telex: FCSKL MA 32956

American Chamber of Commerce in Malaysia
AIA Building
P.O. Box 759
Kuala Lumpur, Malaysia

Embassy of Malaysia Commercial Section
2401 Massachusetts Avenue, NW.
Washington, DC 20008
Tel: (202) 328-2700
Telex: 440119 MAEM UI
61435 MALAYEM 61435

Mexico

American Embassy Commercial Section
Paseo de la Reforma 305
Mexico 5 D.F., Mexico
Tel: (525) 21 1-0042
Telex: 017-73-091 or 017-75-685

American Consulate General—
  Guadalajara Commercial Section
Progreso 175
Guadalajara, Jal., Mexico
Tel: 25-29-98/25-27-00
Telex: 068-2-860

American Consulate General—
  Monterrey Commercial Section
Avenida Constitucion
411 Poniente
Monterrey, N.L., Mexico
Tel: 4306 50/59
Telex: 0382853

American Chamber of Commerce in Mexico—
Mexico City
Embotelladora Tarahumara, S.A. de C.V.
Rio Amazonas No. 43
06500 Mexico, D.F. Mexico
Tel: 591-0066
Telex: 1775481 CCDFME

American Chamber of Commerce in Mexico-
Guadalajara
Apartado 31-72
45070 Guadalajara, Jal., Mexico
Tel: 15-88-22

American Chamber of Commerce in Mexico-
Monterrey
Apartado 2781
Monterrey, N.L., Mexico

Embassy of Mexico Commercial Section
2829 16th Street, NW.
Washington, DC 20009
Tel: (202) 234-6000
Telex: 90 4307 OCCMEX

Netherlands

American Embassy Commercial Section
Lange Voorhout 102
The Hague, the Netherlands
APO New York 09159
Tel: (070) 62-49-11
Telex: (044) 31016

American Consulate General—
Amsterdam Commercial Section
Museumplein 19
Amsterdam, the Netherlands
APO New York 09159
Tel: (020) 790321
Telex: 044-16176 CGUSA NL

American Consulate General—
Rotterdam Commercial Section
Baan 50
Rotterdam, the Netherlands
APO New York 09159
Tel: (010) 117560
Telex: 044-22388

The American Chamber of Commerce
in the Netherlands
2517 KJ The Hague, the Netherlands
Tel: 023-339020
Telex: 41219

Embassy of the Netherlands Commercial Section
4200 Linnean Avenue, NW.
Washington, DC 20008
Tel: (202) 244-5300

Netherland Antilles

American Consulate General—
Netherland Antilles Commercial Section
St. Anna Blvd. 19
P.O. Box 158
Willemstad, Curacao, Netherland Antilles
Tel: (5999) 613066/613350/613441
Telex: 1062 AMCON NA

New Zealand

American Embassy Commercial Section
29 Fitzherbert Terrace, Thorndon
Wellington, New Zealand
FPO San Francisco 96690-0001
Tel: 722-068
Telex: NZ 3305

The American Chamber of Commerce in
New Zealand
P.O. Box 33-246 Takapuna
Auckland 9, New Zealand
Tel: 444-4760
Telex: NZ 2601

Embassy of New Zealand Commercial Section
37 Observatory Circle, NW.
Washington, DC 20008
Tel: (202) 328-4800
Telex: 8 9526 TOTARA WSH

Nigeria

American Embassy Commercial Section
2 Eleke Crescent
P.O. Box 554
Lagos, Nigeria
Tel: 610097
Telex: 21670 USATO NG

American Consulate General—
Kaduna Commercial Section
2 Maska Road
P.O. Box 170
Kaduna, Nigeria
Tel: (062) 213043/213074/213175

Embassy of Nigeria Commercial Section
2201 M Street, NW.
Washington, DC 20037
Tel: (202) 822-1500
Telex: 89 2311 NIGERIAN WSH

Norway

American Embassy Commercial Section
Drammensveien 18
Oslo 2, Norway
APO New York 09085
Tel: 44-85-50
Telex: 18470

Embassy of Norway Commercial Section
2720 34th Street, NW.
Washington, DC 20008
Tel: 333-6000
Telex: 89-2374 NORAMB WSH

Pakistan

American Embassy Commercial Section
Diplomatic Enclave, Ramna 5
P.O. Box 1048
Islamabad, Pakistan
Tel: 8261-61 through 79
Telex: 825-864

American Consulate General—Karachi, Pakistan
8 Abdullah Haroon Road
Karachi, Pakistan
Tel: 515081
Telex: 82-02-611

American Consulate General
50 Zafar Ali Road
Gulberg 5
Lahore, Pakistan
Tel: 870221 through 5

American Chamber of Commerce in Pakistan
3rd Floor, Shaheen Commercial Complex
G.P.O. 1322
M.R. Kayani Road
Karachi, Pakistan
Tel: 526436
Telex: 25620 CHASE PK

Embassy of Pakistan Commercial Section
2315 Massachusetts Avenue, NW.
Washington, DC 20008
Tel: (202) 939-6200
Telex: 89-2348 PARAP WSH

Panama

American Embassy Commercial Section
Avenida Balboa y Calle 38
Apartado 6959
Panama 5, Republic of Panama
Box E
APO Miami 34002
Tel: Panama 27-1777

American Chamber of Commerce in Panama
Apartado 5010
Panama 5, Republic of Panama
Tel: 60-0122

Embassy of Panama Commercial Section
2862 McGill Terrace, NW.
Washington, DC 20008
Tel: (202) 483-1407

Peru

American Embassy Commercial Section
Grimaldo Del Solar 358
Miraflores, Lima 18, Peru
APO Miami 34031
Tel: 44-3921
Telex: 25028PE USCOMATT

American Chamber of Commerce in Peru
3M Peru, S.A.
P.O. Box 1897
Lima 100, Peru

Embassy of Peru Commercial Section
1700 Massachusetts Avenue, NW.
Washington, DC 20036
Tel: (202) 833-9860
Telex: 197675 LEPRU UT

Philippines

American Embassy Commercial Section
395 Buendia Avenue
Extension Makati
Manila, the Philippines
APO San Francisco 96528
Tel: 818-6674
Telex: 66887 COSEC PN

American Chamber of Commerce
  in the Philippines
P.O. Box 1578 MCC
Makati
Philippines, Manila
Tel: 819-7911
Telex: (RCA) 63637 SDTCO PN

Embassy of the Philippines Commercial Section
1617 Massachusetts Avenue, NW.
Washington, DC 20036
Tel: (202) 483-1414
Telex: 44 0059 AMBPHIL

Portugal

American Embassy Commercial Section
Avenida das Forcas Armadas
1600 Lisbon, Portugal
APO New York 09678-0002
Tel: 726-6600
Telex: 12528 AMEMB

American Chamber of Commerce in Portugal
Avenida Marcechal Gomes de Costa 33
1800 Lisbon, Portugal
Tel: 853996
Telex: 12599 AUTOREX P

Embassy of Portugal Commercial Section
2125 Kalorama Rd., NW.
Washington, DC 20008
Tel: (202) 328-8610
Telex: 64399 PORT EMB P

Saudi Arabia

American Embassy Commercial Section
Sulaimaniah District
P.O. Box 9041
Riyadh, Saudi Arabia
APO New York 09038
Tel: (01) 464-0012
Telex: 201363 USRIAD SJ

American Consulate General—
  Dhahran Commercial Section
Between Aramco Headquarters
  and Dhahran International Airport
P.O. Box 81, Dhahran Airport
Dhahran, Saudi Arabia
APO New York 09616
Tel: (03) 8913200
Telex: 601925 AMCON SJ

American Consulate General—
  Jeddah Commercial Section
Palestine Road, Ruwais

P.O. Box 149
Jeddah, Saudi Arabia
APO New York 09697
Tel: (02) 667-0080
Telex: 401459 AMEMB SJ

The American Businessmen of Jeddah,
   Saudi Arabia
P.O. Box 5019
Jeddah, Saudi Arabia
Tel: 651-7968
Telex: 401906 UCAJED SJ

American Chamber of Commerce in Saudi Arabia
c/o Saudi Business Systems
P.O. Box 4992
Dhahran, Saudi Arabia
Tel: 864-5838, 894-8181
Telex: 670418 SABSYS SJ

Embassy of Saudi Arabia Commercial Section
601 New Hampshire Ave., NW.
Washington, DC 20037
Tel: (202) 483-2100

Singapore

American Embassy Commercial Section
30 Hill Street
Singapore 0617
FPO San Francisco 96699-0001
Tel: 338-0251

American Chamber of Commerce in Singapore
11 Dhoby Ghaut
08-04 Cathay Building
Singapore 0922

Embassy of Singapore Commercial Section
1824 R Street, NW.
Washington, DC 20009
Tel: (202) 667-7555
Telex: 440024 SING EMB

South Africa

American Consulate General—
   Johannesburg Commercial Section
Kine Center, 11th Floor
Commissioner and Krulis Streets
P.O. Box 2155
Johannesburg, South Africa
Tel: (011) 331-1681
Telex: 48-3780-SA

American Chamber of Commerce in South Africa
P.O. Box 1616
Johannesburg 2000, South Africa

Embassy of South Africa Commercial Section
4801 Massachusetts Avenue, NW.
Washington, DC 20016
Tel: 966-1650

South African Consulate General—
   Commercial Section
425 Park Avenue
New York, NY 10022
Tel: (212) 838-1700
Telex: 233290

South Korea

American Embassy Commercial Section
82 Sejong-Ro; Chongro-ku
Korea
APO San Francisco 96301
Tel: 732-2601 through 18
Telex: AMEMB 23108

Embassy of Korea
2320 Massachusetts Ave., NW.
Washington, DC 20008

Spain

American Embassy Commercial Section
Serrano 75
Madrid, Spain
APO New York 09285
Tel: 276-3400/3600
Telex: 27763

American Consulate General—
   Barcelona Commercial Section
Via Layetana
Barcelona, Spain
Box 5
APO New York 09285
Tel: 319-9550
Telex: 52672

American Chamber of Commerce in Spain
Paseo de Gracia 95
Barcelona 8, Spain

Embassy of Spain Commercial Section
2558 Massachusetts Avenue, NW.
Washington, DC 20008
Tel: (202) 265-8600
Telex: 89 2747 SPAIN WSH

Sweden

American Embassy Commercial Section
Strandvagen 101
Stockholm, Sweden
Tel: (08) 63.05.20
Telex: 12060 AMEMB S

Embassy of Sweden Commercial Section
600 New Hampshire Avenue, NW.
Washington, DC 20037
Tel: (202) 298-3500
Telex: 89 2724 SVENSK WSH

Switzerland

American Embassy Commercial Section
Jubilaeumstrasse 93
3005 Bern, Switzerland
Tel: (031) 437011
Telex: (845) 32128

American Chamber of Commerce in Switzerland
Bahnhofstrasse 45
8021 Zurich, Switzerland
Tel: 211 24 54
Telex: 812747 Ipco Ch

Embassy of Switzerland Commercial Section
2900 Cathedral Avenue, NW.
Washington, DC 20008
Tel: (202) 745-7900
Telex: 64180 AMSWIS

Taiwan

American Chamber of Commerce in Taiwan
P.O. Box 17-277
Taipei, Taiwan, R.O.C.

American Institute in Taiwan (AIT)
1700 N. Moore Street
17th Floor
Arlington, Virginia 22209
Tel: (703) 525-8474

American Institute in Taiwan (AIT)
7 Lane 134 Hsin Yi Road
Section 3
Taipei, Taiwan
Telex: 23890 USTRADE

Coordination Council for
    North American Affairs
Economic Division
4301 Connecticut Avenue, NW.
Suite 420
Washington, DC 20008
Tel: (202) 686-6400
Telex: 440292 SINOECO

USA-ROC Economic Council
200 South Main Street
P.O. Box 517
Crystal Lake, Illinois 60014
Tel: (815) 459-5875

Thailand

American Embassy Commercial Section
Shell Building, "R" Floor
140 Wireless Road
Bangkok, Thailand
APO San Francisco 96346
Tel: 251-9260/2
Telex: 20966 FCSBKK

American Chamber of Commerce in Thailand
4th Floor, Wanglee Building
297 Suriwongse Road
Bangkok 10500, Thailand
Tel: 234-5173
Telex: LYMAN TH 82978

Embassy of Thailand Commercial Section
1990 M St., NW., Suite 350
Washington, DC 20036
Tel: (202) 467-6790
Telex: 248 275 TTHAI UR

Trinidad & Tobago

American Embassy Commercial Section
15 Queen's Park West
P.O. Box 752

Port-of-Spain, Trinidad and Tobago
Tel: 62-26371
Telex: 22230 AMEMB POS

Embassy of Trinidad and
    Tobago Commercial Section
1708 Massachusetts Avenue, NW.
Washington, DC 20036
Tel: (202) 467-6490
Telex: 64321 TRINOFF

Turkey

American Embassy Commercial Section
110 Ataturk Boulevard
Ankara, Turkey
APO New York 09254
Tel: 265470
Telex: 43144 USIA TR

American Consulate General—
    Istanbal Commercial Section
104-108 Mesrutiyet Caddesi
Tepebasl
Istanbal, Turkey
APO New York 09380
Tel: 1436200/09
Telex: 24306 USIC TR

Embassy of Turkey Commercial Section
2523 Massachusetts Avenue, NW.
Washington, DC 20008
Tel: (202) 483-6366
Telex: 904143 TURKFIN

Union of Soviet Socialist Republic

American Embassy Commercial Section
Ulitsa Chazkovskogo 19/21/23
Moscow, Union of Soviet Socialist Republic
APO New York 09862
Tel: (096) 252-24-51 through 59
Telex: 413160 USGSO SU

U.S. Commercial Office—Moscow
Ulitsa Chaykovskogo 15
Moscow, U.S.S.R.
APO New York 09862
Tel: 001-7-95-255-46-60
Telex: 413-205 USCO SU

U.S.S.R. Trade Representative
    in the U.S.A.
2001 Connecticut Avenue, NW.
Washington, DC 20008
Tel: (202) 232-2917

United Arab Emirates

American Chamber of Commerce in U.A.E.
P.O. Box 155
Dubai, United Arab Emirates
Tel: 971-4-442790
Telex: 45544 CALTX

American Embassy Commercial Section
United Bank Building
Flat No. 702

Corner of Liwa Street and Corniche Road
Abu Dhabi, U.A.E.
Tel: 345545
Telex: 22229 AMEMBY EM

American Embassy Branch Office—
  Dubai Commercial Section
Dubai International Trade Center
P.O. Box 9343
Dubai, U.A.E.
Tel: 471115
Telex: 98346031 BACCUS EM

Embassy of the United Arab Emirates
  Commercial Section
600 New Hampshire Avenue, NW., Suite 740
Washington, DC 20037
Tel: (202) 338-6500

United Kingdom

American Embassy Commercial Section
24/31 Grosvenor Square
London W. 1A 1AE, England
Box 40
FPO New York 09510
Tel: (01) 499-9000
Telex: 266777

American Chamber of Commerce
  in the United Kingdom
c/o The Chase Manhatten Bank, NA
Woolgate HSE

Coleman Street
London EC2P 2HD, United Kingdom
Tel: 01-726-5000
Telex: 8954681 CMBG

Embassy of Great Britain Commercial Section
3100 Massachusetts Avenue, NW.
Washington, DC 20008
Tel: (202) 462-1340
Telex: 892384 WSH
892380 WSH

Venezuela

American Embassy Commercial Section
Avenida Francisco de Miranda and
  Avenida Principal de la Floresta
P.O. Box 62291
Caracas 1060 A, Venezuela
APO Miami 34037
Tel: 284-7111/6111
Telex: 25501 AMEMB VE

American Chamber of Commerce in Venezuela
Apartado 5991
Caracas 1010-A, Venezuela
Tel: 241-0882, 241-4705
Telex: 25214

Embassy of Venezuela Commercial Section
2445 Massachusetts Avenue, NW.
Washington, DC 20015
Tel: (202) 797-3800

Organizations of interest to U.S. exporters

ASEAN-U.S. Business Council
(U.S. Section)
Chamber of Commerce of the United States
International Division
1615 H Street, NW.
Washington, DC 20062
Telephone: (202) 463-5486

Academy of International Business
World Trade Education Center
Cleveland State University
Cleveland, OH 44115
Telephone: (216) 687-3733

Advisory Council on Japan-
U.S. Economic Relations
(U.S. Section)
Chamber of Commerce of the United States
International Division
1615 H Street, NW.
Washington, DC 20062
Telephone (202) 463-5489

Affiliated Advertising Agencies International
World Headquarters
1393 East Iliff Avenue
Aurora, CO 80014
Telephone: (303) 750-1231

American Arbitration Association
140 West 51st Street
New York, NY 10020
Telephone: (212) 484-4000

American Association of Exporters and Importers
30th Floor, 11 West 42nd Street
New York, NY 10036
Telephone: (212) 944-2230

American Enterprise Institute for Public Policy
Research
1150 17th Street, NW., Suite 1200
Washington, DC 20036
Telephone: (202) 862-58001

American Importers Association
11 West 42nd Street
New York, NY 10036
Telephone: (212) 944-2230

American Institute of Marine Underwriters
14 Wall Street, 21st Floor
New York, NY 10005
Telephone: (212) 233-0550

American Management Association
440 1st Street, NW.
Washington, DC 20001
Telephone: (202) 347-3092

American National Metric Council
1010 Vermont Avenue, NW.
Washington, DC 20005
Telephone: (202) 628-5757

American Society of International
Executives
1777 Walton, Suite 419
Blue Bell, PA 19422
Telephone: (215) 643-3040

American Society of International Law
2223 Massachusetts Avenue, NW.
Washington, DC 20008
Telephone: (202) 265-4313

Bankers Association for Foreign Trade
1101 16th Street, NW., Suite 501
Washington, DC 20036
Telephone: (202) 833-3060

Brazil-U.S. Business Council (U.S. Section)
Chamber of Commerce of the United States
International Division
1615 H Street, NW.
Washington, DC 20062
Telephone: (202) 463-5485

Brookings Institution (The)
1775 Massachusetts Avenue, NW.
Washington, DC 20036
Telephone: (202) 797-6000

Bulgarian-U.S. Ecomonic Council
(U.S. Section)
Chamber of Commerce of the United States
International Division
1615 H Street, NW.
Washington, DC 20062
Telephone: (202) 463-5482

Carribbean Central American Action
1333 New Hampshire Avenue, NW.
Washington, DC 20036
Telephone: (202) 466-7464

Caribbean Council
2016 O Street, NW.
Washington, DC 20036
Telephone: (202) 775-1136

Chamber of Commerce of the United States
1615 H Street, NW.
Washington, DC 20062
Telephone: (202) 659-6000

Coalition for Employment Through Exports, Inc.
1801 K Street, NW.

9th Floor
Washington, DC 20006
Telephone: (202) 296-6107

Committee for Economic Development
1700 K Street, NW
Washington, DC 20006
Telephone: (202) 296-5860

Committee on Canada-United States Relations
(U.S. Section)
Chamber of Commerce of the United States
International Division
1615 H Street, NW.
Washington, DC 20062
Telephone: (202) 463-5488

Conference Board (The)
845 Third Avenue
New York, NY 10022
Telephone: (212) 759-09001

Council of the Americas
680 Park Avenue
New York, NY 10021
Telephone: (212) 628-3200

Council on Foreign Relations, Inc.
58 East 68th Street
New York, NY 10021
Telephone: (212) 734-0400

Customs and International Trade Bar Association
c/o 40 Siegel Mandell and Davidson
1 Whitehall Street
New York, NY 10004
Telephone: (212) 425-0060

Czechoslovak-U.S. Economic Council
(U.S. Section)
Chamber of Commerce of the United States
International Division
1615 H Street, NW.
Washington, DC 20062
Telephone: (202) 463-5482

Egypt-U.S. Business Council (U.S. Section)
Chamber of Commerce of the United States
International Division
1615 H Street, NW.
Washington, DC 20062
Telephone: (202) 463-5487

Emergency Committee for American Trade
1211 Connecticut Avenue, Suite 801
Washington, DC 20036
Telephone: (202) 659-5147

Foreign Credit Interchange Bureau—
National Assoc. of Credit Managers
475 Park Avenue South
New York, NY 10016
Telephone: (212) 578-4410

Foreign Policy Association
205 Lexington Avenue
New York, NY 10016
Telephone: (212) 481-8450

Fund for Multi-National Management Education
(FMME)
680 Park Avenue
New York, NY 10021
Telephone: (212) 535-9386

Hungarian-U.S. Economic Council
(U.S. Section)
Chamber of Commerce of the United States
International Division
1615 H Street, NW.
Washington, DC 20062
Telephone (202) 463-5482

Ibero American Chamber of Commerce
2100 M Street, NW., Suite 607
Washington, DC 20037
Telephone: (202) 296-0335

India-U.S. Business Council (U.S. Section)
Chamber of Commerce of the United States
International Division
1615 H Street, NW.
Washington, DC 20062
Telephone: (202) 463-5492

Institute for International Development
354 Maple Avenue West
Vienna, VA 22108
Telephone: (703) 281-5040

International Advertising Association
475 Fifth Avenue
New York, NY 10077
Telephone: (212) 684-1583

International Airforwarders and Agents Association
Box 627
Rockville Center, NY 11571
Telephone: (516) 536-6229

International Bank for Reconstruction and
Development
1818 H Street, NW.
Washington, DC 20006
Telephone: (202) 477-1234

International Cargo Gear Bureau
17 Battery Place
New York, NY 10004
Telephone: (212) 425-27501

International Economic Policy Association
1625 Eye Street, NW.
Washington, DC 20006
Telephone: (202) 331-1974

International Executives Association, Inc.
114 East 32nd Street
New York, NY 10016
Telephone: (212) 683-9755

International Finance Corporation
1818 H Street, NW.
Washington, DC 20433
Telephone: (202) 477-1234

International Insurance Advisory Council
(U.S. Section)
Chamber of Commerce of the United States

International Division
1615 H Street, NW.
Washington, DC 20062
Telephone: (202) 463-5480

International Trade Council
750 13th Street, SE.
Washington, DC 20003
Telephone: (202) 547-1727

Israel-U.S. Business Council (U.S. Section)
Chamber of Commerce of the United States
International Division
1615 H Street, NW.
Washington, DC 20062
Telephone: (202) 463-5478

National Association of Export Management
   Companies, Inc.
200 Madison Ave.
New York, NY 10016
Telephone: (212) 561-2025

National Association of Manufacturers
1776 F Street, NW.
Washington, DC 20006
Telephone: (202) 626-3700

National Association of State Development Agencies
Hall of State, Suite 345
444 North Capitol, NW.
Washington, DC 20001
Telephone: (202) 624-5411

National Committee on International Trade
   Documentation (The)
350 Broadway
New York, NY 10013
Telephone: (212) 925-1400

National Council for U.S. China Trade (The)
Suite 350
1050 17th Street, NW.
Washington, DC 20036
Telephone: (202) 429-0340

National Customs Brokers and
   Forwarders Association of America
One World Trade Center, Suite 1109
New York, NY 10048
Telephone: (212) 432-0050

National Export Traffic League
234 Fifth Avenue
New York, NY 10001
Telephone: (212) 697-5895

National Foreign Trade Council
11 West 42nd Street, 30th Floor
New York, NY 10036
Telephone: (212) 944-2230

National Industrial Council
1776 F Street, NW.
Washington, DC 20006
Telephone: (202) 626-3853

Nigeria-U.S. Ecomonic Council
(U.S. Section)
Chamber of Commerce of the United States
International Division
1615 H Street, NW.
Washington, DC 20062
Telephone: (202) 463-5734

Organization of American States
19th & Constitution Avenue, NW.
Washington, DC 20006
Telephone: (202) 789-3000

Overseas Development Council
1717 Massachusetts Avenue, NW.
Suite 501
Washington, DC 20036
Telephone: (202) 234-8701

Pan American Development Fund
1889 F Street, NW.
Washington, DC 20006
Telephone: (202) 789-3969

Partners of the Americas
1424 K Street, NW.
Washington, DC 20005
Telephone: (202) 628-3300

Partnership for Productivity International
2441 18th Street, NW.
Washington, DC 20009
Telephone: (202) 234-0340

Polish-U.S. Economic Council
(U.S. Section)
Chamber of Commerce of the United States
International Division
1615 H Street, NW.
Washington, DC 20062
Telephone (202) 463-5482

Private Export Funding Corporation
280 Park Avenue
New York, NY 10017
Telephone: (202) 557-3100

Romanian-U.S. Economic Council
(U.S. Section)
Chamber of Commerce of the United States
International Division
1615 H Street, NW.
Washington, DC 20062
Telephone: (202) 463-5482

Sudan-U.S. Business Council
(U.S. Section)
Chamber of Commerce of the United States
International Division
1615 H Street, NW.
Washington, DC 20062
Telephone: (202) 463-5487

Trade Relations Council of the United States, Inc.
1001 Connecticut Avenue, NW.
Room 901
Washington, DC 20036
Telephone: (202) 785-4194

The U.S.-U.S.S.R. Trade and Economic Coucil
805 3rd Avenue, 14th Floor
New York, NY 10022
Telephone: (202) 644-4550

The U.S.-Yugoslav Economic Council, Inc.
1511 K Street, NW., Suite 431
Washington, DC 20005
Telephone: (202) 737-9652

The U.S.A.-Republic of China Economic Council
200 Main Street
Crystal Lake, IL 60014
Telephone: (815) 459-5875

United States of America Business and Industry
   Advisory Committee
1212 Avenue of the Americas
New York, NY 10036
Telephone: (212) 354-4480

Washington Agribusiness Promotion Council
14th & Independence Avenue, Room 3120
Auditors Building
Washington, DC 20250
Telephone: (202) 382-8006

World Trade Institute
1 World Trade Center 55 West
New York, NY 10048
Telephone: (212) 466-4044

Bibliography

A. Market identification and assessment

Addresses to AID Missions Overseas, Office of Small and Disadvantaged Business Utilization/Minority Business Center, Agency for International Development, Washington, DC 20523. Free.

AID Commodity Eligibility Listing, Office of Small and Disadvantaged Business Utilization/Minority Resource Center, Agency for International Development, Washington, DC 20523, 1984 revised. This document lists groups of commodities, presents the Agency for International Development (AID) commodity eligibility list, gives eligibility requirements for certain commodities and describes commodities that are not eligible for financing by the agency. Free.

AID Regulation 1, Office of Small and Disadvantaged Business Utilization/Minority Resource Center, Agency for International Development, Washington, DC 20523. This tells what transactions are eligible for financing by the Agency for International Development (AID), and the responsibilities of importers, as well as the bid proceedures. Free.

AID Financed Export Opportunities, Office of Small and and Disadvantaged Business Utilization/Minority Resource Center, Agency for International Development, Washington, DC 20523. These are fact sheets also referred to as "Small Business Circulars". They present procurement data about proposed foreign purchases. Free.

American Bulletin of International Technology Transfer, International Advancement, P.O. Box 75537, Los Angeles, CA 90057. Bimonthly. This is a comprehensive listing of product and service opportunities offered and wanted for licensing and joint ventures agreements in the United States and overseas. $72 per year.

Annual Worldwide Industry Reviews (AWIR), Export Promotion Services, U.S. Department of Commerce, P.O. Box 14207, Washington, DC 20044; tel: (202) 377-2432. These reports provide a combination of country by country market assessments, export trends, and a 5-year statistical table of U.S. Exports for a single industry integrated into one report. They quickly show an industry's performance for the most recent year in most countries. Each report covers 8 to 18 countries. A single report is $200; two reports within the same industry are $350; and three reports within the same industry are $500.

Big Business Blunders: Mistakes in Multinational Marketing, 1982, David A. Ricks, Doug Jones-Irwin, Homewood, IL 60430. 200 pp. $13.95.

Business America, International Trade Administration, U.S. Department of Commerce. This magazine is the principle Commerce Department publication for presenting domestic and international business news and news of the application of technology to business and industrial problems. Available through the Superintendent of Documents, Government Printing Office, Washington, DC 20402. Annual Subscription, $57.

Catalogo de Publicaciones de la OPS, Pan American Health Organization/World Health Organization, 525 23rd Street, NW., Washington, DC 20037. A free guide of publications, many in of which are in English. This catalog is published in Spanish.

Country Market Surveys (CMS), Export Promotion Services, U.S. Department of Commerce, P.O. Box 14207, Washington, DC 20044. Tel: (202) 377-2432. This report series offers short summaries of International Market Research (IMR) geared to the needs of the busy executive. They highlight market size, trends and prospects in an easy to read format. $10 per copy or $9 per copy for six or more.

Country Trade Statistics (CTS), Export Promotion Services, U.S. Department of Commerce, P.O. Box 14207, Washington, DC 20044; tel: (202) 377-2432. This is a set of four key tables that indicate which U.S. products are in the greatest demans in a specific country over the most recent five-year period. They indicate which U.S. industries look best for export to a particular country and the export performance of single industries. Tables highlight the top U.S. exports, those with the largest market share, the fastest growing, and those which are the primary U.S. market. The CTS is $25 for the first country, and $10 for each additional country up to 25.

Custom Statistical Service, Export Promotion Services, U.S. Department of Commerce, P.O. Box 14207, Washington, DC 20044; tel: (202) 377-2432. Individually tailored tables of U.S. exports or imports. The custom service provides data for specific products or countries of interest, or for ones which may not appear in the standard ESP country and product rankings for a chosen industry. With Custom Statistics one can also obtain data in other formats such as quantity, unit quantity, unit value and percentages. Custom orders are priced by the number of products, countries, or other data desired, and range from $50 to $500.

Developments in International Trade Policy, International Monetary Fund, Publications Unit, 700 19th Street, NW., Washington, DC 20431. This paper focuses on the main current issues in trade policies of the major trading nations. $5.

Direction of Trade Statistics, International Monetary Fund, Publications Unit, 700 19th Street, NW., Washington, DC 20431. This monthly publication provides data on the country and area distribution of countries' exports and imports as reported by themselves or their partners. A yearbook is published annually which gives seven years of data for 157 countries and two sets of world and area summaries. $36 for 12 monthly issues, including the yearbook. Single monthly issue is $14, the yearbook is $10.

Directory of Leading U.S. Export Management Companies, 1984, Bergamo Book Co., 15 Ketchum Street, Westport, CT 06881. $37.50.

Economic and Social Survey for Asia and the Pacific, UNIPUB, P.O. Box 1222, Ann Arbor, MI 48106. Tel: (800) 521-8110. This publication analyzes recent economic and social developments in the region in the context of current trends. It examines agriculture, food, industry, transport, public finance, wages and prices, and external trade sectors. $19.

Element of Export Marketing, John Stapleton, 1984, Woodhead-Faulkner, Dover, NH, $11.25.

Entry Strategies for Foreign Markets—From Domestic to International Business, Franklin R. Root, American Management Association, 1977, 51 pp., $10.

EXIM Bank Information Kit, Public Affairs Office, Export-Import Bank of the United States, 811 Vermont Avenue, NW., Washington, DC 20571. This includes the Bank's annual report, which provides information on interest rates and the Foreign Credit Insurance Association.

Export Development Strategies: U.S. Promotion Policy, Michael R. Czinkota and George Tasar, Praeger, New York, NY, 1982, $27.95.

Export Directory, Foreign Agricultural Services, Department of Agriculture, 14th & Independence Avenues, SW., Room 5918-S, Washington, DC 20230. The directory describes the principle functions of the Foreign Agricultural Service and lists agricultural attaches. Free.

Export Directory: Buying Guide, biennial, Journal of Commerce, 110 Wall Street, New York, NY 10005. $225.

Export-Import Bank: Financing for American Exports— Support for American Jobs, Export-Import Bank of the United States, 1980. Free.

Export/Import Operations: A Manager's "How to" and "Why" Guide, Robert M. Franko, 1979, Professional Business Services, Inc. $35.

Export Statistics Profiles (ESP), Export Promotion Services, U.S. Department of Commerce, P.O. Box 14207, Washington, DC 20044; tel: (202) 377-2432. These tables of U.S. exports for a specific industry help identify the best export markets and analyze the industry's exports product-by-product, country-by-country over each of the last five years to date. Data is rank-ordered by dollar value. The price is $70.00 for each ESP.

Export Strategies: Markets and Competition, Nigel Percy, 1982, Allen & Unwin, Winchester, MA 01890, $30 (cloth), $13.95 (paper).

Exporter's Encyclopedia, annual with semimonthly updates, Dun & Bradstreet International, One Exchange Plaza, Suite 715, Jersey City, NJ 07302. This provides a comprehensive, country-by-country coverage of 220 world markets. It contains an examination of each country's communications and transportation facilities, customs and trade regulations, documentation, key contacts, and unusual conditions that may affect operations. Financing and Credit abroad are also examined. $365 per year.

Exporting: A Practical Manual for Developing Export Markets and Dealing with Foreign Customs, 2nd Edition, Earnst Y. Maitland, 1982, 150 pp., Self-Counsel Press, $12.50.

Exporting from the U.S.A.: How to Develop Export Markets and Cope with Foreign Customs, A.B. Marring, 1981, 114 pp., Self-Counsel Press, $12.95.

Exporting to Japan, American Chamber of Commerce in Japan, 1982, A.M. Newman. $10.

FAS Commodity Reports, U.S. Department of Agriculture, Foreign Agriculture Service, Room 5918, Washington, DC 20250. Tel: (202) 477-7937. These reports provide information on foreign agricultural production in 22 commodity areas. Reports are based on information submitted by Foreign Agricultural Service (FAS) personnel overseas. The publication frequency varies with the commodity. The price is $1 - $460 depending on commodity and whether the report is mailed or picked-up at USDA office.

FATUS: Foreign Agricultural Trade of the United States, U.S. Department of Agriculture, Foreign Agriculture Service, Room 5918, Washington, DC 20250. Tel: (202) 477-7937. This report of trends in U.S. agricultural trade by commodity and country and of events affecting this trade is published six times a year with two supplements. The price is $19 per year.

Findex: The Directory of Market Research Reports, Studies and Surveys, FIND/SVP, The Information Clearinghouse, 500 Fifth Avenue, New York, NY 10036. Tel: (212) 354-2424. Over 10,000 listings. $245.

Foreign Agriculture, U.S. Department of Agriculture, Foreign Agriculture Service, Room 5918, Washington, DC 20250. Tel: (202) 477-7937. A monthly publication containing information on overseas markets and buying trends, new competitors and products, trade policy developments and overseas promotional activities. The price is $16 per year.

Foreign Agriculture Circulars, U.S. Department of Agriculture, Foreign Agriculture Service, Room 5918, Washington, DC 20250; tel: (202) 477-7937. These individual circulars report on the supply and demand for commodities around the world. Products covered include: dairy, livestock, poultry, grains, coffee, and wood products. The frequency of publication varies with the commodity. The price is $3 to $66 depending on commodity.

Foreign Commerce Handbook, Chamber of Commerce of the United States, 1615 H Street, NW., Washington, DC 20062. A publication containing organizations of assistance to U.S. exporters, as well as up-to-date published information on all important phases of international trade and investment. $10.

Foreign Economic Trends (FET), Superintendent of Documents, U.S. Government Printing Office, Washington, DC 20402. Prepared by the U.S. and Foreign Commercial Service. This presents current business and economic developments and the latest economic indications in more than 100 countries. Annual subscription, $70; single copies are available for $1 from ITA Publications Distribution, Rm. 1617D, U.S. Department of Commerce, Washington, DC 20230.

Foreign Market Entry Strategies, Franklin R. Root, 1982, AMACOM, New York, NY 10020, 304 pp. $24.95.

General Economic Problems, OECD Publications and Information Center, Suite 1207, 1750 Pennsylvania Avenue, NW., Washington, DC 20006-4582. Tel: (202) 724-1859. This contains the latest monographs on: Economic policies and forecasts; growth; inflation; national accounts; international trade and payments; capital markets; interest rates; taxation; and energy, industrial and agricultural policies. $144.25.

Glossary of International Terms, International Trade Institute, Inc., 5055 N. Main Street, Dayton, OH 45415; Tel: (800) 543-2453, 68 pp, $17.50.

A Guide to Export Marketing, International Trade Institute, Inc., 5055 North Main Street, Suite 270, Dayon, OH 45415. Tel: (800) 453-2453. $50.

Handbook of International Statistics, UNIPUB, P.O. Box 1222, Ann Arbor, MI 48106. Tel: (800) 521-8110. The handbook examines structural trends in 70 developing and developed countries, including: Changes in the pattern of consumption for specific commodities; long-term patterns of growth; and the export performance of key industries. $22.

Highlights of U.S. Import and Export Trade, Superintendent of Documents, U.S. Government Printing Office, Washington, DC 20402. Statistical book of U.S. imports and exports. Compiled monthly by the Bureau of the Census. $41 per year; single copies, $4.50.

How to Build an Export Business: An International Marketing Guide for Minority-Owned Businesses, Superintendent of Documents, U.S. Government Printing Office, Washington, DC 20402. $10.

International Development, OECD Publications and Information Center, Suite 1207, 1750 Pennsylvania Avenue, NW., Washington, DC 20006-4582. Tel: (202) 724-1857. This contains the latest monographs on: Financial Resources and aid policies, general problems of development, industrialization, transfer of technology, rural development, employment, human resources, imigration, and demography. $173.

International Financial Statistics, International Monetary Fund, Publications Unit, 700 19th Street, NW., Washington, DC 20431. This monthly publication is a standard source of international statistics on all aspects of international and domestic finance. It reports, for most countries of the world, current data needed in the analysis of problems of international payments and of inflation and deflation, i.e., data on exchange rates, international liquidity, money and banking, international transactions, prices, production, government finance, interest rates, and other items. $10 per issue, or $100 per year, including a yearbook and two supplement series.

International Market Research (IMR) Reports, Export Promotion Services, U.S. Department of Commerce, P.O. Box 14207, Washington, DC 20044. Tel: (202) 377-2432. This is an in-depth industry sector analysis for those who want the complete data for one industry in one country. A report includes information such as behavior characteristics, trade barriers, market share figures, end user analysis, and trade contacts. $50 to $250.

International Market Information (IMI), Export Promotion Services, U.S. Department of Commerce, P.O. Box 14207, Washington, DC 20044. Tel: (202) 377-2432. These are special "bulletins" that point out unique market situations and new opportunities to U.S. exporters in specific markets. $15.00 to $100.

International Marketing, 5th edition, 1983, Philip R. Cateora, Irwin, Homewood, IL 60430, $29.95.

International Marketing, Raul Kahler, 1983, Southwestern Publishing Co., Cincinnati, OH 45227, 426 pp.

International Marketing, 3rd edition, Vern Terpstra, 1983, Dryden Press, Hinsdale, IL 60521, 624 pp., $32.95.

International Marketing, Revised Edition, Hans Thorelli & Helmut Becker, eds., 1980, Pergamon Press, Elmsford, NY 10523, 400 pp., $14.25.

International Marketing, 2nd edition, 1981, L.S. Walsh, International Ideas, Philadelphia, PA 19103, $15.95.

International Marketing: An Annotated Bibliography, 1983, S.T. Cavusgil & John R. Nevin, eds., American Marketing Association, 139 pp., $8.

International Marketing Handbook, 1985, 3 Vols., Frank S. Bair, ed., Gale Research Co., Detroit, MI 48226, 3,637 pp., $200.

International Marketing Research, 1983, Susan P. Douglas & C. Samual Craig, Prentice-Hall, Englewood Cliffs, NJ 07632, 384 pp., $27.95.

International Monetary Fund: Publications Catalog, International Monetary Fund, Publications Unit, 700 19th Street, NW., Washington, DC 20431. Free.

International Trade Operations . . . A Managerial Approach, R. Duane Hall, Unz & Co., 190 Baldwin Ave., Jersey City, NJ 07303, $42.50.

Local Chambers of Commerce Which Maintain Foreign Trade Services, 1983. International Division, Chamber of Commerce of the United States, 1615 H Street, NW., Washington, DC 20062. This is a list of chambers of commerce that have programs to aid exporters. Free.

Market Shares Reports, National Technical Information Services, U.S. Department of Commerce, Box 1553, Springfield, VA 22161. These are reports for over 88 countries. They provide basic data needed by exporters to evaluate overall trends in the size of markets for manufacturers. They also: Measure changes in the import demand for specific products; compare the competitive position of U.S. and foreign exporters, select distribution centers for U.S. products abroad, and identify existing and potential markets for U.S. components, parts, and accessories.

Marketing Aspects of International Business, 1983, Gerald M. Hampton & Aart Van Gent, Klewer-Nijhoff Publishing, Bingham, MA, $39.50.

Marketing High-Technology, William L. Shanklin & John K. Ryans, Jr., DC Heath & Co., 125 Spring Street, Lexington, MA 02173, $24.

Marketing in Europe, Economic Intelligence Unit, Ltd., 10 Rockefeller Plaza, New York, NY 10020, monthly. This Journal provides detailed analysis of the European market for consumer goods. The issues are published in three subject groups: Food, drink and tobacco; clothing, furniture and consumer goods; and chemists' goods such as pharmaceuticals and toiletries. $380 for three groups per year.

Marketing in the Third World, Erdener Kaynak, Praeger, New York, NY 10175, 302 pp., $29.95.

Metric Laws and Practices in International Trade—Handbook for U.S. Exporters,U.S. Government Printing Office, Washington, DC 20402, 1982, 113 pp. $4.75.

Monthly World Crop Production, U.S. Department of Agriculture, Foreign Agriculture Service, Room 5918, Washington, DC 20250. Tel: (202) 477-7937. This report provides estimates on the projection of wheat, rice, coarse grains, oilseeds, and cotton in selected regions and countries around the world.

The Multinational Marketing and Employment Directory, 8th edition, World Trade Academy Press,

Inc., 50 East 42nd Street, New York, NY 10017, 1982, two volumes. This directory lists more than 7,500 American corporations operating in the United States and overseas. The directory is recognized as an outstanding marketing source for products, skills and services in the United States and abroad. It is of particular value to manufacturers, distributors, international traders, investors, bankers, advertising agencies and libraries. It is also helpful for placement bureaus, executive recruiters, direct mail marketers, and technical and management consultants. The specialized arrangement of the information expedites sales in domestic and foreign markets. $90.

Multinational Marketing Management, 3rd edition, 1984, Warren J. Keegan, Prentice Hall, Englewood Cliffs, NJ 07632, 720 pp., $31.95.

OECD Publications, OECD Publications and Information Center, Suite 1207, 1750 Pennsylvania Avenue, NW., Washington, DC 20006-4582. Tel: (202) 724-4582. Free.

Outlook for U.S. Agricultural Exports, U.S. Department of Agriculture, Foreign Agriculture Service, Room 5918, Washington, DC 20250. Tel: (202) 477-7937. This report analyzes current developments and forecasts U.S. farm exports in coming months by commodity and region. Country and regional highlights discuss the reasons why sales of major commodities are likely to rise or fall in those areas. The price is $7 per year.

Overseas Business Reports (OBR), Superintendent of Documents, U.S. Government Printing Office, Washington, DC 20402. These reports are prepared by the country specialists in the International Trade Administration (ITA). They include current marketing information, trade forecasts, statistics, regulations, and marketing profiles. Annual subscription, $26. Single copies are available from ITA Publications, Rm. 1617D, U.S. Department of Commerce, Washington, DC 20230.

Product/Country Market Profiles, Export Promotion Services, U.S. Department of Commerce, P.O. Box 14702, Washington, DC 20044. Tel: (202) 377-2432. These products are tailor-made, single product/multi-country; or single country/multi-product reports. They include trade contacts, specific opportunities, and statistical analyses. $300 to $500.

Profitable Export Marketing: A Strategy for U.S. Business, Maria Ortiz-Buonafina, Prentice-Hall, Englewood Cliffs, NJ 07632, $9.95.

Reference Book for World Traders, Annual, Croner Publications, Inc., 211 Jamaica Avenue, Queens Village, NY 11428. A loose-leaf reference book for traders. Gives information about export documentation, steamship lines and airlines, free trade zones, credit and similar matters. Supplemented monthly.

Source Book . . . The ''How to'' Guide for Exporters and Importers, Unz & Co., 190 Baldwin Avenue, Jersey City, NJ 07036.

Trade and Development Report, UNIPUB, P.O. Box 1222, Ann Arbor, MI 48106. Tel: (800) 521-8110. This report reviews current economic issues and longer run development in international trade. $15.00.

Trade Directories of the World, Annual, Croner Publications, Inc., 211 Jamaica Avenue, Queens Village, NY 11428, $59.95 plus supplements.

Trends in World Production and Trade, UNIPUB, P.O. Box 1222, Ann Arbor, MI 48106. Tel: (800) 521-8110. This report discusses the structural change in world output, industrial growth patterns since 1960, changes in the pattern of agricutural output, and changes in patterns of trade in goods and services. Product groups and commodity groups are defined according to SITC criteria. $6.

United Nations Publications, United Nations and Information Center, 1889 F Street, NW., Washington, DC 20006. Free.

U.S. Export Sales, U.S. Department of Agriculture, Foreign Agriculture Service, Room 5918, Washington, DC 20250. Tel: (202) 477-7937. A weekly report of agricultural export sales based on reports provided by private exporters. There is no cost for this publication.

U.S. Export Weekly—International Trade Reporter, Bureau of National Affairs, Inc. $352 per year.

U.S. Farmers Export Arm, U.S. Department of Agriculture, Foreign Agricultural Service, Room 5918 Washington, DC 20250 1980. Free.

Weekly Roundup of World Production and Trade, U.S. Department of Agriculture, Foreign Agriculture Service, Room 5918, Washington, DC 20250. Tel: (202) 477-7937. This publication provides a summary of the week's important events in agricultural foreign trade and world production. Free.

World Agriculture, U.S. Department of Agriculture, Foreign Agriculture Service, Room 5918, Washington, DC 20250. Tel: (202) 477-7937. Provides production information, data and analyses by commodity and country, along with a review of recent economic conditions and changes in food and trade policies. Price: $9 per year.

World Agriculture Regional Supplements, U.S. Department of Agriculture, Foreign Agriculture Service, Room 5918, Washington, DC 20250. Tel: (202) 477-7937. Provides a look by region at agricultural developments during the previous year and the outlook for the year ahead. Reports are published on North America/Oceania, Latin America, Eastern Europe, Western Europe, U.S.S.R., Middle East and North Africa, Subsaharan Africa, East Asia, China, South Asia, and Southeast Asia. Price: $18 per year.

The World Bank Catalog of Publications, World Bank Publications, P.O. Box 37525, Washington, DC 200013 Free.

World Economic Outlook: A Survey by the Staff of the International Monetary Fund, International Monetary Fund, Publications Unit, 700 19th Street, NW., Washington, DC 20431. This report provides a comprehensive picture of the international situation and prospects. It highlights the imbalances that persist in the world economy and their effects on inflation, unemployment, real rates of interest and exchange rates. Published yearly. $8.

World Economic Survey, UNIPUB, P.O. Box 1222, Ann Arbor, MI 48106. Tel: (800) 521-8110. This publication assesses the world economy. It provides an overview of developments in global economics for the past year and provides an outlook for the future. $12.

Yearbook of International Trade Statistics, UNIPUB, P.O. Box 1222, Ann Arbor, MI 48106. Tel: (800) 521-8110. This yearbook offers international coverage of foreign trade statistics. Tables are provided for overall trade by regions and countries. Vol. I: Trade by Commodity. Vol. II Commodity Matrix Tables. Both Volumes $80.

B. Selling & sales contacts

American Export Register, Thomas Publishing Co., 1 Penn Plaza, 250 N. 34th Street, New York, NY 10010, 1984. A listing of more than 25,000 firms, this book is designed for persons searching for U.S. suppliers, for foreign manufacturers seeking U.S. buyers or representatives for their products. It contains product lists in four languages, an advertiser's index, information about and a list of U.S. Chambers of Commerce abroad, and a list of banks with international services and shipping, financing and insurance information. $112.

Background Notes, Superintendent of Documents, U.S. Government Printing Office, Washington, DC 20402. These are four to twelve page summaries on the economy, people, history, culture and government of about 160 countries. $42 per set; binders, $3.75.

A Business Guide to the Near East and North Africa, 1981. Superintendent of Documents, U.S. Government Printing Office, Washington, DC 20402, 28 pp. This guide is designed to provide U.S. business with information on the nature of these markets, how do do business in these areas, and how the Department of Commerce can help in penetrating these markets. $4.75.

Commercial News USA (CN), Monthly export promotion magazine circulated only overseas, listing specific products and services of U.S. firms. Applications for participation in the magazine are available from the District Offices of the U.S. and Foreign Commercial Service, U.S. Department of Commerce.

Directory of American Firms Operating in Foreign Countries, 10th Edition, 1984, World Trade Academy Press, 50 E. 42nd Street, New York, NY 10017, 1600 pp. This directory contains the most recent data on more than 4,200 American corporations controlling and operating more than 16,500 foreign business enterprises. It lists every American firm under the country in which it has subsidiaries or branches, together with their home office branch in the United States. It also gives the names and addresses of their subsidiaries or branches, products manufactured or distributed. $150.

Export Mailing List Service (EMLS), Export Promotion Services, U.S. Department of Commerce, P.O. Box 14207, Washington, DC 20044. Tel: (202) 377-2432. These are targeted mailing lists of prospective overseas customers from the Commerce Department's automated worldwide file of foreign firms. EMLs identify manufacturers, agents, retailers, service firms, government agencies and other one-to-one contacts. Information includes name and address, cable and telephone numbers, name and title of a key official, product/service interests, and additional date. $35 and up.

How to Get the Most from Overseas Exhibitions, International Trade Administration, Publications Distribution, Room 1617D, U.S. Department of Commerce, Washington, DC 20230. This eight-page booklet outlines the steps an exporter should take to participate in an overseas exhibition sponsored by the Department of Commerce. Free.

Japan: Business Obstacles and Opportunities, 1983, McKinney & Co., John Wiley, NY, $24.95.

Management of International Advertising: A Marketing Approach, 1984, Dean M. Peeples & John K. Ryans. Allyn & Bacon, Boston, MA 02159, 600 pp., $48.

Service Industries and Economic Development: Case Studies in Technology Transfer. Praeger Publishers, New York, NY 10175. 1984, 190 pp. $24.95.

Top Bulletin, Export Promotion Services, U.S. Department of Commerce, P.O. Box 14207, Washington, DC 20044; tel: (202) 377-2432. A weekly publication of trade opportunities recieved each week from overseas embassies and consulates. $175 per year. Also available on computer tape.

Trade Lists, Export Promotion Services, U.S. Department of Commerce, P.O. Box 14207, Washington, DC 20044. Tel: (202) 377-2432. Preprinted trade lists are comprehensive directories listing all the companies in a country across all product sectors, or all the companies in a single industry across all countries. Trade lists are priced from $12 to $40, depending on the age of the publication.

World Traders Data Reports (WTDRs), Export Promotion Services, U.S. Department of Commerce, P.O. Box 14207, Washington, DC 20044. Tel: (202) 377-2432. This service provides background reports on individual foreign firms. WTDRs are designed to help U.S. firms evaluate potential foreign customers before making a business commitment. $75 per report.

C. Financing exports

Chase World Guide for Exporters, Export Credit Reports, Chase World Information Corporation, One World Trade Center, Suite 4533, New York, NY 10048. The **Guide,** covering 180 countries, contains current export financing methods, collection experiences and charges, foreign import and exchange regulations and related subjects. Supplementary bulletins keep the guide up to date throughout the year. The **Reports,** issued quarterly, specify credit terms granted for shipment to all the principal world markets. The reports show the credit terms offered by the industry groups as a whole, thereby enabling the reader to determine whether his or her terms are more liberal or conservative than the average for specific commodity groups. Annual subscription for both the **Guide** and **Reports,** $345.

Commercial Export Financing: An Assist to Farm Products Sales, U.S. Department of Agriculture Foreign Agricultural Service, Room 5918, Washington, DC 20250, 1980, brochure. Free.

Export-Import Financing—A Practical Guide, Gerhart W. Schneider, Ronald Press, 1974. This book presents details of foreign trade financing and services available for making international payments. $59.95.

FCIB International Bulletin, FCIB-NACM Corp., 475 Park Avenue South, New York, NY 10016, twice monthly. The Bulletin presents export information and review of conditions and regulations in overseas markets. $175 per year.

Financing and Insuring Exports: A User's Guide to Eximbank and FCIA Programs, Export-Import Bank of the United States, User's Guide, 811 Vermont Avenue, NW., Washington, DC 20571. A 350 page guide which covers Eximbank's working capital guarantees, credit risk protection (guarantees and insurance), medium-term and long-term lending programs. Includes free updates during calendar year in which the guide is purchased. $50 (plus $5 postage and handling).

Financial Institutions and Markets in the Far East, Morgan Guarantee Trust Company of New York, 23 Wall Street, New York, NY 10015. The book discusses export letters of credit, drafts, and other methods of payment and regulations of exports and imports.

A Guide to Checking International Credit, International Trade Institute, Inc., 5055 North Main Street, Suite 270, Dayton, OH 45415.

A Guide to Financing Exports, U.S. and Foreign Commercial Service, International Trade Administration Publications Distribution, Room 1617D, U.S. Department of Commerce, Washington, DC 20230, 1985. Brochure, 40 pp. Free.

A Guide to Understanding Drafts, International Trade Institute, Inc., 5055 N. Main Street, Dayton, OH 45415. Tel: (800) 543-2455, 64 pp, $17.50.

A Guide to Understanding Letters of Credit, International Trade Institute, Inc., 5055 N. Main Street, Dayton, OH 45415, 138 pp., $34.50.

A Handbook on Financing U.S. Exports, Machinery and Allied Products Institute, 1200 18th Street, NW., Washington, DC 20036, $20.

Official U.S. and International Financing Institutions: A Guide for Exporters and Investors, International Trade Administration, U.S. Department of Commerce. Available from the Superintendent of Documents, U.S. Government Printing Office, Washington, DC 20402, $2.75.

Specifics on Commercial Letters of Credit and Bankers Acceptances, James A. Harrington, 1979 UNZ & Co., Division of Scott Printing Corp., 190 Baldwin Avenue, Jersey City, NJ 07036, 1979.

D. Laws and regulations

Customs Regulations of the United States, Superintendent of Documents, Government Printing Office, Washington, DC 20402, 1971. Reprint includes ammended text in revised page nos. 1 through 130 (includes subscription to revised pages). This contains regulations for carrying out customs, navigation and other laws administered by the Bureau of Customs.

Distribution License, 1985 Office of Export Administration, Room 1620, U.S. Department of Commerce, Washington, DC 20230 free.

Export Administration Regulations, Superintendent of Documents, Government Printing Office, Washington, DC 20402. Covers U.S. export control regulations and policies, with instructions, interpretations and explanatory material. Last revised Oct 1, 1984. $65 plus supplements.

Export Marketing of Capital Goods to the Socialist Countries of Eastern Europe, 1978, M.R. Hill, Gower Publishing Company, 200 pp., $50.75.

Manual for the Handling of Applications for Patents, Designs and Trademarks Throughout the World, Ocrooibureau Los En Stigter B.V., Amsterdam, the Netherlands.

Summary of U.S. Export Regulations, 1985, Office of Export Administration, Room 1620, Department of Commerce, Washington, DC 20230.

Technology and East-West Trade, 1983, Summarizes the major provisions of the Export Administration Act of 1979 and its implications in East-West trade, Office of Technology Assessment, U.S. Department of Commerce, Washington, DC 20230 $4.75.

E. Shipping and logistics

Export Documentation Handbook, 1984 Edition, Dun & Bradstreet International, 49 Old Bloomfield Avenue, Mt. Lakes, NJ 07046. Compiled by Ruth E. Hurd, Dun's Marketing Services, 200 pp., $60.

Export-Import Traffic Management and Forwarding, 6th edition, 1979. Alfred Murr, Cornell Maritime Press, Box 456, Centerville, MD 21617, 667 pp., $22.50. This publication presents the diverse functions and varied services concerned with the entire range of ocean traffic management.

Export Shipping Manual, Indexed, looseleaf reference binder. Detailed current information on shipping and import regulations for all areas of the world. Bureau of National Affairs, 1231 25th Street, NW., Washington, DC 20037, $186 per year.

Guide to Canadian Documentation, International Trade Institute, Inc., 5055 N. Main Street, Dayton, OH 45415, 68 pp., $24.50.

Guide to Documentary Credit Operations, ICC Publishing Corporation, New York, NY. 1985, 52 pp. $10.95.

Guide to Export Documentation, International Trade Institute, Inc., 5055 N. Main Street, Dayton, OH 45415, 168 pp., $44.50.

Guide to International Air Freight Shipping, International Trade Institute, 5055 N. Main Street, Dayton, OH 45415, $17.50.

Guide to International Ocean Freight Shipping, International Trade Institute, 5055 N. Main Street, Dayton, OH 45415, $34.50.

Guide to Selecting the Freight Forwarder, International Trade Institute, Inc., 5055 North Main Street, Suite 270, Dayton, OH 45415.

Journal of Commerce Export Bulletin, 110 Wall Street, New York, NY 10005, $200 per year. This is a weekly, newspaper that reports port and shipping developments. It lists products shipped from New York and ships and cargoes departing from 25 other U.S. ports. A "trade prospects" column lists merchandise offered and merchandise wanted.

Shipping Digest, Geyer-McAllister Publications, Inc., 51 Madison Avenue, New York, NY 10010. $26 per year. This is a weekly, which contains cargo sailing schedules from every U.S. port to every foreign port, as well as international air and sea commerce news.

F. Licensing

Foreign Business Practices . . . Material on Practical Aspects of Exporting, International Licensing and Investment, 1981, International Trade Administration, U.S. Department of Commerce, Available from the Superintendent of Documents, U.S. Government Printing Office, Washington, DC 20402, 124 pp., $5.50.

American Bulletin of International Technology Transfer, International Advancement, P.O. Box 75537, Los Angeles, CA 90057, $72 per year, bimonthly. This is a comprehensive listing of product and service opportunities offered and sought for licensing and joint ventures agreements in the United States and overseas.

Forms and Agreements on Intellectual Property and International Licensing, 3rd edition, 1979, Leslie

W. Melville, Clark Boardman Co., Ltd. New York, NY 10014, 800 pp. looseleaf, $210.

International Technology Licensing: Competition, Costs, and Negotiation, 1981, J. Farok Contractor, Lexington Books, Lexington, MA 02173, $23.95.

Investing, Licensing, and Trading Conditions Abroad, Business International Corporation, base volume with monthly updates, $964.

Licensing Guide for Developing Countries, 1978. UNIPUB, 345 Park Avenue South, New York, NY 10010, $25. This book by the World Intelligence Property Organization covers the legal aspects of industrial property licensing and technology transfer agreements. It includes discussion of the negotiation process, the scope of licensing agreements, technical services and assistance, production, trademarks, management, compensation, default, and the expiration of agreements.

Technology Licensing and Multinational Enterprises, 1979, Piero Telesio, Praeger Publishers, New York, NY 10175, 132 pp., $29.95

International Time Zones

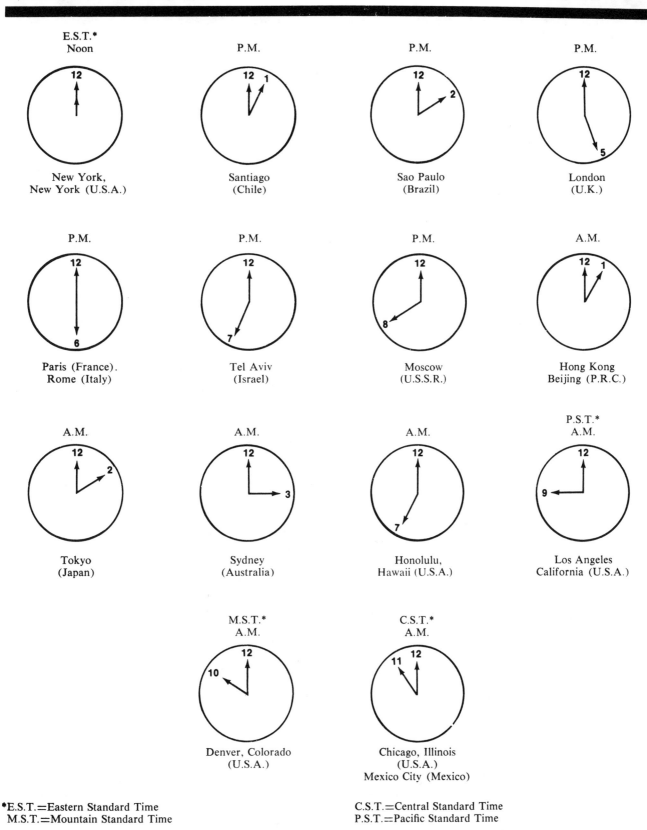

E.S.T.*
Noon

New York,
New York (U.S.A.)

P.M.

Santiago
(Chile)

P.M.

Sao Paulo
(Brazil)

P.M.

London
(U.K.)

P.M.

Paris (France).
Rome (Italy)

P.M.

Tel Aviv
(Israel)

P.M.

Moscow
(U.S.S.R.)

A.M.

Hong Kong
Beijing (P.R.C.)

A.M.

Tokyo
(Japan)

A.M.

Sydney
(Australia)

A.M.

Honolulu,
Hawaii (U.S.A.)

P.S.T.*
A.M.

Los Angeles
California (U.S.A.)

M.S.T.*
A.M.

Denver, Colorado
(U.S.A.)

C.S.T.*
A.M.

Chicago, Illinois
(U.S.A.)
Mexico City (Mexico)

*E.S.T.=Eastern Standard Time
M.S.T.=Mountain Standard Time

C.S.T.=Central Standard Time
P.S.T.=Pacific Standard Time

Commerce Department District Offices

ALABAMA, Birmingham - 2015 2nd Ave. N., 3rd flr., Berry Bldg., 35203. Tel: (205) 264-1331

ALASKA, Anchorage - 701 C Street, P.O. Box 32, 99513. Tel: (907) 271-5041.

ARIZONA, Phoenix - Fed. Bldg. & U.S. Courthouse, 230 N. 1st Ave., Rm. 3412, 85025. Tel: (602)254-3285.

ARKANSAS, Little Rock - Savers Fed. Bldg., Ste. 635, 320 W. Capitol Ave., 72201. Tel: (501) 378-5794.

CALIFORNIA, Los Angeles - Rm. 800, 11777 San Vicente Blvd., 90049. Tel: (213) 209-6707.

Santa Ana - 116-A, W. 4th St., Ste. 1, 92701. Tel: (714)836-2461.

San Diego - P.O. Box 81404, 92138, Tel: (619) 293-5395.

San Francisco - Fed. Bldg. Box 36013, 450 Golden Gate Ave., 94102. Tel: (415) 556-5860.

COLORADO, Denver - Room 119, U.S. Customhouse, 721 19th St., 80202, Tel: (303) 844-3246.

CONNECTICUT, Hartford - Rm. 610-B, Fed. Bldg., 450 Main St., 06103. Tel: (203) 722-3530.

DELAWARE, Serviced by Philadelphia D.O.

DISTRICT OF COLUMBIA, Serviced by Baltimore D.O

FLORIDA, Miami - 224 Fed. Bldg., 51 SW. 1st Ave., 33130. Tel: (305) 536-5267.

Clearwater - 128 N. Osceola Ave., 33515. Tel: (813) 461-0011.

Jacksonville - 3 Independent Dr., 32202. Tel: (904) 791-2796.

Orlando - 75 E. Ivanhoe Blvd., 32802. Tel: (305) 425-1247.

Tallahassee - 107 W. Gaines St., Rm. G-20, 32304. Tel: (904) 488-6469.

GEORGIA, Atlanta - Suite 504, 1365 Peachtree St., NE., 30309. Tel: (404) 881-7000.

Savannah - Fed. Bldg., Rm. A-107, 120 Bernard St., 31401. Tel: (912) 944-4204.

HAWAII, Honolulu - 4106 Fed. Bldg., P.O. Box 50026, 300 Ala Moana Blvd., 96850,. Tel: (808) 546-8694.

IDAHO, Boise - Statehouse, Rm 113, 83720,. Tel: (208) 334-2470.

ILLINOIS, Chicago - 1406 Mid Continental Plaza Bldg., 55 East Monroe St., 60603,. Tel: (312) 353-4450.

Palatine - Harper College, Algonquin & Roselle Rd., 60067. Tel: (312) 397-3000.

Rockford - 515 N. Court St., P.O. Box 1747, 61110-0247. Tel: (815) 987-8100.

INDIANA, Indianapolis - 357 U.S. Courthouse & Fed. Bldg., 46 E. Ohio St., 46204. Tel: (317) 269-6214.

IOWA, Des Moines - 817 Fed. Bldg., 210 Walnut St., 50309. Tel: (515) 284-4222.

KANSAS, Wichita (Kansas City, MO, District) - River Park Pl., Ste. 565, 727 N. Waco, 67203. Tel: (316) 269-6160.

KENTUCKY, Louisville - Rm 636B, U.S. Post Office and Courthouse Bldg., 40202. Tel: (502) 582-5066.

LOUISIANA, New Orleans - 432 Intl. Trade Mart, No. 2 Canal St. 70130. Tel: (504) 589-6546.

MAINE, Augusta (Boston, MA, Districts) - 1 Memorial Circle, Casco Bank Bldg., 04330. Tel: (207) 622-8249.

MARYLAND, Baltimore - 415 U.S. Customhouse, Gay & Lombard Sts., 21202. Tel: (301) 962-3560.

Rockville - 101 Monroe St., 15th Flr., 20850. Tel: (301) 251-2345.

MASSACHUSETTS, Boston - 10th Flr, 441 Stuart St., 02116. Tel: (617) 223-2312.

MICHIGAN, Detroit - 445 Fed. Bldg., 231 W. Lafayette, 48226. Tel: (313) 226-3650.

Grand Rapids - 300 Monroe N.W., Rm. 409, 49503. Tel: (616) 456-2411.

MINNESOTA, Minneapolis - 108 Fed. Bldg., 110 S. 4th St., 55401. Tel: (612) 349-3338.

MISSISSIPPI, Jackson - 300 Woodrow Wilson Blvd., Ste. 328, 39213 Tel: (601) 965-4388.

MISSOURI, St. Louis - 120 S. Central Ave. 63105. Tel: (314) 425-3302.

Kansas City - Rm. 635, 601 E. 12th St., 64106. Tel: (816) 374-3142.

MONTANA, Serviced by Denver D. O.

NEBRASKA, Omaha - 1st Flr., 300 S. 19th St., 68102. Tel: (402) 221-3664.

NEVADA, Reno - 1755 E. Plumb Ln., #152, 89502. Tel: (702) 784-5203.

NEW HAMPSHIRE, Serviced by Boston D. O.

NEW JERSEY, Trenton - 3131 Princeton Pike, 4-D, Ste. 211, 08648. Tel: (609) 989-2100.

NEW MEXICO, Albuquerque - 517 Gold, SW., Ste. 4303, 87102. Tel: (505) 766-2386.

NEW YORK, Buffalo - 1312 Fed. Bldg., 111 W. Huron St., 14202. Tel: (716) 846-4191.

Rochester - 121 E. Ave., 14604. Tel: (716) 263-6480.

New York - Fed. Bldg., 26 Fed. Plaza, Foley Sq., 10278. Tel: (212) 264-0634.

NORTH CAROLINA, Greensboro - 203 Fed. Bldg., 324 W. Market St., P.O. Box 1950, 27402. Tel: (919) 378-5345.

NORTH DAKOTA, Serviced by Omaha D.O.

OHIO, Cincinnati - 9504 Fed. Bldg., 550 Main St., 45202. Tel: (513) 684-2944.

Cleveland - Rm. 600, 666 Euclid Ave., 44114. Tel: (216) 522-4750.

OKLAHOMA, Oklahoma City - 6601 Broadway Ext., Ste. 200, 73116. Tel: (405) 231-5302.

Tulsa - 440 S. Houston St., 74127. Tel: (918) 581-7650.

OREGON, Portland - Rm. 618, 1220 SW. 3rd Ave., 97204. Tel: (503) 221-3001.

PENNSYLVANIA, Philadelphia - 9448 Fed. Bldg., 600 Arch St. 19106, Tel: (215) 597-2866.

Pittsburgh - 2002 Fed. Bldg., 1000 Liberty Ave., 15222. Tel: (412) 644-2850.

PUERTO RICO, San Juan (Hato Rey) - Rm. 659-Fed. Bldg., 00918. Tel: (809) 753-4555.

RHODE ISLAND, Providence (Boston, MA, District) - 7 Jackson Walkway, 02903. Tel: (401) 528-5104.

SOUTH CAROLINA, Columbia - Fed. Bldg., Suite 172, 1835 Assembly St. 29201. Tel: (803) 765-5345.

Charleston - 17 Lockwood Dr., 29401. Tel: (803) 724-4361.

SOUTH DAKOTA, Serviced by Omaha D.O.

TENNESSEE, Nashville - Ste. 1114 Parkway Towers, 404 Jas. Robertson Pkwy. 37219-1505. Tel: (615) 736-5161.

Memphis - 3876 Central Ave., 38111. Tel: (901) 521-4826.

TEXAS, Dallas - Rm. 7A5, 1100 Commerce St., 75242. Tel: (214) 767-0542.

Austin - P.O. Box 12728, Capitol Station, 78711. Tel: (512) 472-5059.

Houston - 2625 Fed. Courthouse, 515 Rusk St., 77002. Tel: (713) 229-2578.

UTAH, Salt Lake City - Rm. 340 U.S. Courthouse, 350 S. Main St., 84101. Tel: (801) 524-5116.

VERMONT, Serviced by Boston D. O.

VIRGINIA, Richmond - 8010 Fed. Bldg., 400 N. 8th St., 23240. Tel: (804) 771-2246.

WASHINGTON, Seattle - Rm. 706, Lake Union Bldg., 1700 Westlake Ave. N., 98109. Tel: (206) 442-5616.

Spokane - P.O. Box 2170, 99210, Tel: (509) 838-8202.

WEST VIRGINIA, Charleston - 3000 New Fed. Bldg., 500 Quarrier St., 25301. Tel: (304) 347-5123.

WISCONSIN, Milwaukee - Fed. Bldg., U.S. Courthouse, 517 E. Wisc. Ave., 53202. Tel: (414) 291-3473.

WYOMING, Serviced by Denver D. O.

Index